Old Age in Modern Society

A textbook of social gerontology

Second edition

Christina R. Victor

St George's Hospital Medical School
London

CHAPMAN & HALL

London · Glasgow · Weinheim · New York · Tokyo · Melbourne · Madras

Published by Chapman & Hall, 2–6 Boundary Row, London SE1 8HN, UK

Chapman & Hall, 2–6 Boundary Row, London SE1 8HN, UK

Blackie Academic & Professional, Wester Cleddens Road, Bishopbriggs, Glasgow G64 2NZ, UK

Chapman & Hall GmbH. Pappelallee 3, 69469 Weinheim, Germany

Chapman & Hall Inc., One Penn Plaza, 41st Floor, New York NY 10119, USA

Chapman & Hall Japan, Thomson Publishing Japan, Hirakawacho Nemoto Building, 6F, 1–7–11 Hirakawa-cho, Chiyoda-ku, Tokyo 102, Japan

Chapman & Hall Australia, Thomas Nelson Australia, 102 Dodds Street, South Melbourne, Victoria 3205, Australia

Chapman & Hall India, R. Seshadri, 32 Second Main Road, CIT East, Madras 600 035, India

Distributed in the USA and Canada by Singular Publishing Group Inc., 4284 41st Street, San Diego, California 92105

First edition published by Croom Helm 1987

Second edition 1994

© 1994 Chapman & Hall

Typeset in 10/12 pt Palatino by EXPO Holdings, Malaysia

Printed in Great Britain by St Edmundsbury Press, Suffolk

ISBN 0 412 54350 8   1 56593 233 1 (USA)

A catalogue record for this book is available from the British Library

Library of Congress Catalog Card Number: 93-74899

∞ Printed on permanent acid-free text paper, manufactured in accordance with ANSI/NISO Z39.48-1992 and ANSI/NISO Z39.48-1984 (Permanence of Paper).

For David and Christopher

Contents

Preface

Old age is a part of the lifecycle about which there are numerous myths and stereotypes. To present an overstatement of commonly held beliefs, the old are portrayed as dependent individuals, characterized by a lack of social autonomy, unloved and neglected by both their immediate family and friends; and posing a threat to the living standards of younger age groups by being a 'burden' that consumes without producing. Older people are perceived as a single homogeneous group, and the experiment of ageing characterized as being the same for all individuals, irrespective of the diversity of their circumstances before the onset of old age.

In this book, detailed statistical material is used to portray the circumstances of older people in modern society in an attempt to evaluate the appropriateness (or otherwise) of the major stereotypes of later life. This volume does not address ageing from a psychological or micro-social perspective. In particular, we do not explore major issues relating to old age. Rather we feel that, from the extensive collection of surveys concerned with the elderly, we can provide a context within which individual elderly people can be studied from more anthropological or biographical perspectives.

The main focus of this book is the exploration of old age within modern western society. In particular the book concentrates upon ageing in Britain. However, where appropriate, research from North America and Europe has been included and it is hoped that the usefulness of the book is not limited by its concentration upon Britain and things British.

The study of ageing is something that transcends professional and academic disciplines. The book is aimed at sociologists, social policy analysts, social workers and health professionals at both undergraduate and postgraduate level. A wider, non-academic, audience may also find the book a useful introduction to the characteristics of older people in a modern industrial society.

C.R. Victor
London

Acknowledgements

The data presented in this second edition derive from a variety of sources and it is a great pleasure to thank formally all those who made data available. The Office of Population Censuses and Surveys granted access to the General Household Survey data which were made available by the ESRC data archive at Essex University. Table 8.3 is reproduced by kind permission of Dr Frank Laczko of Coventry University. As always I thank my husband David Jefferies for his support and encouragement. The arrival of Christopher slowed the preparation of this second edition but has provided me with a new perspective on the study of ageing.

1

Introduction to the study of ageing

Gerontology is the study of ageing and has three core components; the biological, the psychological and the social. Thus gerontology is a multi-disciplinary field of investigation in which each of these perspectives has a valuable contribution to make. The biological approach stresses the impact of ageing upon physiological systems; the psychological concentrates upon mental functions. This book is concerned with the third dimension: the social aspects of ageing.

The study of the social dimensions of ageing, usually referred to as social gerontology, incorporates three distinct aspects (Ward, 1984). The first approach examines ageing as an individual experience by investigating such topics as changes in perceived age identity as the individual progresses through the life course. However, few individuals grow older in isolation from the rest of society. Rather, ageing occurs within a social context ranging from the microscale of the family to the macroscale of the whole society or culture. Thus the second approach to the study of ageing examines the social context which defines ageing and seeks to understand the position of elderly people within society. The third dimension of social gerontology is the examination of the societal consequences of ageing. Demographic change in the composition of the population, such as the ageing of the population, raises a host of policy issues, especially in the economic field, which require investigation and discussion (Johnson and Falkingham, 1992). In this book we shall address each of these aspects of social ageing.

Ageing is a sociologically interesting phenomenon because it takes place within a social context which exerts various constraints upon the individual. For example society may encourage older adults to maintain patterns of behaviour typical of earlier stages in the lifecycle. Alternatively, older people may be encouraged to adopt patterns perceived as 'appropriate' to their age, such as playing bowls or giving up playing vigorous sports such as squash. The constraints operating upon the ageing adult are numerous and include the obvious biological changes which accompany old age as well as social factors such as employment policy, housing, social services, social attitudes and stereotypes of age-appropriate behaviour in later life.

The meaning and impact of the constraints operating upon the older adult are highly dependent upon the social environment in which the individual encounters them. Ageing is not a homogeneous experience which affects every individual within the same society in exactly the same way. The experience of ageing amongst members of ethnic minority groups may differ markedly from that of the host population. This book does not deal in detail with this topic because of the paucity of good quality data. Older adults from different social classes may experience ageing quite differently. We must recognize that ageing is interpreted differently in various societies and cultures and, as we shall see in Chapter 4, the experience of ageing has also varied historically.

We also need to remember in our study of ageing that the older adult is not simply a passive actor in the process of ageing. The interaction between society and the older person is not uni-directional. Rather, there is a continuous interaction between the older adult and society so that the ageing of individuals influences the context within which it occurs and vice versa. For example, older workers may possess unique skills and qualities that society may (or may not) use to advantage.

Terms such as 'the elderly' or 'older people' are often used, by both professionals and the lay public, to describe people in the later phases of life. Throughout this book a variety of terms such as 'elderly people', 'later life' and 'older adult' are used. However we must remain aware that these terms are a 'shorthand' way of identifying the group of interest. They do not imply that the identified group is homogeneous. The term 'elderly population' is often used to describe a group with an age range of 40 years or more. It is totally unrealistic to expect such a group to be homogeneous in either character or attitudes. It is the objective of this book to deconstruct the elderly population into component parts, and to describe the diversity which characterizes old age and the ageing experience in modern society. In this chapter we consider the different approaches which have been adopted towards the definition of old age and we examine the characteristics of these competing perspectives. The chapter then provides a summary of some of the dominant values that characterize society which are of importance for understanding the experience of ageing and the position of the elderly in modern society.

WHAT IS OLD AGE?

'Old age' and 'the elderly' are terms which are common currency in both popular usage and more academic environments. Despite the frequency with which the terms are used the definition of exactly what 'old age' is is problematic. We can identify four main approaches to the definition of old age. These are: biological age, chronology, the political economy approach and as a stage in the lifecycle. Whatever definition of old age is used the term usually implies (implicitly or explicitly) some notion of decline and deterioration in health, vitality, social usefulness and independence.

BIOLOGY AND AGEING

Perhaps one of the most interesting, and fundamental, questions faced by biologists is why organisms age and die. Allied to this is the identification of the features which define biological ageing.

It is common knowledge that different organisms are characterized by variations in the length of the lifespan. The lifespan of a horse is about 40 years compared with 3 years for a rat. Data from biological work indicate that the maximum probable human life span, in an ideal world where all pathology could be eliminated, is 115–120 years. There have been claims from various cultures of life spans considerably in excess of this. However it seems that these have probably been exaggerated either because of inadequate records or by deliberate falsification.

Biologists refer to ageing as 'senescence'. This is a general term which is used to describe decreases in the efficient functioning of an organism with age. It is important to remember that senescence is a natural process which must be distinguished from abnormal processes which bring about pathology and disease. There have been various attempts to define the biological changes and characteristics which accompany growing older in all forms of life. Strehler (1962) considers that ageing is the change which occurs in the post-reproductive phase of life resulting in a decrease in the survival capacity of the organism. Ageing is viewed as an involuntary phase in the development of the organism which brings about a decrease in its adaptive capacities.

Although there is still considerable debate about the precise biological definition of ageing, Strehler (1962) again suggests that four criteria distinguish ageing from other biological processes. These are universality, internality, progressiveness and harmfulness.

1. Universality

For a process to be considered part of ageing it must happen to each member of the population. Thus the observation of an increased prevalence of a medical condition in old age does not necessarily make it part of senescence. For example older people have a higher prevalence of lung cancer but for this to be part of senescence lung cancer would have to occur to everyone in later life.

2. *Internality*

The processes which constitute senescence must come from within the organism and not from external sources such as exposure to radiation or other environmental hazards. Neither should the process be the result of lifestyle factors such as smoking, diet or alcohol consumption.

3. *Progressiveness*

The biological changes which define ageing must occur gradually over time. Thus ageing is a progressive, rather than acute, event whose effects are cumulative and the probability of death and ageing increases with age.

4. *Harmfulness*

The final distinguishing feature of ageing is that the changes must have a deleterious effect upon the organism and its ability to cope with its environment. Thus the final result of ageing is the death of the organism. Biological changes which have a benign effect upon the organism cannot, therefore, be considered part of the ageing process.

Biological theories of ageing

The above comments indicate that senescence is not a single biological process but a combination of factors. To date, biologists have concentrated upon the search for a theory of ageing which is universally applicable to all organisms, and which defines characteristics of ageing common to all members of a species. This strategy has had only limited success and it may well be that in the future biologists concentrate upon describing the characteristics of ageing, some of which will be experienced by all individuals at certain times. However it has proved difficult to distinguish between subclinical disease processes and ageing itself.

Despite the lack of agreed definitions as to what actually constitutes ageing a variety of theories have been proposed as explanations for the process. The notion of ageing as 'wear and tear' is probably the oldest perspective and can be traced back to the ideas of Aristotle. This theory asserts that the human body is like a machine and after extensive use individual parts start to wear out. Thus whilst many people believe that exercise keeps the body in good condition Aristotle's view would suggest that exercise would wear out the body. In a similar vein Weismann in 1882 suggested that death occurred because worn-out tissue could no longer be replaced. A popular, but far too simplistic, version of this view is that each individual has a fixed amount of time allocated and that vigorous exercise or lifestyle will use up this energy, leading to premature death.

Very similar to the fixed energy idea is the declining energy view of ageing, the basic postulate of which is that each individual has a fixed amount of energy or vitality (rather like a battery). Thus ageing is seen as the inevitable result of the using up of the fixed supply of energy. This is a theory of ageing which has a long historical pedigree. Hippocrates, in the fourth century BC, thought that the process of ageing was due to a progressive loss of body heat resulting in a loss of vitality. Implicit within this theory is the view that those who undertake vigorous activity would die younger than those with a less strenuous lifestyle. Ageing brings about a decline in vigour which results in the organism being less able to deal with its environment. This perspective is very similar to the notion of vitalism which was very popular in the Middle Ages. Given that recent evidence indicates that exercise and nutrition can revitalize the energy supply of older people, this theory is currently in eclipse.

Another theory of ageing relates to cross linkage. This theory suggests that chemical reactions within the body create bonds between normally separate molecular structures. This theory is best described by the changes in collagen with ageing. Approximately 25–30% of body protein is collagen. This substance is responsible for maintaining structure in the body and gives the support and strength for body tissues. High concentrations of collagen are found in skin, tendons, bone and muscle and the connective tissues of the body. With ageing, collagen loses some of its elasticity as a result of an increase in the number of cross links. Consequently the connective tissues become less flexible resulting in increasing stiffness in joints. Whilst increased joint stiffness as a result of cross linkage undoubtedly accompanies ageing it is doubtful if changes in cross links are the sole cause of senescence.

One very popular theory of ageing relates to the notion of 'programmed' ageing. This set of ideas suggests that ageing and the maximal life span are programmed into the genes of the particular organism. Thus some scientists have linked ageing with the ability of cells to divide or reproduce themselves. Research indicates that cells have a finite life span with a decreased capacity for division with age. Thus there is an inverse relationship between the age of the organism and the time required for cell division or doubling. Hayflick (1977) has shown that normal human lung cells divide about 50 times and then die. Cells taken from an embryo will divide between 40 and 60 times in a laboratory culture; those from a 28-year-old about 30 times and those from an older person about 20 times (Hayflick, 1977). Cells kept at sub-zero temperatures, when reintroduced to appropriate temperatures, will start dividing from the point at which they were interrupted. This suggests that the maximum number of cell divisions is programmed into the cell. One interesting feature to arise from these experiments is that there is no difference between the sexes in the number of times a cell will divide. Thus it seems that there is no biological basis for the different life expectancy of males and females. These experiments indicate that four stages describe the ageing of a cell. First there is an increase in the time required for the cell to divide. This is followed by a decrease in metabolic activity and an increase in cellular debris. This then results in the decline of the cell culture.

These experiments in cell division have, of course, been conducted in an experimental laboratory and it remains to be demonstrated that cells behave in the same way inside the living being. A further limitation of this theory is that it is difficult to relate actual age changes with patterns of cell division. It would also be hard to demonstrate that specific physiological changes were due to changes in cell division, because of the difficulties of controlling for all the other potential confounding biological factors. However this 'programmed ageing' notion implies that there is an inherent biological clock which keeps track of time and initiates the ageing process when certain limits are met. This is an interesting, if speculative, theory.

Related to these ideas about cell division are the error and somatic mutation theories. The basic concept involved in these two theories is that during the course of cell division errors occur producing faulty cells. These errors and mutations are then reproduced and accumulate throughout successive generations interfering with the ability of the cell to maintain biological functioning. This may result in a loss of function on the part of the organism where the error occurred. Somatic mutation theory relates to alterations in DNA in the course of cell division whilst the error theories relate to changes in RNA, protein and enzyme synthesis.

Other theories of ageing have focused upon the immune system. The role of the immune system within the body is to create antibodies to resist disease, especially infectious diseases. Kent (1977) has suggested that these antigens may produce the process of ageing as well as bringing about disease resistance. Biological evidence indicates that the immune system is at its most efficient at the age of 40 and after this it starts to decline. Proponents of this view point to the increased prevalence of disorders such as maturity-onset diabetes and anaemia, which are immune-based diseases, in support of the explanation of ageing.

The immune system is, however, a very complex system and some theories of ageing have focused particularly upon the auto-immune system. Proponents of this view of ageing suggest that senescence is brought about by the inability of the body to distinguish healthy cells that have been slightly altered by mutation or other changes, responding to them as if they were disease cells and producing an auto-immune reaction. In addition to a decreased ability of the immune system to identify normal cells the immune system may also exhibit a decreased surveillance of antigen cells. Experimental evidence has shown that restriction of food intake in rats extends the life span whilst keeping fish at low temperatures produces the same result. Both restricted food intake and low temperature seem to delay auto-immune reactions. This approach seems to be one of the most promising in terms of explaining the biological basis of ageing and also holds the potential for intervention to retard or delay the ageing process. If the immune system is shown to be instrumental in bringing about biological ageing then immuno-engineering to maintain 'normal' functioning by either selective alteration of diet or environment or therapy to rejuvenate the system may well delay the onset of senescence.

Another theory of ageing is the concept of free radicals. This relates to the tendency of molecules to detach themselves from their origin site and relocate elsewhere, thereby damaging or altering its original function (Harman, 1956). This is a theory of ageing which takes place at a sub-microscopic level and is still highly speculative.

Physiological changes with ageing

Whatever the causes, ageing results in some readily observable changes in the physiological characteristics of the elderly which are summarized below.

1. The skin becomes darker, less elastic and more susceptible to bruising. There is a lessening of fat and a decrease in the number of nerve cells in the skin. This results in a diminished ability to maintain a constant body temperature.
2. Joints stiffen and bones become lighter, more porous and brittle as calcium is decreased.
3. The size and strength of muscles decreases with age. At age 50 biceps strength is only half what it was at age 25.
4. The heart muscle strength decreases and the arteries shrink and harden.
5. The respiratory system becomes less efficient as vital capacity decreases with age. At 70 years of age lung capacity is only half of what it was at 30.
6. The metabolic and gastro-intestinal systems change.
7. Brain weight decreases by about 10% between the ages of 30 and 75.
8. The filtering rate of the kidneys declines. The kidney filtration rate of a 75-year-old is about 60% of that of the same individual at the age of 30. Excess urination is common among the elderly and in males this is usually due to the enlargement of the prostate gland.
9. The sensations of touch, taste and smell decrease with age.

Overall these physiological changes result in a fundamental decrease in the ability of the body to maintain homoeostasis, that is to regulate the functions of the body within the very precise limits required.

Consequently the body becomes less able to adapt to physiological stress and less resistant to disease and pathology.

However, individuals display these physiological characteristics of ageing at markedly different times. Studies of hair-greying and handgrip strength have demonstrated the enormous variation in the chronological age at which different individuals show physiological effects of ageing. Despite this variation between individuals, almost everyone will eventually demonstrate some loss of handgrip strength although these losses are often very difficult to identify without sophisticated equipment. Confirming our attention to changes in hair colour Australian data indicate that some individuals had grey hair by the age of 30 whilst other displayed little evidence of greying by the time they were 60 (Lamb, 1977).

CHRONOLOGY AND AGEING

It is evident that there is no readily agreed biological definition of ageing or of the onset of old age. So a variety of other indicators have been used to define the later phases of the life course. One of the most frequently used measures is chronological, or calendar, age. The use of this measure requires a society to be sufficiently well organized that its members have an idea of their chronological age. Gray and Wilcock (1981) suggest that even as late as the 17th century, people in Britain had only a very rough idea of their age.

As noted above, the physiological manifestations of biological ageing occur at different rates in different people. Consequently the older age groups are very varied in terms of senescence. Although chronological or calendar age is frequently used to define the onset of old age this is, at best, only a very rough guide to the ageing of the individual in biological terms.

The use of chronological age as a criterion for the definition of ageing (or any other phase of the lifecycle) has two distinct dimensions. The first use of calendar age to define ageing is based upon the cultural ascriptions of the society. This requires some knowledge of the socio-cultural context in which it is being applied, particularly the social meanings attributed to particular ages. Thus age is a characteristic with very strong social meanings and a marked element of social construction just as are the terms 'male' or 'Asian'. In modern Britain a 15-year-old girl is considered a schoolgirl whereas in a another society she may be a wife and mother.

The age at which old age is thought to start varies in different cultures and historically. In Samoa old age is usually defined as starting at 50, in Japan and Thailand at 60 and at 65–70 years in most western industrial countries. During the last century, individuals living in Britain would be considered old at much earlier chronological ages than today. There are frequent references, in both literature and the many social investigations carried out in Victorian Britain, to 'old people' whose chronological age was only 40.

There is a second element to the use of chronological age to define 'old age' and this relates to the response of the state to the perceived problems of old age. Increasingly, old age has become defined as the age at which an individual becomes eligible to receive certain sorts of benefits, a pension, or is excluded from participation in the labour market (Phillipson 1982).

The use of chronological age to define old age (or any other phase of life) is based more upon the cultural ascriptions of society than on its function as a surrogate indicator of biological ageing. Despite these limitations, chronological age is an index given increasing importance in modern society, especially where legal definitions couched in terms of chronology have become important in defining particular phases of the lifecycle, such as the age of legal responsibility, majority or retirement.

THE POLITICAL ECONOMY APPROACH TO AGEING

Political economy may be defined as the study of the interaction between government, the economy and various socially defined groups. The central issue in political economy is the distribution of social goods between groups and the mechanisms by which they are allocated (Walton, 1979). This approach to the study and definition of old age is essentially structural and stresses the examination of the differential experience of ageing between varying sub-groups of elderly.

This a macroscale approach to the study of ageing. Estes (1979), Olsen (1982) and Walker (1983) argue that old age is defined neither by chronology or biology but by the relationship between older people and the means of production. The organization of production, social and political institutions, social processes and the social policies pursued explicitly (or implicitly) by society are seen to be, in this approach, the key relationships.

The political economy approach assumes a structural relationship between elderly people and the rest of society, with society constructing the institutions and rules within which old age is defined. From this perspective, the elderly are seen not as a group separate from the wider social context, but as an integral part of society. This approach relates the social and economic status of elderly people to the institutions of society which are either partly, or entirely, organized around the concept of production. Central to this perspective is the notion of structural dependency. In this perspective dependency is viewed as a socially constructed entity best understood in terms of relationships between the dependent group and the labour market. Policies for social security, retirement and pensions assume particular importance because they determine the duration of the working life and assign to specific phases such as retirement (or child-rearing) or to groups such as the long-term sick or handicapped, a dependent status. This dependency is enhanced and reinforced by the exclusion of the elderly (or young mothers) from employment, the major means of economic status in advanced capitalist societies. In Britain the structural dependency hypothesis has both strong protagonists (Walker and Phillipson, 1986; Macnicol, 1990) and opponents (Johnson, 1987).

Guillemard (1983), in France, has suggested that there have been three distinct periods in the social construction and definition of later life. During the 1950s she considers that the predominant approach was the emphasis of old age as period of dependency and as a burden for society. This was replaced by a stressing of activity in the 1960s whilst the 1970s and 1980s have stressed unemployment and the withdrawal of the elderly from the labour market. Whatever the flavour of the individual approach, the social construction of old age results in the individual being labelled and rejected by economic markets, simply on the grounds of age.

Social policies, in the broadest sense, define a minimum standard of welfare and provide useful criteria for defining the onset of old age and describing its status. The social construction of old age is related to both policies for pensions and retirement as well as broader aspects of social policy. Retirement policies are fundamental to this definition, for they mark the boundary between independent and dependent status. The growth of retirement has ensured that an increasing fraction of older workers are excluded from the labour market at a pre-defined age and therefore from access to earnings. This process has progressed rapidly over this century. Since 1931 the fraction of men over 65 classed as wholly retired has increased from less than one-half to 88%. In a comparatively short space of time, the onset of old age has come to be practically defined as retirement age.

The growth and development of retirement policy is related to both the organization of production and the demand for labour. Phillipson (1982) sees the growth of retirement in 20th century Britain as a reflection of the differential labour needs of a capitalist economy. This perspective suggests that the elderly should be seen as a reserve 'army' of labour. In times of slump, older workers, i.e. those aged between 50 and 65 years, are encouraged to leave the labour force to make way for younger workers, as in the government sponsored and created Job Release Scheme. Conversely, in periods of labour shortage the justification for retiring and becoming non-productive may be questioned and the older worker will be encouraged to remain in the labour force for as long as possible.

Viewed from this perspective the process of assigning dependent status upon the basis of a particular chronological age, as in current statutory retirement policies, is a social and not a biological construct. There is no necessary relationship between age and dependency (Walker 1980). In Britain statutory retirement age is 65 for men and 60 for women. The selection of these ages as defining retirement reflected a popular belief that most people become unfit for employment at some point in their 60s (Thane, 1978). However retirement age varies between countries and is subject to change over time. In Denmark both men and women retire at 67 whilst in the USA it is 70. Italy specifies retirement for males at 60 and for women at 55.

The exclusion of the majority of the elderly from the labour market renders most of them dependent upon the state for the majority of their income. The corollary of the growth of retirement has been the development of a pensions policy. On retirement the average person experiences a halving of income (Walker, 1980). This reduction in income occurs because state pensions are extremely low in relation to average earnings. In 1985 the state retirement pension was 22% of the average manual worker's wage. The justification for this differential is that social benefits in advanced capitalist societies are implicitly (or explicitly) designed to preserve monetary incentives and the work ethic. State benefits have never been designed to provide anything other than the most basic standard of living for recipients. Almost all elderly receive some form of state pension, and 70% are totally reliant upon state benefits for all their income (Victor and Vetter, 1986). The low value of the benefits means that in Britain two-thirds live on or below the poverty line (Walker, 1980). In Britain the relationship between poverty and old age has been recognized for at least the last 100 years. The political economy approach challenges this essential 'fact' of ageing by drawing our attention to the causes of poverty in old age, namely the low monetary value of benefits paid to elderly people and their exclusions from the labour market.

The perception of elderly people as a homogeneous group with particular needs different from the rest of the population has dominated social policy formulation for later life. Such policies are essentially ageist in approach, for they contain the implicit assumption that the elderly can be treated as a distinct social group isolated from the rest of society. Social policies are closely related to age, such as defining a specific age for retirement, rather than specific needs such as chronic disability. This reflects an essentially lifecycle approach to the definition of social need. The early studies of Booth in London and Rowntree in York identified a strong link between the stage in the lifecycle and poverty. This has resulted in British social policy being superimposed upon typical patterns of family development and a chronological age scale, rather than responding to the needs themselves such as disability or low wages.

THE LIFECYCLE DEFINITION OF OLD AGE

Another approach to the definition of old age is via the concept of the lifecycle. This is usually conceived as an orderly progression from infancy to old age with biological and socio-cultural factors interacting to govern the sequence of progression. Categories such as old or middle age are, therefore, seen from this perspective as social constructs based upon social cues and norms rather than the more structural approach outlined above.

Although the lifecycle is often perceived as a simple universal progression from one well defined set of social roles to another, it is in reality a highly complex concept. Within the broad term lifecycle it is possible to distinguish between a variety of sub lifecycles related to different aspects of life such the family or work. The family dimension of the lifecycle involves numerous transitions including courtship, newly married, new parents, parents of teenagers, 'empty nesters', retirement and widowhood. Not everyone will experience all these phases of the family cycle; there may also be enormous variations in the age at which individuals experience these transitions. For example, some marry at 18 and have three children by the age of 25; others may not marry until well into their 30s.

Neugarten (1974) describes how the lifecycle has become increasingly differentiated into smaller segments with the emergence of the subgroups of 'adolescence', 'pre-school' and 'middle age' as distinct phases. It was not until industrialization in the 17th and 18th centuries that childhood emerged as a specific phase of life with its own special needs and characteristics (Aries, 1962). Adolescence did not become widely recognized until the early part of this century. More recently middle age has become recognized as a distinctive phase and, increasingly, there is a trend to differentiate between the 'young' elderly (those aged between 65 and 74 years) and the 'old' elderly (those aged over 75 years). There is also the distinction between the 'third age' (those aged 50–74) and the 'fourth age' (Laslett, 1989).

From the lifecycle perspective, in describing someone as old (or juvenile) we are locating them within a specific social environment which expects particular roles and provides opportunities and barriers. These vary throughout the lifecycle. Chronological age serves as the basis for proscribing or permitting various social roles and behaviours. Again we find that the meanings of these social ages varies both between cultures and historically. For example retirement was often dreaded in the early years of this century. As late as the 1950s in Britain, Townsend (1957) was reporting in his studies of Bethnal Green in London that workers would rather take a massive change in job status than retire altogether. However, the emergence of a more positive image of the pensioner and a society in which leisure is a prized asset has radically altered the perception of retirement.

All cultures have rules (either explicit or implicit) which define what are appropriate (and inappropriate) forms of behaviour. These rules are generally referred to as norms and allow us to predict the behaviour of others in specific situations, as well as allowing others to predict our behaviour. For example, in our culture the norm, or expected behaviour, upon being introduced to someone for the first time is to extend our hand and shake hands. This seems perfectly natural to us but in some cultures it would be interpreted as a gesture of hostility, not friendship. Similarly in Britain it is still considered polite for a man to hold open a door for a woman and let her go through first. In Japan, however, the prevailing cultural norm is for a man to go through the door first with the woman following behind.

Norms such as the example of shaking hands apply to all age groups. Some forms of behaviour are, however, only considered appropriate to specific age or sex groups. We are not surprised to see a young child having a tantrum if her mother refuses to give her some sweets. However we would consider it most surprising if a teenager behaved in the same way.

There are a variety of behaviour norms operating within society. Sociologists usually distinguish between norms according to their considered degree of importance. Three types of norm may be identified; folkways, mores and laws.

Most of the rules governing the conventions of everyday life are informally enforced normative values known as folkways. Included within this group are such things as using the right cutlery when eating out. These norms are enforced by such informal mechanisms as ridicule and gossip. Transgression of these norms does not result in any serious harm to the social group so the sanctions for such misdemeanours are usually no more than mild disapproval.

Much age-appropriate behaviour for older people falls into this category. For example, we expect older people not to be interested in sex or romantic involvements and to dress in a conservative fashion. Neither are they expected to engage in heavy manual labour. Informal behaviour rules also provide suggestions about appropriate behaviour towards older people. We are expected to help old ladies across the street, give them our seat on crowded buses and trains and carry their shopping or luggage. Similarly, older adults have social obligations. In particular they are expected to show an interest in their grandchildren. The erring or uninterested grandparent would be subject to considerable social sanction and gossip, both from within the family and from the wider social world.

A more serious group of behaviour norms are termed mores. These are generally considered very important to the welfare of the social group and transgression of these behaviour rules carries serious sanctions. Broadly speaking, mores define what is considered morally correct in a specific culture at a specific point in time.

Some examples of mores or moral values are the expectations that citizens will not murder or steal. We expect people to be faithful to their spouse and to express loyalty to their country. Some age norms fall into this category. A divorce between older people who have been married for many years is perceived as much more shocking than amongst younger people.

The line which divides informal folk values from mores is not always easy to define. The definition of these two categories tends to vary over time. It is probably better to think of these as representing a continuum of behaviour that attracts increasing levels of disapproval, rather than as two discrete categories.

Society is a highly complex organization. In order to ensure its orderly functioning there is a need for a formalized system of social control. Laws define the strictest types of behaviour norms. Some laws, such as those prohibiting bigamy, rape or murder, are firmly rooted in mores and are, usually, effective. However some laws may conflict with the prevailing mores, such as the former prohibition of alcohol in the United States. Some age norms are laws. For example no one can vote in a British election or marry without their parents consent until they are 18. The purchase of cigarettes or frequenting of a public house, but not the purchase of alcoholic drinks, is permissible at the age of 16 years.

Roles within society, and their sequence of occurrence, are 'age graded'. This means that they are linked to specific ages. Systems of age stratification are found in most societies and cultures. It is via these linkages that chronological time is transformed into 'social' time. This results in social expectations of age appropriate behaviour and the timing of social events and transitions throughout the lifecycle. These notions of social time result in systems of age stratification in which different age groups occupy varying positions in society. These positions extract differential rights, duties and obligations.

One method of researching informal age norms is to look for regularities in lifecycles and consider how life events occur in relation to age. In the USA there has been a remarkable consistency through the 20th century in both women's ages at marriage and the birth of their first child. Carter and Gillick (1970) have shown that for age at first marriage the variance around the mean has decreased for successive groups in the 25 years preceding 1966.

Neugarten, Havighurst and Tobin (1968, p. 230) have identified empirically that non-institutionalized age norms are well recognized by the population, and appropriate behaviours are ascribed to them. In a study of residents in a Mid-Western city she demonstrated that adulthood was seen as consisting of four periods; young adulthood, maturity, middle age and old age (Neugarten and Peterson, 1957). Progression from one stage to the next was defined by five dimensions: health, career, family responsibilities, psychological and social. Subjects could easily respond to questions such as 'What is the best age for a woman to marry?'

Greatest agreement amongst respondents was observed on the timing of major role transitions such as marriage or retirement. Most middle-class men and women felt that men should be prepared to retire between the ages of 60 and 65 and that the right age for a man to marry was 20–25.

Individuals are aware of such norms in their own timing of life events, and make role transitions when they think they have reached the most appropriate age or when they think they ought to. Individuals are aware of how their pattern of timing varies from the norm with such comments as 'I married late' or 'I had my children late'. Age norms are evident in other areas, such as employment. Sofer (1970) demonstrates that executives had a clear notion of career development at specific ages and defined their own success, at least in part, as to how they related to these norms.

Merton (1957) developed a typology to describe behaviour of individuals based upon their acceptance of culturally prescribed goals and normative expectations regarding the achievement of these goals. This was later modified to explain individuals' conformity to or deviance from the expected timing of major life events. Using this typology, conformity is defined as having socially acceptable goals and arriving at these at the correct time such as marrying at the 'right' age. Innovation occurs when the individual accepts the major socially defined goals but is unable to follow the prescribed timetable. For example, women may leave their careers for a few years to have children; when they return they are then several years 'behind' their contemporaries. Persons who decline the accepted goals and timetables are labelled as retreaters, whilst rebels question the validity of the goals and timing of events. Such people wish to reorder the system and question its utility. Acceptance or rejection of these goals and timing has implications for the ageing of individuals. Gubrium (1974) suggests that those who view these events as under their control and are in sequence with the timetable perceive themselves as younger than those who are either behind schedule or do not feel in control.

These expectations and social cues are not, however, universal. They vary between societies, between sub-groups within a single society and historically. American studies suggest a greater consensus about the appropriate age behaviours of women as compared with men. Amongst the upper or middle classes, major life events are seen as being appropriate to later chronological ages than among working-class subjects. Consequently age is a ambiguous characteristic, which is often difficult to define but which is increasing in importance as a dimension of differentiation in modern industrial society.

We saw earlier that most of us consider that there is a right age for certain kinds of behaviour. Following on from this we should consider whether there are any particular norms or forms of behaviour which are only relevant to older people. Work from the United States by Havighurst and Albrecht (1953) suggests that there are few behaviour norms which apply only to older people. Most norms, especially those with negative connotations, seem to apply to all age groups. Sitting around doing nothing, or failing to keep in touch with family and friends, is disapproved of irrespective of age. Where specific norms associated with the elderly were identified, these focused upon the family, church and income.

Lack of positive norms about what is expected in old age leads Rosow (1974) to argue that this results in boredom and aimlessness amongst older people. However Bengtson (1970) sees lack of a clearly prescribed role as giving older people a flexibility of action and freedom of behaviour which is denied to other age groups. This debate has not been resolved.

CULTURAL VALUES AND THE STUDY OF AGEING

All societies have a set of values which dominate its social organization. These give each society a distinctive character and make it different from other types of culture. Society is usually characterized by variations in the status accorded to different age groups. In order to place our study of the aged and ageing in context we will briefly describe the dominant values and themes in our own culture. These cultural values apply to most western industrial societies, although the emphasis placed upon different dimensions exhibits some variation between countries.

Independence

Self reliance, autonomy and independence are highly valued characteristics which pervade all aspects of life. The importance of this set of values is reflected in aphorisms such as 'People should stand on their own two feet' and 'I wouldn't accept welfare; that's charity' or 'I've never asked anyone for anything in my life'. We are constantly taught that dependency, in any of its diverse manifestations, is a sign of weakness. Dependent people are frequently derided for their lack of character and are given such derogatory labels as idler, scrounger, workshy or good-for-nothing. Those dependent upon welfare benefits for their income are seen by many as scroungers or as living off the charity of taxpayers. In the 1980s the spectre of the 'dependency culture' has loomed large in the collective consciousness. This is reflected in the attention which is paid, by both the media and government, to the financially insignificant problem of welfare benefits fraud whereas comparatively little attention is given to the much more extensive problem of the non-claiming of benefits or to tax evasion and fraud.

Two sets of reasons, adaptive and maladaptive, seem to explain this emphasis upon independence as a source of self esteem. Taking a pride in remaining independent and not wanting to be a burden upon others are adaptive reasons. Older people feel that they can preserve their self-respect (and maintain the respect of others) by not impinging upon the freedom of loved ones and not having their loved ones impinge upon their freedom in return. As a widow of 83 living alone in the East End of London said, 'I can go to bed when I like and come back when I like. There's no one to say "where've you been?" (Townsend, 1964, p. 37). Maladaptive reasons for the preservation of independence, often at all costs, centre upon the fear and mistrust of others. In this context, independence becomes a defence against the possibility of neglect and mal-treatment. By following a policy of isolation, the older person avoids any possibility of rejection by others, but often at great cost to her/his own quality of life.

The pattern of socialization in modern society continues to stress the need for independence, without any concession to the fact that as we grow older some of us will be unable to preserve our autonomy and will require the assistance of others. This identifies a crucial social aspect of ageing, for we do little to help people heavily imbued with the notion of independence to accept a more dependent status. Similarly at a societal level, we have not yet worked out a response to the problem of dependency amongst other sectors of the population, such as the long-term unemployed, the sick or the handicapped.

The work ethic

A second major organizing principle of modern western society is the work ethic. This is, obviously, linked to the notion of financial independence noted above. Western industrial capitalist societies place a great deal of social importance on work and paid employment. It is generally held that being busy is a good thing and something which is to be encouraged. In order to maximize the potency of the work ethic, welfare benefits paid to those without work are usually below the general level of wages. The payment of benefits at a subsistence level was one of the major organizing principles of the British welfare state (Victor, 1986). Those who reject the work ethic are viewed as 'scroungers' by the rest of society. Thus groups such as the unemployed are seen by many as being workshy or lazy and undeserving of support via the system of welfare benefits (Victor, 1985). Additionally, work is a major form of social status and social class from which the elderly are usually excluded. As we shall see in a later chapter, older people are largely excluded from the formal labour market and cannot be part of the wider work-orientated society. There is a clash between the circumstances that many elderly find themselves placed in, unproductive and with much enforced leisure time, and the prevailing social ethos which stresses activity and productiveness.

Youth orientation

Within many western societies, especially the United States, the virtues of youth, and to a much lesser extent of young people, are extolled. Youth is perceived as a time of energy, enthusiasm, resourcefulness, resilience and inventiveness compared with the decline and stagnation which is seen as characterizing later life. The emphasis upon youth has grown enormously since 1945 so that it is now dominant in large areas of popular culture such as music, fashion, leisure and, to some extent, even language.

A common stereotype is that the best years of one's life are those of youth. Adulthood, and especially old age, are perceived as regressive. Because of these strongly held beliefs, many people experience fear as they age. This is preyed upon by many advertisers who reinforce the desire to stay young. A cursory glance through almost any mass publication journal or newspaper will reveal a whole host of advertisements for products to keep us young looking, by ridding us of grey hair or wrinkles or by the attentions of a cosmetic surgeon. Consequently ageing becomes problematic in a society where youth is valued and old age devalued.

Progress

Allied to the stress upon youth as a time of achievement is the emphasis placed upon progress. This perspective stresses the future rather than the past. Terms such as 'old fashioned' and 'outdated' have highly negative orientations for, almost without question, we accept that new is inherently better than old. The rate of social change and progress within society may affect the status of older people. In a rapidly changing society, the old may no longer fulfil the functions of elder statesmen and guardians of a group's knowledge. Rather the skills of older people are seen as devalued and obsolete and they are thought to be unable to gain new skills.

SOCIALIZATION AND THE ELDERLY

These cultural values are all-pervasive and are transmitted from one generation to the next. The way that an individual learns their culture is termed socialization. Through this process, individuals learn the skills, values, attributes and roles which enable them to become fully participating members of their particular social group and society. It also teaches the individual how to adapt to new roles and to relinquish old roles as they progress through the life course.

Socialization is usually equated with childhood. Whilst this is the period when much of our socialization takes place, it is a continuing process. We are constantly having to learn new roles such as when we get a new job, marry or are bereaved. As we adopt new roles we drop other, less favoured, roles. Thus socialization is a continuous process of adopting and discarding roles. The newly qualified computer graduate will probably drop the role of student and adopt the role of computer specialist. A recently bereaved older person discards the role of wife and acquires the role of widow.

Old age is seen as a time of great loss of social roles. As we shall see, both retirement and widowhood are major role losses which accompany old age whilst grandparenthood is one of the roles which is adopted in later life. Other role losses experienced in old age relate to the loss of friends through death, decreased income and increasing infirmity.

In addition to experiencing specific role loss, older people also suffer from ambiguity about their general social role. This may arise where there are no clear guidelines or requirements for a given role. This is seen by some as a characteristic of later life. As society we have not yet clearly established what we consider to be the main functions and roles of elderly people. However, role ambiguity is not confined to later life. There is considerable ambiguity about the role of women in modern society. Are they to get married, stay at home and raise children, or should they pursue an independent and career-orientated life style?

For many of the social roles which we are called upon to play we prepare well in advance. This is known as anticipatory socialization. For example a student planning to be a computer scientist, as well as reading for her/his degree, may work in the holidays with a computer firm and subscribe to a variety of computer journals. Where no such preparation for a new role is available, and what we learn now is useless in the next situation, then the individual may experience discontinuity. The transition to old age is seen as being characterized by severe discontinuity. During adult life the individual has learnt to develop independence and find fulfilment in her work or family. In contrast, in old age she must be dependent, submissive and a passive receiver of what other people think is best for her.

STATUS SYSTEMS

Status defines our position in society. At various times an individual occupies a variety of different statuses. For example at school a young girl has the status of a student and at home that of a daughter. With each status goes a variety of rights and obligations. These are the roles accorded to each status group.

We can differentiate between two different types of status: ascribed and attained. Ascribed status is assigned to us by the wider society. Sex is an ascribed status, as is being born a member of the Royal Family. Achieved status is gained by our own efforts, such as becoming a wife, a doctor or a criminal.

Age is a very important criterion for establishing status. All societies have some differentiation according to age group, ranging from three or four categories to the seven ages of Hippocrates and Shakespeare. Age status refers to the rights and obligations awarded to individuals upon the basis of age. The transition from one age status to the next is via a 'rite of passage'. Van Gennep (1960) in his book *Rites of Passage* distinguishes three phases in this event: separation from the former status, transition and incorporation into the new status. Rites of passage serve to ease the difficulties of the transition and incorporate the individual into the new group. One of the most universal rites of passage is the transition to adulthood, often achieved via a marriage or initiation ceremony.

The transition from adulthood to old age receives comparatively little formal recognition in modern society. One obvious reason for this is the gradual and variable nature of the onset of old age. Additionally this is a transition which is viewed very negatively by most individuals so it is hardly surprising that they are not over-eager for public acknowledgement. The nearest equivalent we have of a transition to old age ritual is retirement.

SOCIAL CLASS STRATIFICATION AND THE ELDERLY

Societies are not collections of equally ranked individuals. Rather they are usually arranged, with various degrees of formality, into a series of groups or strata. Stratification involves the ranking of individuals into higher and lower positions. In examining the position of elderly people in modern society it is necessary to locate them within the system of social stratification. We noted earlier that age is one aspect upon which societies are stratified. However in Britain the major dimensions of stratification relate to wealth, power and prestige, rather than to age or ethnicity.

In comparison with many countries Britain is very rich. Yet within the country there are huge and persistent inequalities between the rich and poorest members of society (Townsend, 1979). Further, there is little evidence that the gap is closing. Elderly people, because of their reduced incomes, are often towards the poorer end of the distribution of wealth (Johnson and Falkingham, 1992). However there are a small but significant minority of affluent older people who have been the focus of recent attention.

There are two main types of power; individual and social. Individual power refers to the extent to which the individual is able to control her/ his own destiny and lifestyle. Because of reduced resources, many elderly people are unable to exercise full control over their lives, and consequently become less than autonomous members of society. Social power refers to the ability to control and influence the behaviour of others. This type of power is differentially distributed amongst the elderly; some older people are in positions of enormous power as judges or members of Parliament. However these are the exceptions. The majority of older people are excluded from this power system. Thus the majority of elderly people suffer a double disadvantage because they have neither individual nor social power.

A third facet of stratification is prestige. This broadly relates to the degree of social recognition and respect one receives from others. Usually, but not always, occupation is the major determinant of prestige. Retirement may bring about a decline of prestige because of the exclusion of the older person from the labour market. It seems that many older people still relate to their former occupation. Rarely do older people describe themselves as simply retired. Rather they are much more likely to state that they are, for example, a retired bus driver.

These dimensions of stratification are united in the concept of social class. A social class may be thought of as a group of individuals with comparable degrees of social standing and regard. The meaning of the term 'social class' depends upon the theoretical perspective from which the researcher is working. Consequently any discussion of social class can become confined to the discussion of technical issues of meaning and measurement. At the most general level there are two main approaches to the definition of class. The first approach conceptualizes class in terms of gradations of status. The second looks at class in terms of relationships to either the means of production, a Marxist approach, or the labour market, a Weberian analysis.

Social class is the dimension which is probably the most important axis of stratification in British society (Reid, 1977). Social gerontologists have always been rather reluctant to incorporate social class within their analysis of later life. There has often been a rather naive assumption that the profound inequalities which characterize the earlier phases of the lifecycle are not maintained during old age. In this text we shall pay particular attention to the examination of the relatively neglected topic of social class and its relationship to the experience of ageing (Arber and Ginn, 1991a).

The most frequently used approach to the measurement of social class in Britain is a gradational classification of occupational status. Typical of this approach is the typology of social class devised by the Registrar General which divides the population into four major classes. Social classes 1 and 2 identify the professional and managerial occupation groups; class 3n is the intermediate non-manual occupations whilst class 3m describes the skilled manual occupations. The unskilled and semi-skilled working-class occupations are grouped into classes 4 and 5.

Throughout this book we shall be using the above typology to examine social class and its influence upon the ageing experience. However, there are a number of problems in applying this classification to older people. Firstly, because the elderly are largely excluded from the labour market, it has been argued that it is inappropriate to classify them in terms of occupational status. Hence our analysis of social class and later life is based upon a retrospective indicator of the class position of the older person. Second, classifications based upon last, rather than main, occupation may be inappropriate because last occupation may not be representative of the main occupation during the working life of the older person. Thirdly, the status evaluation of occupations varies over time. Consequently, it is possible that the status ascribed to jobs held by many now elderly people will have changed over their lifetime. For example, the status of a clerk in the 1930s could have been very different from that in 1980. Further difficulties arise when we try to apply these social class classifications to older women (see Arber and Ginn, 1991b). As few of the population of now elderly women were employed we have to classify them on the basis of their husband's occupation. Thus, older women's class position, using this typology, is based upon retrospective and indirect information. Fourthly, there is a more general problem in accurately assessing an individual's social status from their occupations or other social signs such as dress or style of conversation.

In response to these criticisms we must accept that there is little we can do about changes in the status evaluation of different jobs over time. However it seems to be exceptionally naive to assume that because elderly people are no longer in paid employment they cease to identify with their previous occupational group. Rarely do people describe themselves as retired. Rather, they are much more likely to define themselves as a retired teacher or bus driver. It also seems unlikely that vast numbers of older people retire from jobs which are not typical, in broad status terms, of their main lifetime job. Individuals may demonstrate considerable mobility between jobs during their working life. However, it seems highly improbable that these changes would take the individual outside the broad grouping of 'skilled manual' or 'professional' in which they were located. Consequently, it is felt that the occupational typology of social class has considerable meaning in later life and can be used as a means of exploring the influence social class may have upon the experience of old age.

CONCLUSION

Gerontology is concerned with the study of ageing and is an area of interest that has experienced a considerable expansion in the post-war period, largely in response to the perceived 'problem' of an ageing population. Within this broad area of study, three main traditions have emerged: the biological, the psychological and the social. This book concentrates upon the social dimensions of ageing within modern industrial society.

Old age, whilst it is a term which is widely used, is a concept that is difficult to define. Biological definitions of the onset of old age are not yet well developed, although many of the theories such as vitalism have been rejected because of their simplistic approach. However, even within the social study of old age, biomedical models which conceptualize old age as a time of inevitable decline have had a very important influence upon the development of the subject.

Chronological definitions of old age are essentially 'shorthand' terms that either imply a proxy for a biological view of old age or reflect the influence of social ascriptions or statutory provision such as the provision of retirement pensions. These definitions of old age are both culturally and historically specific.

The third, and more recent, approach to the definition of old age has been via the development of a political economy of old age. This approach rejects the individualistic perspective to the study of ageing and seeks to examine the social construction of old age and dependency within the wider arenas of the economic and political structures and interests of society. This approach considers that the experience of ageing and later life can best be understood by looking at the position of the elderly in relation to the labour market and the relationships and social structures that this produces. This approach, therefore, sees the growth of retirement as a response of a capitalist system to a 'surplus' of labour. It is a perspective which encompasses an examination of the politics of ageing and gives a high priority to the issues of class structure and how these relate to, and condition, the experience of old age. It is a perspective which requires the elderly to be studied as part of the wider society rather than adopting an approach which sees the elderly as a separate group. This critical gerontology seeks to point out the social construction of many of the 'objective' facts about ageing, as well as seeking to stress the essential diversity of the experience of ageing.

The fourth approach to the definition of old age is via the notion of the lifecycle. This approach places its main emphasis upon the social definition of stages, such as old age, via the operation of social cues and norms. Whilst it is true that there are regularities to be observed in individuals' family and employment careers, the lifecycle is a restricted approach to the definition of old age. It gives the impression of being deterministic and presents society as a functional organism with a will of its own.

Of the main approaches to defining old age the political economy perspective seems currently the most helpful. This perspective forces the gerontologist to adopt an approach which places the understanding of ageing within the mainstream of society rather than encouraging a perspective which envisages old age as a separate state somehow divorced from the mainstream of society. It also confronts the essential social definition of ageing and the accepted facts about ageing. The political

economy view rejects the individual biomedical approach which has concentrated upon the medicalization of ageing. Thus this approach expands
the scope and nature of the areas considered to be the legitimate interest
of the social gerontologist. Adoption of a political economy approach to
the study of ageing also serves to stress the diversity of the ageing experience, and moves away from a narrow focus which presents the elderly as
a homogeneous group characterized by similar needs and expectations.
In Chapters 6–12 we shall consider just how varied the elderly
population is.

2

Approaches to the study of ageing

Social gerontology does not possess an extensive theoretical framework in its own right. The systematic development of theory, and its subsequent application, are activities that have been absent from many social scientific studies of ageing. Frequently, researchers have been content simply to describe aspects of behaviour in later life, or the characteristics of various sub-groups of the elderly population, without trying to organize the findings into a coherent theory of social ageing.

As Fisher (1978, p. 194–195) wrote:

> Social gerontology has not succeeded in creating a body of theory....
> Probably, gerontology will never be a theoretical discipline in its own right, but rather a consumer of theory from other sciences. Its major function seems to be that of an applied social science.... Its major role, perhaps, has been to destroy the myths which so thickly encrust the study of ageing, to oppose the age prejudice which has grown so strong....

This failure to formulate a systematic theory of social ageing is perhaps not surprising given the complexity of the field and its relatively recent development as a substantive area of study. However social gerontology has not been immune from the broader sociological paradigms such as social interactionism, social exchange theory and functionalism. In the rest of this chapter we shall summarize the main sociological theories and frameworks which have been used to study ageing.

OLD AGE AS A SOCIAL PROBLEM

Whilst not a specific theory as such, the consideration of old age as a social problem is one that has consistently informed social gerontological research, especially that carried out in Britain. Fuller and Meyers (1941, p. 320) define social problems as 'what people think they are, and if conditions are not defined as social problems by the people involved in them they are not problems to those people although they may be problems to outsiders or to scientists'. Problems may be defined as being perceived either by the individual (a subjective definition) or by society at large (an objective definition).

Elderly people as a group for which specific social policies were required did not emerge in Britain until the 1890s (Thane, 1983; Mac-Intyre, 1977). Prior to this older people were not differentiated from the rest of the pauper classes because under the Elizabethan Poor Law, old age *per se* was not a problem; rather destitution, irrespective of age, was the criterion by which relief was allocated. As the 1909 Majority Report of the Royal Commission on the Poor Law (His Majesty's Stationery Office, 1909, part 4, paragraph 304) observed 'the practice of considering the aged as a class by themselves for the purposes of poor relief is one of modern growth'.

Why then did elderly people emerge as a specific problem group at this time? Demographic changes are an insufficient explanation because the major period of growth in the percentage of older people in the population did not occur until the early part of the 20th century (see Chapter 6). Thane (1983) suggests that the awareness of the elderly as a particular problem group arose from three inter-related factors. Firstly, there was a growing awareness of the complexity of the causes of poverty. Increasingly, poverty was being seen as resulting from a variety of causes of which old age was a contributory factor, rather than simply being the result of idleness or fecklessness. The social surveys of Booth in London and Rowntree in York were important contributors to the ideological shift in the perceived causes of poverty. In particular these reports were important because they exposed the high rates of poverty in old age and related these to inadequate wages, rather than considering poverty as a failure of the individual. However, the important distinction between the 'deserving' and 'undeserving' poor continued to enjoy popularity.

The second major factor governing the identification of older people as a distinct 'problem' group was the increasing difficulty older workers had in remaining in the labour market. Economic difficulties and changes in methods of production combined to drive many older workers into retirement. Thus Quadagno (1982, p. 139) quotes a notice from the manager of the Barrow Steel Company which stated that 'no men to be engaged in any department who are older than 50 years of age...'. Commensurate with this exclusion of older people from the workforce was the growth of retirement as a social concept. Twenty years before the introduction of a state old age pension, approximately one-third of males aged over 65 were not working. This indicates the strength of the forces working to exclude older workers from the labour market (Quadagno, 1982). This was a trend which was not confined just to Great Britain but was manifest throughout the industrial countries of western Europe.

Thirdly, there were concentrations of elderly in particular locations, usually rural, brought about by the migration of younger people. These concentrations of older people increased their general visibility within society and drew attention to the problems of old age for both the individual and society as a whole.

There are two distinct forms of the 'old age as a social problem' perspective: the humanitarian and the organizational (MacIntyre, 1977). The humanitarian perspective emphasizes an interest in the problems of old age for the individual. One focus of attention is on how society can best respond by providing services, on an individual basis, to ameliorate the worst effects of old age. This conceptualization of old age as a social problem is part of the liberal philosophical tradition. The organization approach is concerned with the problems for society of an ageing population.

There is an extensive British academic tradition of work in the humanitarian framework. At the most general level this type of research tradition has concentrated upon describing the circumstances of the poorest and most disadvantaged sections of the community as a means of changing attitudes towards these groups by the rest of society. The surveys of Booth in London and Rowntree in York provide some of the earliest examples of this tradition of academic research. This type of approach has been applied frequently in social gerontology and relies heavily upon the biological model of ageing with its emphasis upon decline and deterioration in function.

Within this tradition, ageing is not defined as the problem. Rather, the focus of attention is upon the individual elderly person. Research has been very heavily orientated towards medical and health matters. Where other issues have been addressed the focus has been on describing the differences between elderly people and other age groups, rather than looking at either continuities between age groups or differences within the elderly population. Few of the investigations carried out considered the contributions made by the elderly. Thus they usually portray a very one-sided picture. Five main areas of investigation have dominated empirical work (Johnson, 1978).

1. **Morbidity studies.** These are usually epidemiologically based studies which seek to determine the incidence and prevalence of social, mental and physical disabilities amongst elderly people, in either community or institutional settings. Such studies have been conducted at national (Hunt, 1978) and local levels (e.g. Bond and Carstairs, 1982).
2. **Quality of life.** These are concerned with various aspects of old people's environment such as access to facilities, housing quality and related aspects. The bulk of these studies have concentrated

upon housing either in the community, in sheltered housing, or residential homes (Willcocks, Peace and Kellaher, 1987).

3   **Personal relationships.** This category includes the vast bulk of sociological studies of ageing. Empirical investigations of family relationships (Townsend, 1964), friendship patterns (Jerrome, 1990), social isolation, loneliness and social networks (Wenger, 1983) have received the most attention. Little attention has been given to the positive contribution made by the elderly either to their families or to the community.

4   **Use of services.** This type of investigation has pursued a narrow objective in that it seeks to describe old people's use of, and need for, specific social and medical support services such as home helps or meals on wheels (Bond and Carstairs, 1982). Also included are studies which have looked at the misallocation of elderly to institutional care (Townsend, 1964).

5. **Retirement and employment.** These surveys have looked at the creation and growth of retirement (Phillipson, 1982; Laczko and Phillipson, 1991) adjustment to retirement, early retirement and the contribution of older workers to the labour market (Parker, 1980). These have been based upon the premise that retirement is a male problem. There are still few studies of retirement as a female issue.

The second manifestation of the 'old age as a social problem' perspective is as an organizational problem for society. This tradition emphasizes the ideology that old age is a 'burden' for society. This perspective, which has been highly distinctive of many British government reports especially those produced in the 1940s and the 1980s, was prompted by demographic concerns particularly the very low birth rates of the pre-war years. Forward projection of these rates suggested that there would insufficient young people entering the workforce to provide for the increasing number of elderly (often referred to as the demographic time bomb).

Beveridge, in his 1942 report upon social security provision, saw old age as a one-way drain on resources from other more important areas of social need. He wrote that 'It is dangerous to be in any way lavish to old age, until adequate provision has been assured for all other needs such as the prevention of disease and the adequate nutrition of the very young'. These comments indicate that the primary focus of social policy as manifested by the creation of the post-war welfare state was towards the young and was designed to encourage an increase in the numbers of children being born by providing 'incentives' to parents in the form of family allowances and other benefits. The Royal Commission (1949) on population went even further by stressing that the old consumed without producing, thereby reducing the overall standard of living. This report recommended ways of reducing the social costs of old age by getting the elderly people to do more to maintain themselves. Nowhere in the report was there any recognition of the past contributions which they had made to society, nor indeed any awareness of their current contributions, especially in terms of informal care.

This emphasis upon elderly people as a burden which society cannot afford has re-emerged in the 1980s and is illustrated by the debate about the ability of the nation to 'afford' the various health and welfare benefits provided for them. Demographic and ideological factors explain the re-emergence of this perspective. As with the immediate post-war period, there has been considerable worry about the perceived ageing of the population. In particular there have been fears expressed about the growth in numbers of the very elderly (i.e. those over 85 years of age). Decreasing fertility rates and family size have raised fears about the possible lack of workers in the future to maintain the elderly population (and other dependent groups).

Ideological factors have also influenced this debate. In Britain the elderly consume about half of the current social security budget. With the election of a Conservative government which is deeply committed to the reduction of public expenditure, combined with economic recession and high unemployment, the ability of the nation to 'afford' the 'burden of the elderly' has been questioned. Questions have also been raised of the possibility of conflict over welfare and other transfers between the generations (see Johnson *et al.* 1989). In addition the philosophy of the 'new right' is centred upon the responsibility of the individual to provide for her/his old age. Both the ability of, and the appropriateness of, the state providing for old age have been questioned.

DISENGAGEMENT THEORY

One of the earliest theoretical perspectives used by gerontologists was disengagement, which was originally formulated in *Growing Old* by Cumming and Henry (1961). Expressed in its simplest form this perspective states that, independent of other factors such as poor health or poverty, ageing involves a gradual but inevitable withdrawal or disengagement from interaction between the individual and her/his social context. This withdrawal is undertaken in preparation for the ultimate act of disengagement, the death of the individual. By disengaging from activity the individual prepares her/himself for death. At the same time, society also prepares the individual for the later phases of life, by withdrawing the pressure to interact. Whether this process is initiated by the individual, or others in her/his social system, the end result is that the elderly person plays fewer social roles and experiences a deterioration in both the quality and quantity of her/his relationships.

Disengagement therefore implies a triple loss for the individual: a loss of roles, a restriction of social contacts and relationships and a reduced commitment to social mores and values. Successful ageing, from the viewpoint of disengagement theory, implies a reduction in activity levels and a decrease in involvement, until the individual withdraws from all previous activities and becomes preoccupied with self and ultimate death. At the heart of this theory is the loss of the major life role. For males this is implicitly seen as employment, whilst the major female role loss is in the sphere of the family. For males the role loss is seen as more problematic, because it is usually much more abrupt than changes in family structure.

Central to this theory is the assumption that both the individual and the wider society benefit from the process. Withdrawal for the individual may mean a release from social pressures which stress productivity, competition and continued achievement. For society, the withdrawal of older members permits younger, more energetic individuals to take over the roles which need to be filled. Disengagement therefore is seen as a way of permitting an orderly transfer of power between generations. The mutual withdrawal of the individual and society from each other is presented as a necessary condition for both successful ageing and the orderly continuation of society.

Such an underlying premise identifies this theory as part of the functionalist tradition of sociology. This approach views the elements of society as being functionally interdependent, with the individual and society always seeking to maintain a state of equilibrium between themselves. Specific behaviour patterns within a social system can be viewed as either functional or dysfunctional. Functional patterns help to maintain and integrate the social network whilst dysfunctional patterns lead to breakdown and disintegration. Thus disengagement would be seen as functional or useful, because it facilitates a smooth transfer of power from the old to the young.

The empirical evaluation of disengagement as a theory of ageing must address three core aspects of the theory. Firstly, disengagement is a lifelong process; for most individuals, it takes place over a period of time rather than suddenly. Throughout the life course the individual is continually acquiring and dropping particular social roles. Secondly, there is an implicit statement that disengagement is inevitable because death and biological decline are inevitable. Thirdly, disengagement is seen as adaptive for both society and the individual.

There is some empirical evidence to support disengagement theory although not all of the aspects noted above have been subject to investigation. Clearly, older people do experience a loss of roles with ageing, whether through retirement, the death of a spouse or the departure of older children from home. However, most of the evidence is, at best, ambiguous. Insufficient attention has been paid to the strategies of substitution and compensation used by the elderly to compensate for losses of role. The widowed may remarry, or the elderly may replace a widespread and loose-knit pattern of interaction with more intense, locally based networks.

There is little good empirical evidence to support the assertion that the withdrawal of the elderly from employment and other roles is socially adaptive. It could be just as convincingly argued that it is bad, since some of the most knowledgeable and experienced members of society are being removed, by either voluntary or mandatory methods, and are replaced with less competent younger persons.

There have been several other criticisms of this approach. One has been its relative simplicity. It seems highly likely that disengagement, if it exists, will require a much more complex and sophisticated explanation including many aspects of psychology and biology. Another difficulty is the assumption that, at the individual level, the desire for disengagement encounters no competition from desires which seek to prolong engagement. This seems to be very improbable given the complex nature of human behaviour. Central to the theory is the notion that, if an individual withdraws from a particular interaction then behavioural norms will wither away. This seems unlikely. Research evidence indicates that once a norm has been internalized more than the mere absence of interaction is required to make it wither away. A further difficulty with this theory is the implicit value judgement that disengagement is 'a good thing' for both society and the individual. Blau (1973) argues that disengagement theory has been used to 'avoid confronting and dealing with the issue of older people's marginality in American society' and to condone indifference towards the problems of older people. The presumed inevitability of the process, with its basis in the bio-medical and sickness model of ageing, has also been subject to considerable criticism. Whilst disengagement theory has been highly influential upon the development of social gerontology, empirical testing and debate have exposed its essential frailty.

Estes, Swan and Gerard (1982) consider that the popularity of disengagement theory has had a marked influence upon the formulation of policy for elderly people in the United States. They argue that this concept of old age prescribes either no policy response to ageing or interventions which achieve the separation of the older person from society. Disengagement theory has formed the justification and intellectual basis for age-segregated policies and the separation of the elderly from other forms of welfare development. The notion of disengagement has been used to legitimize policies which have sought to exclude elderly people from social arenas. Additionally Fisk (1986) suggests that the existence of disengagement theory has enabled professionals dealing with the elderly to rationalize their often negative stereotypes. This theory has further enabled the erection of 'barriers' between the elderly and other social groups and the professionals dealing with them.

ACTIVITY THEORY

Diametrically opposed to the notion of disengagement is activity theory. Developed by Havighurst (1963) this perspective maintains that normal and successful ageing involves preserving, for as long as possible, the attitudes and activities of middle age. Thus, to compensate for activities and roles the individual surrenders with ageing, substitutes should be found.

Activity theory assumes that the relationship between the social system and the ageing individual remains stable. The norms for old age are seen as being the same as those for middle age. Older persons should be rated in terms of a middle-age set of values and ageing is a continuous struggle to remain middle-aged. According to exponents of this view, any behaviour exhibited by older people that would not be appropriate for the middle-aged should be considered as maladjustment. Lemon, Bengtson and Peterson (1972) isolate the two central assumptions of activity theory.

1. Morale and life satisfaction are related to social integration and high involvement with social networks.
2   Role losses such as widowhood or retirement are inversely correlated with life satisfaction.

To date the empirical evidence in support of these assumptions has been ambiguous. Lemon, Bengtson and Peterson (1972), in their study of a retirement community, found no evidence to support these assumptions. However Palmore (1965) demonstrated a relationship between morale, activity, and personal adjustment.

A further difficulty with this approach is that it says nothing about those who lose the battle to remain middle-aged. Again, one may question the value judgements inherent in the theory that interaction and activity in old age is a 'good thing'. The social policy implications of this perspective are rather more positive than disengagement theory, for it argues for the integration of the elderly as full members of society.

DEVELOPMENT THEORY

Dissatisfaction with both these approaches to the study of ageing has led to the search for other ways of theorizing about ageing. Some gerontologists have stated that an understanding of later life requires a knowledge and understanding of what happened to the individual at earlier phases in the lifecycle. Gerontologists have turned to the theories of Freud, Buhler, Jung and Erikson to try and understand ageing.

Of the various developmental theories that of Erikson (1950) is the most complete. He describes life as being composed of eight phases; early infancy, late infancy, early childhood, late childhood, adolescence, late adolescence, the productive years and late life. The function of each of these stages is, according to development theorists, to master developmental tasks which will be required in the next phase.

Developmental theorists have concentrated upon youth and early infancy. However their work identifies three key issues for the ageing individual. Firstly, old age is seen as a time of summing up of the individual's life. It is a stage in the lifecycle when each person must come to terms with what s/he has achieved (and not achieved) in life. Secondly, old age is seen primarily as a time of adjustment during which the individual must come to terms with new social realities such as retirement or widowhood. Thirdly, and related to this, the individual must adjust to being cut off from familiar roles, identities and relationships because of retirement, widowhood or the death of friends.

These theories offer the gerontologist a way of looking at the adaptation of individuals to the later phases of life. In particular, they encourage the researcher to explain the older person's current life style in terms of her/his earlier history. Later life is viewed as a progression from earlier phases. This approach does not outline a 'desired' or 'right' way of ageing as with disengagement or activity theories. Rather, a diversity of approaches and adaptations to the problem of ageing will be displayed, depending upon the history of the older person. Development theories see old age as a time of challenge which posses new possibilities for the individual. The response to these new circumstances may be either positive or negative.

Whilst offering a stimulating perspective upon ageing, these theories are not yet well developed and there are disadvantages to the approach. First, these theories are highly abstract in their approach. Second, they say very little about those who have arrived at the later phases of life without mastering the tasks of the earlier stages. They are also rather deterministic. The approach implies that if the individual has made a mistake in one of the earlier phases there is little, or nothing, she can do to correct it and put her life back into order. A particular problem is the difficulty of generalizing across the population, as the experience of ageing will vary widely between males and females, or between Asians and Whites. A further limitation of this approach is that it is culturally and historically specific. Thus whilst these approaches offer an innovative way of looking at ageing they are very difficult to test empirically.

CONTINUITY THEORY

Developmental approaches to the study of ageing have largely been used by gerontologists interested in the psychological dimensions of later life. Sociologically inclined gerontologists have turned to continuity theory. Sociologists have argued that the experiences an individual has at a particular time are preparatory for the roles and functions to be assumed at the next phase of the lifecycle. This is the well established sociological tradition of the continuity of socialization. For example, both formal and informal child rearing patterns are seen as contributing to the socialization process which prepares children for the assumption of adult roles. Lifecycles, therefore, are seen to have patterns in which there is considerable continuity from one phase to the next.

Continuity theory holds that, in the course of growing older, the individual will attempt to maintain stability in the life style she has developed over the years. This approach implies that ageing can only be properly understood by examining the relationship between biological, social and psychological changes in the individual's lifestyle and previous behaviour patterns. Continuity theory suggests that in the process of ageing, the person will strive to preserve the habits, preferences and lifestyle acquired over a lifetime. Ageing is, therefore, a constant battle to preserve favoured lifestyles.

This perspective clearly identifies retirement as being problematic for the individual, as nothing in previous experience will have prepared her/him for retirement. Career and job skills become redundant, work is replaced by leisure and the constant drive for achievement and success no longer dominates life. Major role changes such as widowhood or children leaving home are also perceived as being problematic because of the lack of anticipatory socialization.

Both disengagement and activity theory suggest that successful ageing is achieved by movement in a single direction. Continuity theory, in contrast, starts from the premise that the individual will try to preserve the favoured lifestyle for as long as possible. It then suggests that adaptation may occur in several directions according to how the individual perceives her/his changing status. The theory does not assert that one must disengage, or become active, in order to cope with the ageing. Rather the decision regarding which roles are to be disregarded and which maintained will be determined by the individual's past and preferred lifestyle. Unlike activity theory, this approach does not assume that lost roles need to be replaced.

Continuity theory, therefore, has the advantage of offering a variety of adjustment patterns from which the individual can choose. The disadvantage is the problem of trying to test it empirically. Each individual's pattern of adjustment in old age or retirement becomes a case study in which the researcher attempts to determine how successfully the individual was able to continue in her/his previous lifestyle. Building a generally applicable theory from this basis is, therefore, difficult.

SYMBOLIC INTERACTIONISM

Symbolic interactionism, as developed by Mead (1934), is one of the fundamental sociological theories. Proponents of this view argue that it is the acquisition of language which distinguishes humans from other life forms. Through language we live in both a symbolic environment as well as a physical one. Consequently, individuals may be stimulated to act by both symbolic and physical stimuli. Additionally, individuals may stimulate others through language and are influenced by what is said to them. Communication with others is, therefore, a means of both transmitting and receiving cultural norms and values. It is via the communication of symbols that we learn vast numbers of social meanings and ways of acting. Thus this type of approach implies that most adult behaviour is learnt from symbolic communication with others, rather than by trial and error.

Berger and Luckmann (1967) argue that individuals experience society as both objective and subjective reality. In the process of social interaction, the individual is both an actor and a reactor. Through the communication of symbols individuals learn the values and meanings of their culture and therefore ways of acting from others. Essential to the interactionist perspective is the view that individuals construct realities or social worlds in a process of interaction with others. Meanings are socially defined but the social actor defines the social world as well as being defined by it.

The symbolic interactionist perspective on ageing considers that the outcome of ageing is derived from the reciprocal relationship between the individual and her/his social environment. Old people, like other social actors, construct their own social reality. Consequently this approach sees ageing as a dynamic process that is responsive to both structural and normative contexts and individual capacities and perceptions. This perspective is essentially a microscale approach to the study of ageing for it stresses the need to understand the nature and impact of ageing at the individual level. Thus an understanding of the impact of ageing requires an understanding of the meaning and interpretation of the events which accompany old age.

There are, as yet, few empirical examples of the use of the symbolic interactionist perspective in the study of old age. Fairhurst (1976) used this method to study rehabilitation of the elderly in geriatric departments, focusing upon such issues as how the identity of the old person is managed and negotiated, and how the members of the geriatric team interact with one another. An Australian researcher used similar techniques to examine the role of retirement and old age clubs in facilitating the status passage of the elderly from employed to retired (Russell, 1981). We could use this type of approach to study, for example, the negotiation of gender roles by elderly couples and how these change in response to variations in the health status of the couple as they age. It is, therefore, a very flexible approach which has considerable potential for the study of ageing.

AGEING AS EXCHANGE

Symbolic interactionism concentrates upon the nature of the individual–society relationship; exchange theory provides a more detailed explanation of why individuals behave as they do in particular situations. The notion of social behaviour as exchange can be traced back to the anthropological work of Mauss (1954). He considered that interaction constituted an exchange of material and non-material goods and services. The sociological studies of Homans (1961) and Blau (1964) have also studied the exchange relationship.

The centrality of exchange in the relationships of older people has been recognized since the writings of Simmons (1945) who argued that the ability of the older person to maintain reciprocal relationships was the key to the status of the aged. It is, however, only fairly recently that Dowd (1980) has proposed an explicit theory of ageing as social exchange, which seeks to explain the decreased social interaction of later life. The basic premises of exchange theory are as follows.

1. Society consists of social actors pursuing common goals.
2. In pursuit of these goals actors enter into social relationships with other actors. Participating in such interactions entails costs such as time or effort.
3. In order to achieve their goals actors will pay these costs.
4. All actors seek to minimize costs and maximize gains.
5. Only interactions which are economic will be preserved.

From this perspective Dowd (1980) interprets interaction between groups or individuals as an attempt to maximize rewards and minimize costs. Interaction is sustained because, and only as long as, it is profitable for the participating actors. Power derives from the imbalance of the exchange, i.e. when one actor values the rewards to be gained from interaction more than the other. Thus one participant achieves power through the inability of the other to reciprocate.

As the power of older persons, relative to their social environment, is gradually diminished, so interaction declines until all that is left of their stock of power and prestige is the ability to comply. Dowd (1980) considers that the only social currency the older person can bring to the exchange relationship is esteem and compliance. Thus where the worker was once able to exchange skill and knowledge in return for wages (s)he has to comply with statutory retirement in return for a subsistence welfare income. The older worker has to cope with the outdating of her/his skills. This too can bring imbalance to the exchange relationship. The difficulty for the older person is that this unbalanced power relationship becomes institutionalized and then becomes the norm for future exchanges.

This theory explicitly rejects the functionalist notion of reciprocity between individual and society in which both sides benefit from interacting. Rather, the exchange theory approach calls for an explicit analysis of both sides of each social transaction (or exchange) to determine who benefits most and why. The great value of an exchange model study of ageing is the multidisciplinary origin of the model, its dynamic nature and its ability to incorporate processes of both role and resource allocation. As yet there have been few empirical applications of this theory because of its relatively recent formulation. However this may prove to be one of the more fruitful areas in the development of social gerontology theory in the future.

LABELLING THEORY

It has been suggested that old age may usefully be conceptualized within the framework of the labelling theory of deviance (Berger and Berger, 1976). Labelling theory derives from social interactionism. In a youth and health conscious society, old age is socially defined, or labelled, as a deviant condition. The groups so classified must confront the various forms of stigmatization which this label entails.

The basic assumption of labelling theory is that the concept of self is derived from interaction with others in the social environment. We often think of ourselves in terms of how other social actors define and react to us. This may result in changes in the way we think and act. Thus the behaviour of older people is seen to depend largely on the reactions of significant others in their immediate social world. The reactions of these significant others will depend upon how they define and classify the elderly. Therefore the behaviour of the elderly is seen as being socially determined by the norms of the social group to which they belong.

Working from this basis Zusman (1966) has formulated a social breakdown syndrome. The four basic components of the model are:

1. the individual's susceptibility to psychological breakdown;
2. the labelling of the individual as incompetent or deficient;
3. the adoption by the individual of this label and the learning of the behaviour associated with it;
4. the identification of the individual with this role.

Using this as a framework Kuypers and Bengtson (1973) suggest that:

1. older people are likely to be susceptible to and dependent upon social labelling because of the way social life is organized in later life;
2. this creates a vulnerability to, and dependence on, external sources of self-labelling, many of which communicate a stereotypical image of the elderly as useless, dependent and marginal;
3. the individual who accepts this negative labelling is inducted into the dependent negative position, learning to act as the elderly are supposed to and losing previous skills, confidence and independence;
4. the external label is accepted and the person defines her/himself as inadequate, thereby creating a vicious circle.

From this basis the two proponents suggest that with suitable inputs the model can be used to foster a more positive image of ageing. These inputs include:

1. the liberation of individuals from an age specific view of status and the use of economic or productive positions as the means of defining status;
2. the improvement of services to older people; their capacity for adaptation could be enhanced by the improvement of the poor environmental conditions which many elderly experience such as bad housing, or low income;
3. assisting the elderly to develop and maintain confidence in their ability to manage their own lives by giving some measure of self-determination in the development of social care programmes (a policy also proposed by Clarke, 1984).

THE ELDERLY AS A MINORITY GROUP

Some sociologists argue that the most appropriate way to study the elderly is as a minority group experiencing all the problems characteristic of groups that are discriminated against. Here the term 'minority group' does not refer to numerical size but to the marginality of the group to society as a whole. The elderly, like other minority groups such as Asians or Afro-Caribbeans, are distinct from the wider society because of a common biological trait. Palmore and Whittington (1971) propose this perspective by indicating the negative stereotypes of, and discrimination which accompanies, old age. Breen (1960) argues that the elderly show the characteristics typical of a minority group such as low income, unequal opportunity and an inferior status. As with racial minorities discrimination against the old is promoted by the relative ease with which the undesirable trait can be observed.

Although not describing older people as a minority g
Peterson (1965) argued that the elderly comprise a speci
These authors consider that a sub-culture emerges when
group interact more with each other than with other meml
This tendency for a group to interact mainly with itself is l
by the operation of two social processes. Firstly, the existen
problems, such as poor housing, common interests or sha
may encourage the group to interact more with each other than those outside the group. Second they may be excluded, either formally or informally, from interaction with the wider society. To varying degrees, both of
these pressures operate upon older adults in modern western industrial
societies. Features such as the exclusion of older people from the employment market, their dependence upon others for their income and their
marginality to the mainstream of life have been used to support the viewpoint that the elderly constitute a specific sub-culture.

The obvious weakness of this view is that the theory does not apply
universally for the elderly are a highly diverse group. Some older people
are ascribed considerable power and prestige in areas such as the law and
politics. Additionally, though poverty is common in old age, not all the
elderly are poor (Falkingham and Victor, 1991, Walker, 1980). Neither are
the elderly characterized by residence in age-segregated communities, or
by patterns of social interaction confined within their own age groups.
Thus, given the heterogeneous nature of the elderly population, this
perspective is of only limited utility as a conceptual framework.

AGE STRATIFICATION THEORY

Society is often conceptualized as being stratified, or divided, along a
number of dimensions such as social class or ethnic status. Age stratification theory uses chronological age as the defining variable (Riley,
1971; Riley, Johnson and Foner, 1972). Thus the elderly, teenagers and
the middle-aged are seen as distinctive status groups. Every society
divides individuals into age groups or strata and this stratification
reflects and creates age-related differences in capacities, roles, rights
and privileges.

Three basic issues dominate age stratification theory. The first is the
meaning of age and the position of age groups within any particular
social context. Secondly, there are the transitions which individuals experience over the life cycle because of these social definitions of age. Thirdly,
there are the mechanisms for the allocation of roles between individuals.

Age stratification models are obviously flexible. This approach may be
used to look at a variety of age groups, not just the elderly. However we
must remember that, whilst all societies can be characterized by age stratification, the social meaning that individual societies ascribe to different

age groups will vary. These models are both culturally and historically specific.

Age stratification theory is related to theories of social class stratification. However, unlike class stratification, mobility across the strata in the age stratification model is inevitable, universal and irreversible because of the natural progression of time. Social mobility, the class stratification corollary of age mobility, is not inevitable. Linked to this demographic aspect are the age-related differences in roles and behaviour which constitute the structural elements of the model. Thus individuals of varying ages behave differently, have different abilities, hold different values and may be motivated by different attitudes.

The model of age stratification has two distinct elements; structure and process. The structural component relates to the way that roles and behavioural expectations are age-graded. The process dimension of the model is concerned with the mechanism of allocation whereby people are matched with roles.

Age stratification models suggest that age is one variable that determines the particular roles an individual will play in society. The link between age and social roles may be either formal or informal. Formal age grading of roles is typified by the establishment of formal rules, which, for example, demand compulsory school attendance in Britain up to the age of 16. We also saw earlier that there are informal rules operating to influence age-appropriate behaviour. Age also may indirectly influence role allocation by reflecting social, biological or psychological characteristics. Biological factors limit the roles of both mother and professional athlete.

The existence of age norms guiding the allocation of social roles is probably universal to all cultures. However the precise nature of these age norms reflects the culture, history, values and structure of specific societies. For example, over this century there have been substantial variations in some aspects of the lifecycle. Child-bearing and -rearing are now confined to a much shorter period than previously. This has been matched by an increase in the duration of the 'empty nest' phase of the lifecycle. Similarly, within specific societies the size, composition and history of particular cohorts influences both the timing and order of the major life events. The existence of compulsory national service will 'delay' the major life transitions such as marriage, going to university, or starting a career for those conscripted.

These age norms in behaviour may originate in tradition, factual regularity, or negotiation. Whatever the origin, they are based upon assumptions, either explicit or implicit, about age-related abilities and limitations. These norms may, however, vary with social class, ethnicity or sex. For example, members of the working class traditionally marry at an earlier age than members of the professional classes. Similarly age at first marriage is usually older for males than for females. Because of these variations, age norms have different realities and meanings for varying social groups. Despite this, age is a universal criterion for role allocation, and all individuals experience points in the lifecycle at which they must choose from different age-related options.

The social world is a complex entity and any individual has multitude of roles to play. An individual could be involved in the roles of spouse, mother, sibling or employee. All of these roles stress different aspects of the individual's persona. In the broadest sense, competing social roles differ in three main ways. First, roles will emphasize varying qualities. Some roles are defined in terms of the task undertaken, such as the worker role, whilst others are defined more in terms of emotional content, such as wife or husband. Second, social roles vary in the type of reward offered, such as money, prestige, status, emotional support or satisfaction. Third, roles are evaluated according to the values of the society. For example, in capitalist societies strongly imbued with the Protestant work ethic the role of the retired or the mother staying at home looking after small children may be ascribed little value. Similarly, the retired person may be ascribed little status in a society which places its major emphasis upon economic activity and financial independence.

The age-grading of roles within an age stratification system creates age differences and inequalities. Each age group is evaluated, both by itself and others in the society, in terms of the dominant social values. This differential evaluation of roles will produce an unequal distribution of power and prestige across the age groups. Thus when societies value the accumulated experience and wisdom of the old, and allow them to undertake roles which capitalize upon this experience, then the aged will be accorded a position of respect.

Age stratification suggests that the role transitions which we experience are timetabled by age norms rather than being selected by us. To understand these transitions we have to have a knowledge of the process of socialization by which individuals learn to accept specific roles and role transitions. Age stratification makes socialization a lifelong process as people move between a sequence of roles as they age.

The value of this approach is that it allows the gerontologist to look at any age group in terms of its demographic characteristics and its relationships with other groups. However the system of age stratification in any society is complex and dynamic and linked in with other systems of stratification such as class or ethnicity. Thus the task of understanding the effects of age stratification is complicated by these interactions. Furthermore the usefulness of this approach is weakened by the use of chronological age rather than 'actual' ageing speeds of the members of the cohorts. This is very much a macroscale approach to the study of ageing for, whilst it tells us about the attributes of different cohorts, it is of limited value in explaining individual behaviour. This approach can often be seen as being deterministic and allowing little freedom of action for the individual social actor.

CONCLUSION

Theoretical formulations in the social sciences display a marked variation in terms of complexity and sophistication. This chapter has indicated that the theories used by social gerontologists reflect these varying levels of sophistication and complexity. We have also indicated that most of the theory used by gerontologists to inform their work has been derived from other disciplines such as sociology or psychology. Thus there are sometimes difficulties in applying the concepts involved across disciplinary boundaries. Additionally it is important for the European reader to remember that the majority of these theoretical approaches have been developed in North America, which may limit their utility and explanatory power when applied elsewhere.

The earliest formulations in social gerontology such as activity and disengagement theory, although not derived from other academic disciplines, were simplistic in approach. Considerable empirical evaluation of these two theories indicates that neither is sufficient to explain the experience of ageing. Indeed these perspectives seem to be as much if not more philosophical than theoretical. Both activity and disengagement theory appear to be prescriptive recommendations about how to live in the later years of life, rather than theories attempting to explain human behaviour. Nevertheless, these two theories have had considerable impact upon the development of gerontology and the formulation of social and medical policies for later life. In particular, disengagement theory has been used to justify the age-segregated policies for the elderly that characterize many modern industrial societies.

The utility of a particular theory in explaining old age requires considerable empirical investigation. Of the theories described in this chapter, continuity theory is probably the hardest to evaluate because it does not readily lend itself to empirical study. Hypotheses about ageing suggested by this theory require the researcher to have extensive knowledge of the subject's previous lifestyle.

Social gerontology has not been isolated from the wider developments of theory within the social sciences. Theories of human behaviour developed by other scientists have been adopted by gerontologists. Symbolic interactionism, labelling theory, exchange theory and age stratification approaches all offer considerable scope for future evaluation and testing.

Of such developments the symbolic interactionist approach may prove to be one of the most useful theoretical perspectives for the gerontologist to employ. This approach has the advantage of viewing ageing as a dynamic process. It is also value-free: it does not offer a philosophical mandate about how to live the later years of life. A particular advantage of this theory is that it suggests that the influence of negative labelling, low expectations and negative stereotypes of old age can be overcome by more positive attitudes from the rest of society.

Given the complexity of social gerontology, it seems unlikely that a single perspective will adequately explain the experience of ageing. It seems probable that a composite theory of ageing will develop using aspects of a number of these different viewpoints. However, before we are able to formulate a composite theory of social ageing, these competing approaches require much more empirical investigation to test their explanatory power. In particular we need to develop cross-cultural and cross-national perspectives in the study of ageing in order to increase the power of any future theoretical developments in social gerontology.

3

Methodological aspects of the study of ageing

In this chapter we consider the nature of age differences in behaviour and discuss the implications these have, in methodological terms, for the study of social gerontology. Subsequently we summarize the major methodological issues that are particularly relevant to the study of ageing. The chapter is concluded by a brief review of the major types of research design used by social gerontologists.

THE NATURE OF AGE DIFFERENCES

The basic task of the social gerontologist is to identify and account for age differences in, for example, political behaviour or social attitudes. This task is not quite as straightforward as it might seem at first sight, for age differences in behaviour may arise for three major reasons. The observed differences may reflect the process of ageing (an age effect). Alternatively, a seemingly age-related change in attitudes may be the result of either cohort or period effects. This complicates the study of social ageing and creates the potential for the misleading interpretation of research findings.

Age effects

As people grow older they develop both physically and psychologically. This may result in changes in behaviour or attitudes. Such developments mean that, in often very subtle ways, an individual of 65 is different from the same person at age 30. These developmental changes are termed age effects and are divided by Ward (1984) into two types: intrinsic and reactive.

Intrinsic age effects are changes that naturally, and inevitably, accompany the ageing process, irrespective of the social context. In contrast reactive age effects are fashioned by the social environment within which ageing takes place. Reactive age effects are, therefore, both culturally and historically specific. Although conceptually distinct, in practice it is often extremely difficult to differentiate between the two different types of age effect.

For example, the observation of increased religious awareness amongst the elderly may be interpreted either as an inevitable accompaniment of impending death (an intrinsic age effect) or as a consequence of the social definition of ageing (a reactive age effect). To define an age effect as intrinsic it must be manifest in a variety of cultures and be constant over time. These are stringent requirements which few age-related differences have yet been able to satisfy.

Cohort effects

Observed differences between age groups may be due not to the ageing process itself but to generational or cohort effects. This type of effect reflects the influence of historical time and events, rather than developmental time, upon the attitudes of groups of individuals. A cohort consists of a group of individuals born at similar times whose members experience the same historical events at roughly the same point in the life-cycle. This creates the potential for 'generational consciousness' (Mannheim, 1952). A cohort or generation is also a very difficult entity to define but the term is usually, but not exclusively, applied to a time-span of between 5 and 10 years.

There are two important points to be considered when looking at cohort effects. First, events experienced by one cohort may not be experienced by subsequent groups. The generation born in 1900 lived through the great inter-war depression whilst the 1950 cohort did not. The sequence of historical events experienced by each successive cohort is unique. Second there is variation within, and between, cohorts in their experience of the same historical event. A single event like the First World War will be experienced by several cohorts at different stages of development. Individuals born in 1900 experienced the depression as adults whilst those born in 1920 were children. Those born in 1920 experienced the Second World War as young adults whilst those born in 1935 were young children during the war.

Society, therefore, may be envisaged as a series of cohorts moving through time each of which has been influenced by a unique configuration of events. The cohort born in 1900 has experienced two world wars, lived through the depression in early adulthood and experienced the culture shock of the 1960s 'permissive society' in old age. The cohort born in 1940 grew up with the welfare state, experienced the permissive society as young adults and experienced mass economic recession in early middle age.

The central thesis of the cohort explanation of age-related differences in behaviour is that it is these shared experiences which influence the norms, values and attitudes of cohort members. This results in differences in social attitudes and beliefs between cohorts. Using this type of argument, the increased religious awareness of older people would be interpreted as the result of being brought up in a more religious environment, not of having become more religious with age. The liberal views of many of those now in their early middle age may well reflect the permissive values of the 1960s. Conversely, the more conservative views of students in the 1980s may well reflect the deterioration in economic opportunities, especially for young people.

There have been few empirical studies of the effect of events upon the subsequent development of a cohort. One of the few was made by Elder (1974) who investigated the effect of the depression upon a group of children born in Oakland in California in 1920–21. He observed extensive differences within his sample in terms of the effects of the depression. Whilst for many this was a time of great deprivation, some groups were far less affected. Thus we must be careful not to interpret historical events as a monolithic experience which was the same for all. Experiencing the depression as children seems to have had little influence upon subsequent attitudes to work, financial and material success or job security. However he did observe that those who had experienced great material deprivation as children were much more satisfied with their living standards as adults than those who had been better provided for in childhood. In Britain the tendency for older people to evaluate their standards of living in terms of the conditions they experienced as young adults rather than current standards has been documented (Victor, 1985). Future generations of elderly, who have experienced a more affluent standard of living, may not accept with such passiveness a low standard of living in old age.

The idea of the cohort effect is underpinned by two main assumptions. Firstly, it is assumed that the experience of the same historical event produces a universal effect across the whole cohort. This is a questionable assumption, as Elder's study demonstrates. He indicates that the depression was not a monolithic experience for all those who lived through it. Any one historical event is likely to be experienced in many different ways because cohorts consist of sub-groups differentiated in terms of class, gender or ethnic origin. A historical event will provoke a variety of responses, of varying degrees of intensity, within a single generation.

The second assumption is that historical events, especially when experienced early in life, influence behaviour through the life-course. There is very little empirical evidence to support this assumption. However, it seems that the norms and attitudes absorbed when young remain remarkably resistant to change. Thus, although some of the variations in attitudes observed between age groups may result from cohort effects, we must wary of stereotyping whole generations with uniform attitudes or beliefs.

Period effects

The third explanation given for observed variations in behaviour between age groups is period effects. This view suggests that certain processes and events may stimulate changed attitudes throughout the whole of society and not just a single age group. For example, attitudes in British society are now markedly more liberal towards the role of women.

If we looked at members of a particular cohort there would probably be changes with age in such attitudes. These might be considered age or cohort effects when in fact they were period effects: events and trends influencing the attitudes of all age groups. Pampel (1981) indicates that the relative position of the elderly in American society has improved over the last 30 years, partly in response to changes in the nature of the elderly population, but mostly in response to period effects operating across the whole of society, which have provided a more positive social environment within which to experience ageing.

Interpreting age, cohort and period effects

The interaction between these three factors makes the task of the social gerontologist in explaining, identifying and interpreting age differences extremely complex. Thus when presented with an observed difference in, for example, political attitudes the gerontologist has to consider whether this observation is due to age, cohort or period effects.

Glenn (1974), taking the example of the more conservative attitudes of the old compared with the young, observes that this finding may be subject to a variety of interpretations. Biological ageing, which results in a decrease in energy and loss of brain tissue may result in increased cautiousness and resistance to change; this could be interpreted as an intrinsic age effect. Accumulated family responsibilities and possessions as one passes through the lifecycle may lead to an increase in conservative values. This could be seen as a reactive age effect. The elderly population of today were brought up in a more conservative society. Consequently their more conservative attitudes could be interpreted as a cohort effect. This example illustrates well the problems that the gerontologist faces in attempting to enumerate and explain age effects.

METHODOLOGICAL ISSUES

Given the complexities of social gerontological research it is vital that great care is taken in the design, implementation and interpretation of such research. Ideally every single study needs to take into account the three competing explanations of age differences described above. There are now several texts concerned specifically with research in social gerontology (Peace, 1990; Lawton and Herzog, 1989; McCauley, 1987) where further details about the major methodological issues pertinent to the study of ageing may be found.

THE DIVERSITY OF THE ELDERLY POPULATION

The elderly population is highly diverse, demonstrating differentiation in terms of sex, ethnic status and social class. These parameters need to be controlled for in any research design so that we can identify with precision the effects of ageing from all the other interacting variables. The 20-year age difference between a 40-year-old and a 60-year-old person is often given great significance whilst the similar gap in age between a person of 70 and one of 90 is usually overlooked. It is important to remember that the group commonly referred to as 'the elderly' usually consists of at least three separate groups. For this reason Neugarten (1974) likes to distinguish between the 'young' elderly , those under 75, and the 'old' elderly, those over 75. The young elderly are characterized by better health, higher education, greater affluence and a higher degree of political activism than the old elderly. It is important that any social gerontology research design is sufficiently comprehensive for the potentially confounding influence of these variables to be taken into account.

BIAS

Social research may be influenced by two forms of bias. The first definition of bias describes systematic errors within the research and the way it has been carried out. This is, therefore, a precise technical concept and term and some of the ways for minimizing its effects are described below. The second aspect of bias relates to prejudice in the interpretation of the findings, because of the ideological orientation of either the researcher or the funding body. When reading any research report the gerontologist should be aware of the possibilities of prejudice in the way that the findings are presented and interpreted. (S)he should also be aware of the nature of the body funding the research and any interest they may have in the findings proving a particular case. Researchers can minimize the potential for bias, or systematic errors, in the data by careful research design. Bias, because it is a systematic error, affects some parts of the data more than others. This may lead to erroneous results and the subsequent misinterpretation of findings. Thus it is distinguished from random errors, which occur with equal frequency throughout the sample and its sub-groups and which, therefore, may not bias the reported results.

There are a number of potential sources of technical bias within any research study. Bias may result because of errors in sample selection (see below). Thus the findings may not be representative of the target population. Bias may also be introduced by non-response, refusal to participate in a study or the loss of members over a follow-up period. Bias may also be introduced by errors in the collection, recording, coding or analysis of the data.

RELIABILITY

Reliability refers to the extent to which the same result is reproduced when a measurement is repeated. The terms reproducibility, replication and repeatability are also used to describe this concept. We may wish to consider the extent to which any particular index of disability will produce the same results when administered to the same subject by two different interviewers. It is important to remember that just because a particular instrument gives the same measurement twice it does not imply that the procedure is a satisfactory one.

There are a number of potential threats to reliability. Variations in observed measurements may be the result of changes in the characteristic itself. Measures of blood pressure may, for example, vary markedly for the same individual due to entirely natural factors. Disability assessments made in a test setting, or in a patient's own home, may produce widely varying results. Reliability may vary between interviewers, if they are not adequately trained, and between different methods of data collection. Thus postal questionnaires and direct interview surveys may produce different responses for the same individual for the same question. Methodological work undertaken by the author indicates that there seems to be little difference in the reliability of responses given by the elderly to either postal questionnaires or direct interviews. Older people are very reliable reporters to factual questions such as the receipt of social and medical services (Victor, 1984). There is no evidence to suggest that reliability problems overall are any greater in surveys of older people than they are with other population groups. However there may well be difficulties in investigating particular topics such as finances with older people.

VALIDITY

The validity of any measure is the extent to which the technique used actually measures the characteristic the researcher is interested in. Thus validity is concerned with, for example, the extent to which any scale for the measurement of functional capacity is actually measuring this, and not recording gender differences in housecare activities. Poorly designed applied disability scales that require respondents to report on their ability to undertake a wide variety of household and domestic tasks may not be valid measures of functional capacity. Validity is important because if a measure is not valid then we cannot be sure that variations in scores between individuals actually reflect variations in the distribution of the variable under consideration.

Validity is, however, a rather difficult concept to evaluate as it consists of at least three aspects:

1. **relevance** – this is the extent to which the measure collects the type of data the researcher is interested in;
2. **completeness** – the extent to which the measure collects all the information of relevance;
3. **accuracy** – the credibility or reliance which can be attached to the measurements collected.

Texts upon research methodology deal with problems of validity in more detail. However it is an aspect of research design which the gerontologist (or any other social scientist) should bear in mind when evaluating research findings.

SAMPLING

A crucial problem in social gerontology, as in other social research enterprises, is sampling. Seldom is it necessary to interview an entire population to answer a specific research question. Rather, it is the usual practice to study a representative sample of the population of interest. The definition of this population will depend upon the specific research question under investigation. To give one example, a survey of the elderly living at home will require a sample of the entire elderly population normally resident in the community. In contrast a study of satisfaction with the hospital service will require a sample of those in contact with the service. Thus it is crucial that the population the researcher studies is accurately defined.

Obtaining appropriate samples is often difficult, especially if the researcher is interested in the general population of elderly, because there are few readily available lists of elderly people (or indeed any other age group). One list often used by researchers in Britain as a sampling frame is the electoral register. This lists, for each electoral area, the name and address of those individuals eligible to vote in elections. However it does not list the age of voters. The list is updated annually by the local authority. As a sample source this has several well known deficiencies, especially the under-representation of those in multi-occupied dwellings, members of ethnic minority groups and those with high rates of residential mobility.

The electoral roll is used as the basis for selecting citizens for jury service. Currently, individuals over 70 may exclude themselves from jury service and are identified on the register. However not all the over 70s choose to so identify themselves. It is unclear exactly what fraction do exclude themselves from jury service. However it is probable that those who do exclude themselves are in some way different from the general population of those aged over 70. For example, they may be less healthy than those who indicate that they are available for jury service. Thus any sample selected from the electoral roll may be subject to bias and may not be representative of the total population in which the researcher is interested.

In Britain primary medical treatment is provided free under the National Health Service (NHS). Most of the population register with a general medical practitioner (GP). Older people are identifiable from the age–sex registers kept by many, but not all, GPs or from the lists held by the local Family Health Services Authority. However access to such data is fraught with ethical and practical difficulties, especially for the non-clinically-qualified researcher. In addition the researcher must also take into account the inaccuracies inherent in this sampling frame, especially the presence in the records of patients who are either dead or have left the area.

Samples of older people drawn from membership lists of clubs and organizations will usually over-represent the healthy and the middle class. Studies based upon lists derived from those in institutions or receiving social services will over-emphasize the chronically ill and dependent. Observations based upon such samples must not be inferred as being attributable to all the elderly but may only safely be extrapolated to the population under investigation.

Social gerontologists often use as samples populations for which lists are readily available. However these are often of questionable validity and limited utility for the study of ageing in the general population. The student of social gerontology must pay great attention to the selection of the sample which (s)he is going to study. In interpreting research, attention must be paid to the samples upon which specific studies are based for this is of crucial importance in assessing the generality of the results. It is incorrect to make inferences about the characteristics of the general population of older people from studies carried out on samples of the elderly resident in institutions.

RESPONSE RATES

Many social investigations of the older people collect data by the use of questionnaire surveys. Such questionnaires may be administered either by using an interviewer or by post. When discussing the results of a survey the social gerontologist must pay great attention to the response rate. This is usually defined as the percentage of the total sample for whom a questionnaire was completed. The response rate is of import- ance because it indicates what percentage of the study group failed to complete an interview. It is not correct to assume that those who do not respond to a survey possess characteristics identical to those who do respond. Non-responders may well be an unrepresentative fraction of the sample. Consequently the measured results may be subject to bias. For example non-responders may be less (or more) healthy than responders.

The researcher can estimate the degree of bias in the results brought about by non-response if (s)he knows something of the characteristics of the non-responders. There are few data available about the characteris- tics of non-responders in surveys of the elderly. However evidence from a survey in Wales indicates that non-response to a postal survey increases with age and disability (Victor, 1984). Oppenheim (1966) suggests that in postal surveys non-responders are similar in characteristics to those who respond late. However the survey undertaken by the author did not support this suggestion.

It is also of interest to know why subjects refuse to participate in a survey. Knowledge of the reasons for non-response can help the researcher to design research instruments that are intended to maximize response, especially from those least keen to participate. There are few data available about what factors discourage older people from partici- pating in surveys. In a study of the use of a postal questionnaire with older people the author found no evidence to suggest that the length of the schedule encourages non-response (Victor, 1984). This finding is probably equally valid for direct interview surveys. Non-response does seem to be encouraged when the subject does not feel that (s)he is an appropriate subjects for interview. In a survey of elderly people after dis- charge from hospital Victor (1984) found that a substantial number of non-responders refused to participate in the study because they did not feel that it applied to them, as they had only been into hospital for tests or elective surgery. This feeling that the study does not apply to them may explain the above-average non-response rates amongst elderly people selected for participation in surveys of the general population such as the government sponsored General Household Survey.

In order to minimize potential sources of bias in the data response rates of at least 80% are recommended (Moser and Kalton, 1975). However response rates for surveys of the elderly have varied enormously both between studies and between types of survey. Response rates in inter- viewer-administered surveys of the elderly have varied from 96% (Vetter, Jones and Victor, 1984a) to 48% (Herbst, 1981). Response rates for postal surveys have ranged from 94% (Wilcock, 1979) to 68% (McDonnell *et al.* 1979).

DISSEMINATION OF RESEARCH

Gerontologists, like other researchers, are reliant upon the co-operation of many individuals to undertake their research. This includes those who participate in the research as well as those who allow their patients or premises to be used. Thus the gerontologist has a considerable responsibility to disseminate back to these individuals and more widely the results of the research in which they participated or cooperated. This may be achieved in a variety of ways, including sending out copies of the research reports, holding seminars for local groups as well as the more traditional academic pursuits of writing books and articles and presenting papers at conferences.

RESEARCH DESIGNS

There are a variety of different styles and designs of research which the gerontologist may use to answer her/his particular research question. These are summarized below, as are the salient advantages and disadvantages of each approach.

Cross-sectional research

Most research in social gerontology is cross-sectional in design. This means that inferences about the effects of ageing are made by comparing the characteristics of groups of people of different ages at a single point in time. For example people between the ages of 65 and 74 may be compared, in terms of their attitudes towards divorce, to those aged 75 and over. This may reveal that older subjects hold a much more negative view of divorce than the younger sample members.

This type of research design assumes that observing people of different ages at a single point in time has the same effect as observing a single group as they move through the lifecycle. This assumption is questionable because people of different ages at the same point in time vary along dimensions other than age, such as social class, gender or ethnic minority status. This research technique, whilst it can show differences between age groups, cannot state whether such difference are due to age, cohort or period effects.

The popularity of cross-sectional research arises because, compared with longitudinal studies, it is comparatively cheap and easy to undertake. Although it has limitations, cross-section research is not entirely inappropriate for the study of ageing, for such data may be subject to 'cohort' style analysis. The existence of surveys repeated over a period of years using similar questions, such as the General Household Survey, can facilitate the examination of trends over time.

Longitudinal research

The central concern of social gerontology is the nature of age changes. Longitudinal research design is usually the most appropriate approach for the gerontologist and involves following a sample of respondents over a period of time. The length of follow-up may range from a few months to a entire lifetime, depending upon the topic under investigation.

To illustrate the basic differences in approach between cross-sectional and longitudinal studies we can consider the example of a researcher interested in investigating the effect of retirement. A cross-sectional study design would involve the comparison of a group of workers and retired people at a single point in time. Such a study might observe differences between the two groups but could not state, with precision, whether the differences were due to the effect of retirement or variations between the two groups. A longitudinal research design would select a sample of workers and collect data from them whilst they were employed and as they moved into retirement. Thus we would be able to state with some certainty if attitude and behaviour changed in retirement.

Longitudinal research is, however, not without its own logistic, administrative and scientific difficulties. This research technique involves repeated contact with, and the tracing of, sample members. This is expensive, labour-intensive and time-consuming. Taking part in such a study requires a high level of commitment from sample members and researchers involved in the project. Enthusiasm for the study, by either researchers or researched, may well decrease over time. We do not know how participation in a long-term follow-up survey influences sample members. For example, a sample involved in a long-term health study may have been representative of the population at the time of selection. Repeated interviews and health checks over a period of years may influence the characteristics of the group and render them no longer representative of the population.

Apart from the practical problems of maintaining contact with sample members, there are statistical problems over how those who die or drop out of the study should be presented in the analysis. Deaths and refusals to participate in subsequent rounds of the survey will reduce the numbers involved and may bias the results. Those who drop out of the study, or who are lost, may be older or less healthy than the rest of the sample, thereby making the remaining sample no longer representative of its original population.

Whilst the scientific merit of this method of studying ageing is generally recognized, few such studies have been funded in Britain. Here the major longitudinal studies undertaken have been concerned with child development. However in Edinburgh there was a 5-year longitudinal study of the clinical effects of ageing (Milne, 1985). This was a small study with an initial sample of 489 subjects, which had decreased to 261 at the end of the study. However in both Europe and North America there have been several extensive studies of ageing.

The case study

Another methodological approach to the study of ageing is the case study. As its name implies this is an in-depth study of a single case. Typically, such studies are pursued over a long period of time and are highly intensive. The case under study may be a single person, or a detailed account of a social process or event, such as case conferences for the allocation of services to older people. Such studies often provide considerable insight into the social aspects of ageing. The disadvantage is, however, that it is difficult to generalize from the findings of case studies unless the individual cases can be coordinated into a substantial integrated sample.

Participant observation

This is a technique often used by sociologists in which the researcher becomes part of the group, or event, that (s)he is studying. A classic example of this approach is the study of gangs in the 'Little Italy' district of Boston by W.F. Whyte (1955). This approach could be used, for example, to study the interaction amongst residents of an institution by a researcher who was employed as a staff member in the home under study. Staff–patient interaction, or the 'culture' of different types of institutional setting or professional group dealing with older people are all aspects of gerontology which could be approached by participant observation.

However, there are number of problems to this approach. First, the researcher has to gain access to the group under study. This may prove very difficult. Perhaps there is a role here for older researchers/volunteers to work in this field. If the researcher wants, for example, to look at life on a long-stay geriatric ward prior approval of senior medical staff, nursing staff, paramedical staff, management and unions may be required. The researcher must also try to guard against having any influence upon the group or events that (s)he is studying. Also (s)he must be wary of becoming too involved with the group under investigation and compromising her/his objectivity. This is referred to in the research methods literature as 'going native'.

Secondary data analysis

Although not a research design in itself, secondary data analysis can be a useful technique for the gerontologist to employ, especially in times when research funds are in short supply. This approach involves the re-analysis of data collected for a specific purpose to consider further research questions. Such data usually consists of cross-sectional material, although longitudinal studies may be available. In Britain the surveys undertaken by the Government such as the General Household Survey (GHS), the Family Expenditure Survey (FES) and the Labour Force Survey (LFS) are subject to considerable secondary analysis by the academic community. These surveys are undertaken on a regular basis and, because they often use very similar questions, may be used to examine trends over time for a variety of issues. Other *ad hoc* surveys and data from surveys in Europe and North America can also provide a fruitful source of data for the social gerontologist. In Britain many such surveys are lodged at the ESRC Data Archive at the University of Essex.

The major limitation of secondary analysis for the gerontologist is that most surveys rarely contain sufficient numbers of older people and non-response rates tend to be highest amongst the older age groups. This criticism is less relevant to the major government-sponsored surveys, which often include substantial numbers of older people. The researcher must remember who collected the data set and why as this has an important influence upon the conceptualization of old age presented by the data.

CONCLUSION

In this chapter we have seen that observed age differences in behaviour may be attributed to three mechanisms; age effects, cohort effects and period effects. For an age difference to be classified as an intrinsic age effect the causative mechanism must be an inevitable consequence of growing older which is neither culturally nor historically specific. Reactive age effects are fashioned by the social context in which ageing is experienced and therefore demonstrate variation between, and within, cultures. An alternative explanation for age differences in behaviour is to be found in period effects. There are those who doubt the existence of period effects and they do seem to be the most difficult to evaluate. Cohort effects are probably responsible for some of the observed variations between groups in social behaviour and attitudes. However we have shown that it is unwise to group whole birth cohorts together upon the basis of an assumed common experience. Cohorts are sub-divided in terms of a number of parameters including class, ethnicity and gender. These variables will influence the experience of a particular historical event such as the inter-war depression or the progressive society of the 1960s. In attempting to offer cohort explanations for age-related variations in attitudes, we must remember that the group commonly referred to as 'the elderly' includes at least three separate cohorts.

It is common to see these three explanations for age differences as competing perspectives that are mutually exclusive. This is rather extreme and it seems likely that many age differences reflect the influence of both cohort and reactive age effects. As yet there has been insufficient cross-national, cross-cultural and historical research for us to determine whether any of the observed age-related changes are intrinsic age effects. In designing specific research studies the social gerontologist must use appropriate research designs, measurement techniques and samples so that (s)he may unambiguously identify the contribution made by cohort and ageing effects to observed age-specific variations in behaviour.

As with other forms of social research, it is important that the gerontologist minimizes the bias within the data by selecting appropriate samples and achieving adequate response rates. Simply because the subjects of investigation are older people does not excuse the poor research design, inadequate questionnaires and low response rates that some investigators have reported.

Social gerontological research can be undertaken using a variety of designs and approaches. The precise research design to be employed depends upon the question that the researcher wishes to answer. As with other social research enterprises the gerontologist must be aware of the limitations imposed by the type of sample population and measurement techniques employed. Populations should not be researched simply because they are readily available. In particular, studies based upon samples of volunteers should be avoided as data based upon such study groups tell us nothing about the wider population of older people. Erroneous generalizations and extrapolations should not be made from inappropriate study populations. Perhaps one reason why old age is viewed in such a negative way by society is that many early research studies were based upon samples drawn from institutions, thereby giving a highly biased picture of the nature of old age. As gerontologists we have a responsibility to see that research is properly designed, conducted and interpreted so that we do not contribute to the validation of the myths and stereotypes of later life.

4

Historical and cultural perspectives on ageing

The experience of ageing varies between different types of society and within the same society at different points in time. Depending upon the structure of the society and its attitudes towards older people, the aged may be better or worse off. Before examining the position of the elderly in modern industrial society, we consider their position at earlier periods in time as illustrated by the societies of the ancient world and pre-literate societies. We then examine the theory of ageing and modernization. This provides us with a context in which to evaluate the social position of the elderly in our own society. To begin the chapter we examine historical variations in life expectancy.

HISTORICAL VARIATIONS IN LIFE EXPECTANCY

Life expectancy, that is the age to which the average person may expect to live, has varied over time. Evidence for the calculation of life expectancy in earlier times has been collected from archaeological and palaeo-demographic sources such as burial records, analysis of skeletons and administrative records. These records are incomplete and rather speculative. Consequently, we should regard life expectancies for earlier historical periods as approximate guides to the average lifespan.

Prehistoric times

There are few data available about life expectancy in the very earliest times. Expectation of life at birth in prehistoric times was probably about 21 years (Acsadi and Nemeskeri, 1970). Although the data are very patchy, males had a longer life expectancy than females.

Ancient societies

Some evidence about life expectancy is available for the societies of the ancient classical world. At birth, the average Egyptian male could expect to live to about 22 years of age. Those who survived early childhood could have expected to live to 25 whilst those who reached 25 could expect to live to the age of 48.

In Rome, life expectancy at birth was 30 years for a male and 23 years for a female. This lower female life expectancy presumably reflecting the hazards associated with childbirth. There were variations in life expectancy between the different groups which made up ancient Rome. Male and female slaves could expect to live, on average, for 17 years. In the professional classes the comparable life expectancies were 40 and 23 respectively. Based upon an analysis of burial records the Roman scientist Ulpianus produced a life table for both males and females. These data, which are shown in Table 4.1, probably represent the earliest known actuarial calculations.

Table 4.1 Expectation of life in ancient Rome at various ages (Ascadi and Nemesker, 1970)

Age	Years of life expected
0–20	30
35–40	20
49–50	10
60+	5

Medieval England

The expectation of life at birth in medieval England was, as Table 4.2 shows, much affected by the famines, wars and epidemics that characterized that period. This resulted in fluctuations in life expectancy between birth cohorts. An individual born in the period 1276–1300 could expect to

Table 4.2 Expectation of life in mediaeval England (Ascadi and Nemesker, 1970)

| Life expectancy at age | Birth cohort | | | |
	Pre-1276	1346–75	1401–25	1426–50
0	35.3	17.3	23.8	32.8
20	28.7	23.9	29.4	27.4
40	17.8	18.1	19.3	20.4
60	9.4	10.9	10.5	13.7

live for 31 years. This compares with only 17 years for an individual born in the period 1346–1375. During the entire feudal period average life expectancy at birth rarely exceeded 30–35 years. Expectation of life at age 60 years shows much less variation because it was less influenced by the hazards noted above. Indeed life expectancy for those who reached 60 years of age increased by about 4 years during the 200 years between 1200 and 1400.

The pre-industrial period

There were no significant changes in life expectancy in the years leading up to the Industrial Revolution. Males still continued to have a longer life expectancy than females. Rural areas probably had a better expectation of life than urban areas. In 1662 Graunt, using bills of mortality for London, calculated that the expectation of life at birth in the capital was 18.2 years. His analysis showed that 36% of the population of London died before their fifth birthday whilst 60% had died before the age of 25.

The Industrial Revolution

With the advent of industrialization in the early 19th century, there was relatively little change in life expectancy. Table 4.3 shows that life expectancy at birth for both males and females in England in 1841 had increased by only 8 years during the previous 400 years. Improved maternal mortality rates are reflected in the comparability of life expectancy for males and females. Having attained the age of 60 people could then expect to live well into their 70s and possibly longer.

These life expectancies were characteristic of Europe as a whole. In France, during the period 1817–31, the average male could expect to live for 38 years and the average female to 40 years. In Britain the life expectancies were 40 years and 42 years respectively.

Table 4.3 England and Wales: life expectancy in 1841 (Ascadi and Nemesker, 1970)

Life expectancy at age	Males	Females
0	40.19	42.18
20	39.88	40.81
40	26.56	27.72
60	13.50	14.40

THE POSITION OF ELDERLY PEOPLE IN HISTORICAL SOCIETIES

The study of old age in historical societies is difficult. There is little readily available documentary evidence, for written records often fail to differentiate between older people and other groups of adults. Legend, myth and literature depict old age in ancient times but it is doubtful if these portraits bear much resemblance to the reality.

There are several further limitations to the study of old age in antiquity. The position of the old is usually described from the perspective of the ruling social classes; few references relate to the aged poor. Most accounts consider old age from the male point of view; the data rarely allow us to comment about the role and status of old women in the ancient world.

Both ancient China and Israel were societies typified by respect for the old and a linking of old age with wisdom. In the Taoist religion of China the ultimate objective of man was a long life and their teachings stated that, after the age of 60, man was released from worldly desires and became a spiritual being. Amongst the ancient Jews old age was seen as the ultimate reward of virtue with the very old ascribed the role of God's intermediary and chosen ones. Older males, in both societies, exercised considerable political power. In Israel the Sanhedrim, the supreme court and legal body, was composed of older males. Respect for the old permeated throughout both societies and people would often pretend to be older than they really were in order to benefit from this.

Ancient China and Israel were both centrally organized, authoritarian hierarchies. This mode of social organization was mirrored by the family. In China total obedience was given to the oldest male and the patrician's authority did not lessen with age. Despite their generally oppressed state, the status of women increased with age. It was common for older women to control the raising of the grandchildren. Despite its elements of matriarchal descent, ancient Israel was also strongly patriarchal. The family was ruled by the oldest male who exercised considerable authority over the household and all its dealings.

Chinese literature of this period never depicts old age as a burden or a curse. This contrasts with the earliest known Western text that relates to old age. Ptah-hotep, a philosopher and poet of ancient Egypt, wrote in 2500 BC:

How hard and painful are the last days of an aged man! He grows weaker every day; his eyes become dim, his ears deaf; his strength fades; his heart knows peace no longer; his mouth falls silent and he speaks no word. The power of his mind lessens and today he cannot remember what yesterday was like. All his bones hurt. Those things which not long ago were done with pleasure are painful now; and taste vanishes. Old age is the worst of misfortunes that can afflict a man.' (de Beavoir, 1972, p. 104)

The Egyptians saw old age as a burden both for the individual and society. Considerable effort was expended in the search for a method of controlling the decline in physical prowess which characterized old age. One such method advocated by the Egyptians was the use of the glands of young animals as a method of rejuvenating the aged.

In ancient Greece deformed or unwanted children were disposed of. However, there is no evidence to suggest that the elderly were dealt with in a similar way. Semantics would suggest that, in the classical world, old age was also attached to the notion of honour. The Greek words *gera* and *geron*, which mean great age, also convey the privilege of age and the rights of seniority. In Homer old age is associated with wisdom; the passage of time bringing experience as well as physical decline. The city states, which constituted the world of classical Greece, were governed by *gerusia* or council of elders and age was generally a qualification necessary for assuming power. In Sparta old age was honoured and the 28 members of the *gerusia* were selected from the oldest and wealthiest members of the city.

Amongst the wealthy the lot of the old is inextricably bound up with property rights. If property is not underwritten by a stable society and institutions, but has to be protected by force of arms, the old are vulnerable. When, however, property is underwritten by the law the physical prowess of the owner becomes irrelevant. Rights, rather than individual abilities, become the criteria by which status and power are defined. Since wealth usually increases over time, this type of arrangement favours the old at the expense of the young. The old then exercise political control to maintain the ruling order and status quo. This was true of both the Greek city states and Rome once they had established strong and unchanging institutions.

The history of ancient Rome illustrates very well the close relationship between the state of the old and the stability of society. At some points in their history the Romans disposed of their old people by drowning them. Once the major social and legal institutions were established, and property guaranteed by law, there was no question of removing the older members of society. A Roman's wealth came from land, trade and money-lending and usually increased over his lifetime. It was the wealthy who were the chief sources of power and this group contained a high proportion of old men. Until the second century BC the republic was ruled by a conservative, self perpetuating oligarchy dominated by elderly people.

Whilst the regimes of Ancient Greece remained aristocratic and conservative, the laws of Solon gave power to the old in Athens. The advent of democracy in the time of Cleishenes reduced the privileges of the older generation but they still retained some power. Judges were confined to those over 60, as were the *exegetes*, the interpreters of the law. Overall, however, their authority was weakened and they were shown little respect in public or private life. Similarly the collapse of the ruling oligarchy in Rome resulted in a decline in the power of elderly people.

Both Plato and Aristotle considered old age and came to rather different conclusions. The philosophy of Plato considered that the soul was divorced from the body. Thus the physical decline which accompanied old age did not affect the soul. Plato saw old age as a time of release from physical desires, when man could concentrate upon the spiritual aspects of life. Old age was seen by Plato as a time of peace and liberation. Under Platonic philosophy the role of the old was to command and of the young to obey. In his Republic many of the important functions of the state are given to men aged 50–70.

The philosophy of Aristotle was predicated upon the assumption that man existed in a union between body and soul. Any deterioration in physical ability influenced the entire being. Therefore, the body had to remain healthy for old age to be considered happy. Wisdom he thought developed up to the age of 50 and then declined. Experience is seen, not as a means of progress, but rather of decay. In Aristotle's ideal state the old were removed from all positions of power except the priesthood where they had little more to do than offer wise advice.

With the collapse of the Roman oligarchy the power of the old withered. From the time of the Gracchi onwards the power of the Senate decreased and the Emperor ruled without recourse to them. Concurrently legal reform circumscribed the power of the father over his family.

In response to this decrease in power of the elderly Cicero wrote his essay *Cato the Elder on Old Age*. Cicero identifies four major reasons why old age was perceived as a time of decline. These were: the withdrawal of older people from work; physical deterioration; a reduction of interest in physical pleasures; and the awareness of impending death. He refutes these statements and strongly argues that the old could accomplish much in society because of their wisdom, maturity and good council. He suggests that physical deterioration does not affect these mental abilities. He also considers the loss of interest in the pleasures of the flesh to be one of the greatest advantages the old have over the young.

The end of the ancient world is defined of the rise of Christianity and the invasion of the barbarians. History tells us little about the place of the elderly in barbarian society. Julius Caesar reported that they killed those sick and old who wished to die. As the society was orientated around fighting, to die of old age was probably seen as a source of great shame. The Dark Ages were a period of destruction and confusion and it seems that there was little place for the person rich in experience and wisdom. When feudal society began to emerge from this period of confusion it seems that this mode of social organization also had no role for elderly people.

The effect of the rise of Christianity upon the social role of elderly people is difficult to assess. However, the Church did make one positive contribution to improving the lot of the elderly. From about the fourth century onwards the Church built hospitals and stressed the importance of giving alms. Although elderly people are not specifically mentioned it seems likely that they benefited from this charity. The writings of St Paul are more pertinent as they evaluate the status of older people in both prestige and responsibility.

AGEING AND MODERNIZATION

The position of the elderly in pre-industrial society is usually described as one of respect and authority. Typically, pre-industrial society is depicted as the 'golden age' of ageing and the elderly. This is usually contrasted with their position in modern society where older people are thought to be worse off because they are consigned to meaningless retirement, neglected by their family and ignored by the prevailing youth culture.

One of the first to advance the idea that industrialization resulted in a decrease in the status of the old was Burgess (1960). He argued that urbanization and industrialization combined to undermine the extended family and replace it with the nuclear family as the primary unit of society. This, he argued, isolated elderly people from both society and the family.

These ideas were developed further by Cowgill (1974a, b) and Cowgill and Holmes (1972). These authors advanced the argument a stage further and included societies in different stages of development. They studied ageing in 14 different societies ranging from pre-literate to modern industrial. Implicit within this approach was the assumption that pre-literate primitive cultures were equivalent to pre-industrial western societies. These societies were arranged along a linear continuum according to their degree of 'modernization'.

The process of modernization was defined by four parameters; improvements in medical technology; the application to the economy of science and technology; urbanization; and mass education. Cowgill and Holmes (1972) argued that improvements in health care lead to an ageing of the population. The decrease in the potency of death results in an ageing of the working population and a decrease in job opportunities for the young. Thus inter-generational tensions are created by the competition for jobs. Retirement then becomes a social substitute for death and creates job opportunities for the young. However, the dominance of the prevailing work ethic results in a 'devaluing' of retirement. Additionally economic and technological developments devalue the employment skills of the old. Urbanization attracts young people from the rural areas, resulting in a break-up of the extended family. Finally, the development of mass education reduces the hold older people have over younger people. Changes in these four factors contributed, it was argued, to a decrease in the status of the elderly in modern society.

Cowgill suggests that these processes combine with other characteristics of developing societies to produce a lower status amongst the elderly compared with pre-industrial societies. In such developing social settings, youth and progress are extolled. The traditions and experience of the elderly are seen as irrelevant. The model suggests that the role of elderly people becomes devalued and their reduced power and prestige places them at a disadvantage. The old become socially and physically abandoned and live a marginal existence on the fringes of society.

Implicit within this theory is the notion that pre-industrial societies are uniform and are characterized by a positive attitude towards the elderly. Secondly, it assumes there has been a before-and-after situation within societies with regard to the position of the elderly and that there has been a smooth, uniform, linear transition from one type of society to another. These assumptions, as we shall see below, are rather simplistic when compared with the complex realities of human patterns of social organization.

The elderly in pre-industrial society

It is virtually impossible to establish precisely the number and percentage of elderly people in pre-industrial societies. The further we go back in history, the fewer old people there are and old age is ascribed at early chronological dates. Amongst the Arawak of British Columbia, the Adamanese of Burma, the Bontoc Indians of the Philippines, as well as various groups of Eskimos, few people lived to the age of 50 or over. Simmons (1960) suggests that fewer than 3 per cent of the populations of pre-literate societies were aged over 65.

Although there were fewer old people in primitive societies, some individuals lived to similar ages as now. There are scattered references in the anthropological literature to the great ages achieved by people in such diverse settings as the Hopi, Iroquois and Chippewa Indians of North America, the Abipone of South America and the Chin of Burma. Whilst evidence of longevity is found in most primitive societies, this should be regarded as exceptional from the general pattern of a short lifespan and the early onset of old age.

As well as comprising a smaller percentage of the entire population the elderly age group demonstrated a rather different profile from that seen in modern industrial societies. Amongst pre-literate societies the sexes were evenly balanced in the older age groups. This balance reflects the very high mortality rate associated with child-bearing in such societies.

Although the definition of old age has varied both over time and between cultures, every known society has an identified category of people who are classified, either by chronology, physiology or generation, as old. In all cases these people have different rights, privileges and duties from those enjoyed by their juniors. It is almost universally true that societies divide the aged into two categories: those who are still able to fend for themselves and those who are totally dependent for their well-being on other members of the social group.

In examining cultural variation in ageing, anthropologists assume certain universal parameters within which this variation manifests itself. First, like other social groups, older people are not passive actors in a system which is determined by external influences. Rather the elderly interact, in both pre-industrial and modern societies, within the limits established by factors which they cannot control. The aged in any society are constantly adapting to altering social conditions and strive to shape events to suit their own goals. Second, the old have to adapt within the confines established by their social setting such as the nature of the environment or the demographic and economic structure of the society. Third, common goals of all older people are assumed to be the attainment of physical and emotional security, social respect and reassurance that they are contributing to the life of the family and wider social group.

In attempting to achieve these goals two factors are influential. First is the relationship between the costs the old people represent to the group and the contribution they make; second, the degree of control old people maintain over resources required by others to achieve their own goals. In some settings specific powers or privileges accrue to old people collectively. In others, old people may not obtain power simply because of age but they may gain substantial power as individuals. The position of the old within any particular social group may be expressed in terms of the relationship between the contributions of the aged balanced against the costs incurred by the group, and compounded by the degree of control the old exercise over power or scarce resources.

Perhaps the most crucial factor in determining the status of older people in primitive societies was the actual type of social organization. The position of older people in nomadic groups contrasts sharply with more settled agricultural societies. In social groups consisting of a few hundred people existing by hunting or fishing, where there is constant mobility, the basic position of older people is determined by the simple relationship between their costs and their contributions. Under the extremely harsh conditions of life that typify nomadic hunting and fishing social groups, the veneration of the old is a luxury which can be ill afforded. Consequently, neglect and abandonment of elderly people were common practices. Simmons (1945) reported that the practice was customary amongst 18 out of the 39 tribes he studied.

The roles of men and women in nomadic hunting and fishing groups differ markedly. For men, old age tends to be defined by the withdrawal from the activity of hunting and fishing. Amongst the Siriono Indians of Bolivia this often occurs between the ages of 30 and 40 years. Since old men can no longer hunt and contribute to the food stocks of the tribe, old age in such social groups is despised. Old hunters are made to feel unwanted and useless.

Women fare a little better in this type of social group. This may be because women do not have to hunt; rather they are expected to walk and gather berries and look after the domestic chores. These are activities which can be sustained for longer than the more arduous activities of hunting. Additionally older women may look after the children, or the sick, thereby freeing younger women for more productive activities.

Amongst the Bolivian Siriono tribe children neglect their parents and overlook them when the food is being distributed. Those who cannot hunt or fish are relegated to a position of obscurity and are abandoned when they are too ill to keep up with the group. Similarly the Fang tribe of the upper Gaboon, Hopi, Creek and Crow Indians and the Bushmen of South Africa all abandoned their elderly, often in a hut constructed specially for the purpose. Simmons (1960, p. 73) quotes a missionary, James Moffat, who reported an old Hottentot woman he found in the desert who said 'my own children... have left me here to die...'. The Eskimo would persuade the old to go and lie in the snow and await death, whilst the Yakuts of Siberia expelled them from the family group and forced them to become beggars and slaves.

Amongst some other nomadic societies the elderly were put to death, often with great ceremony. This was much a less common practice than simple abandonment or neglect. The Koryak of North Siberia would kill the old as well as the incurably ill. De Beauvoir (1972) describes how the Chokchee tribe of Siberia engaged in the ceremonial slaughter of the aged. A great feast would be held in their honour and the whole community ate seal meat and drank whisky. The condemned man would then be strangled from behind by his son or younger brother.

Many societies distinguish between those who are old, but still healthy, and the frailer elderly. An example of this is the semi-nomadic Hottentots of Africa. The elderly are important to the social life of the tribe. They serve as the guardians of the tribe's culture and preside over rites of passage such as widowhood, convalescence or adolescence. However despite this importance, they are neglected once their faculties start to deteriorate. After a feast at which all the village came to say goodbye the old person would be escorted to a remote hut where (s)he would die of hunger or be killed by wild beasts. The Ojibway Indians, who lived near

Lake Winnipeg, would either abandon their frail elderly or ritually put them to death.

There seems to be little cultural variation in the situation of the frail elderly; they are almost universally regarded as a burden. The Chippewa abandoned them to die when the burden of supporting them endangered the existence of the group or family. Where provision is made for their care, such as in Tongan society, this is usually done very grudgingly.

Not all pre-literate nomadic tribes engaged in the ritual slaughter or abandonment of the elderly. The Yaghan of the Tierra del Fuego region, amongst the most primitive of all known tribes, display great love and affection for their old. Amongst the Aleuts of the Aleutian Islands to abandon the old would be a disgrace. In this group the young often sacrifice themselves for their parents.

Societies characterized by permanent residence and stable food supplies can be more magnanimous towards those who become dependent. Ancient Israel, China and the Incas of Peru developed sophisticated rules for the sharing of food which accorded special treatment to the old and feeble. Aged Incas were fed and clothed from the public storehouse and this right was enshrined in law. Aztec dependants were cared for out of the public purse; a fraction of the tributes that came in from the provinces and the spoils of war were allocated for widows, orphans, the sick and the old.

In stable farming economies opportunities for the elderly to make an economic contribution exist in ways which are impossible in simple hunting societies. In Inca Peru older people unfit for full work were employed as scarecrows to frighten the birds and rodents from the field. Older Chippewa women supervised younger workers and older Andamanese cared for the young and sick and supervised such activities as the moving of camps and the construction of canoes.

Amongst non-nomadic social groups the position of the elderly is also related to their ability to exercise power or control over other members of the social group. In many societies older people gain access to positions in which the customs and laws of the group give them substantial political power.

Within any society it is possible to differentiate two types of politically powerful position that the elderly may occupy. First, power may be ascribed automatically to everyone (or almost everyone) of a specific culturally defined age level. An example of this would be age-stratified social groups where the elders exercise power as a group, as in several East African tribes. In such arrangements the elderly use their accumulation of experience, skill and tact in the political, civil and legal affairs of the group. This, however, requires a form of social organization in which wisdom and knowledge are related to old age. This type of social organization may be mirrored within the family, the group being ruled by the oldest male.

The second type of powerful position associated with old age is where it is held by some old people to the exclusion of others. Simmons (1960) notes that 56 out of the 71 tribes he studied had old chiefs and that older members of the tribes invariably fulfilled the function of councillors to the chief. No tribes had rules which excluded rulers because of their age. However age *per se* was not the sole qualification for such positions. Usually only older males, who have previously demonstrated qualities of leadership would be appointed. Alternatively such leaders could be selected from the households of the wealthy members of the tribe. Amongst the Kirghiz of Afghanistan there is a hierarchy of three levels of political office; camp head, lineage head and Khan or head of the entire group. Access to each of these positions is based upon a combination of wealth, ability, and seniority. The holders of these offices are drawn from the oldest, as well as the wealthiest, household heads.

Amongst many groups the position of the elderly is bound up with their control over knowledge, particularly that relating to the ritual and religious practices of the tribe. Whilst there is great variation in the degree to which older people may exercise political power, there is much less variation in the way older people monopolize knowledge, particularly that relating to ritual or religious practice. The Kikuyu of Mount Kenya are respected because of their wisdom. The elders are viewed as pious, holy beings who are detached from the world. Thus they act as judges because they are thought to be free of passion and capable of impartial decisions. Old women are much respected, especially when they have no teeth; then they are considered full of wisdom and are buried with ceremony when they die, instead of being left to the hyenas.

The old often acquire high status and privilege because of their memories. An example of this is the Miao who reside in the high forest country of China and Thailand. It is the old who pass on the traditions of the group and it is this ability which is the source of their esteem. Here the elderly act as the bearers and interpreters of culture and thereby provide cultural continuity.

The role of memory is of great importance to the Moslem Mendes of Sierra Leone. To be a chief a man must know the history of the country, the lives of the founders and the genealogy of the tribe. This knowledge is passed on from their ancestors. The tribe live in great intimacy with the spirits of their immediate forefathers. As the elderly are closer to the spirits than the rest of the household, they act as mediators between the spiritual and secular worlds.

Healing and medicine are specializations of the elderly amongst many social groups, being based upon a both spiritual power and practical medical skills. Amongst the !Kung San, the old act as healers, using their divine powers to cure various maladies. Older women often fulfil the roles of midwife and paediatric nurse amongst many primitive groups.

Older people will also be respected if they are seen as the guardians of the tribe's technical, legal or social knowledge. Elliot (1886) describes how, amongst the Aleuts of the northern Pacific, old men would take it upon themselves to educate the children. Older people's knowledge may enable them to settle disputes as well as, perhaps, having technical expertise in such areas as navigation or canoe building. The power of aged men of the Tiv in Nigeria stems from their cultural contribution. Officially all the old are respected. However, in practice, an old man has no influence unless he possesses knowledge or ability. Naturally these roles as guardians of culture and knowledge are diminished when traditions and knowledge are transmitted in a written, rather than oral, form.

In traditionally orientated societies the elderly may be ascribed significance if they are seen as links with the past, or with the supernatural. Older people often take on the roles of priests or leaders of religious rites; functioning as intermediaries between man and the unknown. This function relies upon qualities other than sheer physical prowess. Amongst the Polar Eskimos the elderly were reputed to be able to produce storms or calms. For the Aranda of the Australian forests the old were the directors of the tribe's religious life. Only they could touch the *churinga*, the holy stones, that are the symbols of mythical ancestors. Amongst the Zande of the Sudan the domination of the aged man is rooted in his supernatural powers.

The role of the elderly is related to their ability to control scarce resources within the social group. In hunting and gathering tribes goods belong to those who acquire them. Access to land is 'free'. Those who labour to produce goods from the land own them. The old, who can no longer produce for themselves, are rendered dependent upon others for their livelihood. The situation is more complex in agricultural or pastoral societies. In such settings fields or herds may be conceived of as being the property of a specific individual. Ownership rights are underwritten by the custom and practice of the group. Hence property is based upon right, rather than physical strength that may deteriorate with age. In these settings the elderly may employ younger members to work for them. Access to these goods may be dictated by the elderly, thereby strengthening their position. Property may give the elderly power over other age groups and may be used to extract deference from them. In such situations the young may be dependent upon their elders for such scarce resources as farmland and in order to obtain them will defer to their older kin.

An example of this is given by the Gwembe Tonga of Zambia. This tribe lived in the area flooded in the 1950s to create the Kariba dam. Men secured their position by acquiring land and livestock. Wives were acquired with the land and it was the labour of these women and their children that provided men with support in their old age.

Amongst the Etal Islanders the maintenance of control over property is crucial to a successful old age. Older people, rather than give all their wealth to the younger generation, try to maintain sufficient resources to ensure continued care in old age, usually by the threat of disinheritance.

Finally, the position of the elderly may depend upon the extent to which they are situated within an extended family structure. This may give them positions of respect as well as social and economic security. The extended family links the elderly person into a system of mutual dependence and obligation. Amongst the Lepcha of the Himalayas age is honoured within the family and children take care of their parents. However the elderly without children are rejected and viewed as a curse.

The anthropological evidence suggests that all societies distinguish a category defined as old age. There is little evidence to support the view that pre-literate cultures were characterized by a 'golden age' of the elderly or a universal reverence for the old. Rather, the position of the elderly in pre-literate societies was dependent upon the inter-relationship of the factors summarized below:

1. the type of social organization i.e. nomadic or settled;
2. the physical status of the elderly person;
3. the importance to the society of the experience of the older people;
4. the value of the contribution older people can make to economic, family or cultural activities;
5. the extent to which older people may exercise control over knowledge, ritual or religious practices;
6. the extent to which older people retain 'status' from activities from which they have now retired;
7. the extent to which older people exercise direct control over the destiny of others by the control of scarce resources or political power.

Ageing and modernization: a historical approach

The theory of modernization is premised upon the assumption that preliterate societies may be used as approximations for western industrial society at previous points in history. We have demonstrated that it is insufficient to compensate for the lack of knowledge about the status of the old in western countries at previous points in time by using preliterate societies as analogies. When classifying societies on a continuum ranging from pre-literate to industrial we are simply undertaking an exercise in taxonomy. The criteria by which these definitions are arrived at are set entirely by criteria relevant to the modern industrial society.

Attributes found in exclusively in pre-industrial societies are excluded from the analysis. Societies which are the same on a classifying variable, such as the fraction of the population employed in agriculture, may exhibit substantial variation in other dimensions.

A fundamental criticism of the theory of ageing and modernization is that it is ahistorical. As an alternative to this approach several authors have used historical methods to examine the relationships between ageing and modernization (Fisher, 1978; Achenbaum, 1978; Quadagno, 1982). Thomas (1976) examined old age in early modern England. He rejects the idea of a 'golden age' and suggests that, in fact, old age was a time of degradation from which the only protection was wealth. In France, Stearns (1977) demonstrates that the traditional attitude towards the old was disdain rather than veneration or respect.

Quadagno (1982) examined the position of the elderly in Britain during the 19th century with respect to each of the major dimensions of modernization theory. Her analysis indicates that there was no golden age and no simple transition from pre-industrial to industrial society. The theory of ageing and modernization argues that industrialization brought about a decline in household-based production. A direct consequence of this was a decline in the status of the old. This view has as its premise the romantic notion that the old held both power and prestige in situations of the non-industrial production of goods. Quadagno (1982) demonstrates that the assumption was invalid for Britain and that changes in household methods of production were extremely complex. She argues that the extended family unit was a response to the fragility of the economy and not a means for promoting the veneration and power of the old.

A development of the ageing and modernization theory argues that an increase in state welfare brings about the neglect of the old by their families. Obviously this stance is based upon the assumption that non-familial support of the elderly is unique to industrial society. In the case of Britain this assumption is invalid. State-sponsored support for the old developed in England with the establishment of the Poor Law during the reign of Elizabeth I. Taking the example of the development of pensions Quadagno (1982) argues that there is no evidence that the development of state support for the old weakened the role of the family.

Modernization theory conceptualizes retirement as a feature unique to industrial society. Records for peasant societies refute this assumption. What is unique about its manifestation in modern society is the existence of a state bureaucracy to transfer financial resources between generations. The theory of modernization does not consider the meaning of work and the value attributed to the work undertaken by older people. Most historical data support the view that the work done by older people was very hard, low paid, irregular and degrading. The casual nature of these marginal occupations probably accounts for the popularity of the state pension.

CONCLUSION

The available evidence indicates that life expectancy was, at earlier times in our history, very short. However even within the societies of the ancient world it is important to remember that life expectancy demonstrated important variations between the sexes, social classes and urban and rural residents. One of the 'facts' about ageing which we take for granted as being 'natural' is the greater life expectancy of females than males. However we can see that, in historical times, the converse pattern was true, males demonstrating greater life expectancy than females.

The decreasing status of the elderly with increasing modernization is a theory which has had a substantial impact upon gerontology and the way that society thinks about old age. It is a very romantic notion to think of the elderly, in previous times, as being well treated. Perhaps it allows us to justify, or at least condone, our relative neglect of the elderly. The examples described above demonstrate that modernization, as a social theory, is both seriously flawed and not verified by empirical investigation. Under modernization theory the decline of the family mode of production is seen as leading to the inevitable isolation of the old and a decrease in their power. However this theory is founded on a highly romanticized view of the family and the position of the elderly within it. It is also suggested that non-family support of the elderly is unique to post-industrial society. However, in England at least, there was a basic method of providing for the destitute outside of the family via the Elizabethan Poor Law. Certainly the available historical evidence does not support the view that an increase in state support for the old, via the introduction of pensions, resulted in a neglect of the old by family members.

Thus we can conclude that probably at no time in the past, in Britain at least, was there a time when the old were venerated for themselves. Rather, where the elderly did seem to be in an exalted position this was essentially a result of their control of the power and wealth structures. Theories such as modernization, which appeal to our romantic notions of history, are not based upon any concrete theoretical or empirical grounds. In particular the use of pre-literate societies as analogies for industrial societies such as Britain in pre-industrial times is ill-founded and naive. Consequently in trying to look at the role of the elderly in history we should abandon our romantic illusions and accept the reality that ageing was, for most people, a time of pauperism, degradation and dependency.

5

Images of ageing

Images of ageing exist at two levels; the individual and the societal. In this chapter we shall examine both dimensions. To fully understand the meaning of ageing requires an understanding of its impact upon the self-image of the individual. In addition, we need to know how the wider society perceives the place of older people and the relative status or stigma associated with old age. We also consider some of the more commonly held stereotypes about old age and consider how these views are formed and perpetuated.

INDIVIDUAL IMAGES OF AGEING

Each of us holds an image of ourselves. This self-image is based upon a number of attributes which we ascribe to ourselves such as intelligence, good looks or a short temper. This sense of self-image and identity is reinforced by interaction with others in our social environment. One important aspect of self-image is subjective age identity, as distinct from chronological age. Subjective age identity relates to how old a person feels and what broad age group, such as teenagers or the middle-aged, they identify with.

Subjective age identity

Within western industrial society there is a broad consensus that people become 'old' at about the ages of 60/65 years. This is, however, not necessarily reflected at the individual level. People over these chronological ages may reject labels such as 'old' or 'elderly'. An American study revealed that only a fifth of those aged 60–69 consider the labels 'old' or 'elderly' appropriate to them (Ward, 1984). Even among those aged over 80 years, a third rejected these labels and defined themselves as young or middle-aged.

What conditions or circumstances influence people to adopt (or reject) a particular age identity? For example, what precipitates the dropping of the label 'middle-aged' and the adoption of the identity of an older person? Survey data from America indicate that seven factors identified the transition to old age (Ward, 1984). These were:

1. a specific health problem;
2. retirement;
3. physical and/or mental deterioration;
4. chronological age;
5. restrictions in physical activity;
6. change in social contacts;
7. illness or death of spouse.

Two sets of factors, physical health status and changes in social role, dominate the definition of age identity and the transition to old age. Health and activity seem to be the most important parameters defining age identity. Data from Europe confirm the prominence of physical health and related activities in the definition of old age (Vischer, 1978; Thompson, Itzin and Abendstern, 1990).

Those in good health (or who perceive their health as good), or with high activity levels, continue to perceive themselves as middle-aged. Often older people can identify a particular incident such as a fall, stroke or heart attack which made them feel that they were growing old. However health problems need not be acute to bring about a feeling of ageing. Tiring easily, or difficulties in driving or walking, may be frequent small reminders to people that they are not as young and fit as they once were. However such observations are not exclusive to elders and may apply equally well to athletes who may observe such deterioration in 'fitness' in their 30s!

Why is health linked to age identification? Two factors would seem to explain this inter-relationship; body image and physical activity. First, health and body image are inextricably linked. Body image and appearance is, in turn, linked to images of youth and ageing. Appearance is obviously an important part of our personal identity. The manifestation of grey hair or wrinkles may be the first signs of ageing observed by an individual. Second, health is linked with physical activity. The inability to pursue what the individual perceives as normal activities may stimulate the development of a new sense of age identity, that of an older person.

Role changes such as retirement and widowhood are the second major group of factors governing the transition to old age. Retirement is an unambiguous change of role which indicates a shift of identity from economic independence to financial dependence. This is a crucial transition in a society which is strongly influenced by notions of economic independence. Women who have not been formally employed in the

labour market reject the label 'retired' as for them it has no real meaning. For this group of women, widowhood and other family events
such as the arrival of grandchildren (or great grandchildren) seem
more important as markers of old age. Retirement and widowhood
have some similarities in that they are both rites of passage, are suggestive of a change in status from independent to dependent, may be
linked with an implied lack of fitness and declining health and bring
about a reduction in income.

We should also not forget the obvious influence of chronological age
upon subjective age identification. Data from the American Duke longitudinal study of ageing illustrates that the older a person actually is the
more likely (s)he is to place her/himself as belonging to an older age
group (Palmore, 1970). An 80-year-old is much less likely to consider her-
self middle-aged than a person of 60. Other demographic characteristics
such as sex or socio-economic status do not seem to exert any significant
influence upon subjective age identification.

In America ethnic status has a very strong relationship with age identification. African-American members of the Duke study were significantly
more likely to consider themselves as older than their chronological age.
It is difficult to establish whether this is a real difference in age perception
between Negroes and Whites or simply a reflection of the poorer health
of African-Americans compared with their White counterparts. For
Britain there is no evidence currently available about age awareness and
its variation within different ethnic sectors of the population.

The most important aspects in the self-perception of ageing and changes
in age identity are related to health, physical activity, chronological age,
retirement and widowhood. At first sight these parameters seem to have
little in common. However, these factors all relate to implied changes in the
individual's normal pattern of living. The onset of a disabling illness,
retirement or the death of a spouse are all events which are suggestive of
major changes in the lifestyle of the individual. The adjustment necessary
to cope with these changes may stimulate the reassessment of subjective
age identity and provoke the transition between age groups.

Self images of older people

As well as having a subjective age identity individuals maintain an
image of their own traits, attributes and characteristics. It is unclear as to
how the process of ageing influences these self-images. The majority of
older people perceive themselves as friendly, wise, alert, adaptable,
open-minded and good at getting things done; attributes similar to those
described by younger people. This suggests that self-image probably
remains remarkably stable over time regardless of changes in the social
world of the ageing individual.

Evidence to support the idea that self-image remains very stable despite the ageing of the individual is available from a survey of the retired in Britain (Age Concern, 1974). This demonstrated that most older people did not feel that they had changed as they got older. Where they reported changes these were defined in terms of health and mobility rather than more personal characteristics.

One very important manifestation of self-image is personal appearance. Most older people report that there has been no change in the way they think about their dress. Indeed a substantial minority felt that this was now more important to them than when they were younger, perhaps as a way of denying the inevitable advance of ageing (Age Concern, 1974).

The image of society held by the elderly

As well as holding an image of their own individual attributes older people (or any other age group) hold an image of the way they feel the rest of society perceives them. Older people in Britain feel that they are generally well treated by the rest of society (Age Concern, 1974). Overall the sample studied felt that they received good treatment in shops, on buses and in other public places. Few elderly felt that people had stopped caring about them as they grew older. The view that society took more care of its older members than at previous points in time was almost universally expressed by the elderly. The provision of welfare benefits and pensions, bus passes, local authority services and the construction of sheltered housing were all cited as evidence to support the view that the elderly are well treated by the rest of society.

ATTITUDES TOWARDS OLDER PEOPLE

Society expresses certain attitudes towards the elderly and these are explored below. First, we look at general social attitudes and stereotypes of ageing and the functions and creations of stereotypes. Second, we examine particular manifestations of these in popular culture.

Social stereotypes of old age

The term 'ageism' has been coined by gerontologists to describe pejorative images of older people. Ageism may be determined as systematic stereotyping and discrimination against people because they are old. Ageism is similar to sexism or racism in that it is discrimination against all members of a particular group. Implicit within the term is the notion that the old are in some way different from ourselves (and our future selves) and are not subject to the same wants, needs and desires as the rest of society. Unlike sexism and racism, ageism is generally much more covert and subtle in its manifestation. The failure to provide renal dialysis, or treatment in coronary care units to older people and inclusion in screening programmes simply because of their age are appraisals of the old which merit the term 'ageist'.

A stereotype is a distorted representation of a group of people and may be either negative or positive. Some commonly held stereotypes are that English people are snobs, Irish people dull-witted and spectacle-wearers bright. Whatever the group, the stereotype is a source of partial or misinformation which represents a set of ideas or beliefs (or ideology) about a group of people. There are many commonly held stereotypes about old age some of which are listed below.

1. All elderly people are alike.
2. Elderly people are socially isolated and lonely.
3. Most older people are in poor physical and mental health.
4. Retirement is more problematic for men than women.
5. Elderly people are isolated from their family and neglected by them.
6. Elderly people are not interested in, or capable of, an active sex life.
7. The old cannot learn.
8. Intelligence decreases with age.

It is commonly believed that elderly people lead a rather gloomy existence characterized by social isolation, beset with health problems and suffering considerable emotional stress. In a similar vein retirement is seen as leaving a vacuum which it is impossible to replace. On a more personal level, the old are assumed to be neither capable of, or interested in, an active sex life. This is one stereotype which is now being challenged (Gibson, 1992).

We have a stereotypical view of older people which represents them as incapable of running their own lives. They are viewed as passive recipients of a range of services from food parcels to community service volunteers or to young offenders digging their gardens or redecorating their homes. Our images of later life contain the implicit assumption that, whatever their pre-old-age characteristics, older people are incapable of competent social functioning, devoid of critical faculties or intellect and incapable of exercising informed choice over their own lives. One typical expression of this patronizing attitude is the tendency to equate older people with children.

Although the realities of ageing do not fit the commonly held stereotypes, the myths about ageing continue to find common currency and expression in everyday life. An American study looked at what adults under 65 perceived as the main problems of ageing. These expectations were then compared with the experience of a sample of the over-65s (National Council on Aging, 1975). At the most general level, virtually none of the non-elderly adults could envisage the years after their 60th birthday as being the best years of their life. At least a third saw them as the least desirable time of life. However, each phase of life was perceived as having its own advantages as well as disadvantages. The most frequently nominated disadvantages of the seventh and eighth decades were illness, decreased mobility, poverty and loneliness. However the advantages ascribed to this phase of the lifecycle were similar to those of youth; lack of responsibilities and a greater freedom to enjoy life.

Public expectations about later life saw old age as a time of fear of crime, poverty, poor housing, inadequate medical care, poor health and lack of social interaction. Elderly people consistently rated these features as much lesser problems than the non-elderly population. The discrepancies between the perceptions of the two groups were enormous. For example, 60% of the non-elderly thought that loneliness was a serious problem of old age compared with 12% of elderly people. Similarly, 54% thought that not feeling needed was a serious problem compared with 7% of older subjects.

If these stereotypes are so far from the feelings and perceptions of the elderly what function do they perform? Stereotypes about ageing, or any other group such as women or teenagers, are a shorthand method of communicating the particular social value of specific social groups and influence our social interaction with them by suggesting appropriate forms of behaviour. Current stereotypes about ageing teach us to ignore the old because they are essentially a non-productive group within a society which places its strongest emphasis upon the roles of economic productivity and independence.

As well as influencing our behaviour towards the target group, stereotypes communicate appropriate forms of behaviour to the group themselves. Modern stereotypes of ageing inform older members of the community that successful ageing is best achieved by invisibility, and that they should be grateful for the pensions and benefits which are given to them by the rest of society. Criticism of the levels at which these benefits and pensions are paid would be considered inappropriate.

What are the sources of our stereotypes about ageing and elderly people? Stereotypes about ageing (and obviously other groups) originate from two major sources; the societal and the individual. At the most fundamental level stereotypes are related to ideas about social status and social stratification. Social status refers to a position in society which involves certain duties and privileges whilst social role involves the performance of these functions. Elderly people are, in most western industrial societies, ascribed a low-status social role which stresses old age as a dependent phase in the lifecycle. Hence the development of a negative stereotype of ageing.

One of the most obvious sources of stereotypes is lack of information about the stereotyped group. Those who have the least knowledge about ageing probably hold the most negative views about later life. Despite the increase in the proportion of elderly people in modern societies, there is still a great lack of understanding about the realities of ageing amongst both the general population and those responsible for the development of health and social policies. It is possible that some of the early research undertaken by social gerontologists may have contributed to the creation of these negative stereotypes of old age. Several early studies of ageing were based upon samples resident in institutions, rather than the wider community, thereby giving a very false image of the abilities and status of the older members of society.

Lack of information is only a partial explanation. Ageism is also implicated in the generation of negative stereotypes of later life. By seeing elderly people as different in some indefinable but distinct way from ourselves, that is by adopting ageist attitudes, society can conveniently ignore the real difficulties that this group may experience. Ageism is as an ideology which condones and sanctions the subordination of older people within society.

The second source of negative ageing attitudes and stereotypes is more individualistic. This relates to fears about growing old and its anticipated problems experienced by specific individuals. However by exaggerating fears of ageing in younger people we may prevent them from enjoying the natural process of development, maturation and ageing. Perhaps more importantly we may prevent them from planning the later phases of the lifecycle to their best advantage. By constantly exhorting individuals to work harder and be independent we may generate social and psychological problems for individuals in later life when they are excluded from the labour market.

The majority of individual fears about ageing relate to the notion of independence. Self reliance and personal autonomy are much prized attributes, especially in the realms of finance, housing and family relationships, as is seen by the way we often perceive those who are dependent as inferior or stigmatize those who depend upon social security as scroungers or workshy.

Stereotypes assume an extra importance because they also influence the way the defined group perceive themselves. Given the overwhelming negative stereotype of old age, affluent and healthy older people perceive themselves as exceptions in a mass of poverty and ill health, rather than as evidence of the inapplicability of the stereotype. Similarly, active older people are seen, not as manifestations of the myths about ageing, but again as exceptions from the norm. This is what Hess (1974) terms 'pluralistic ignorance'. This strategy allows the maintenance of stereotypes in the face of contradictory evidence because our own experiences are perceived as exceptional. We may perceive all older people in a very negative fashion even though the older people with whom we are acquainted are active and independent and do not conform to the expectations suggested by our stereotypical beliefs.

Old age is a master status trait. This means that, as with labels such as black or homosexual, it becomes the major identifying characteristic of the individual. One is not a person who happens to be old (or gay) but an 'old person' and is assumed to have various other characteristics such as poor health or deteriorating mental abilities because of this label.

Adoption of the master status trait, in our case the label 'elderly', may influence the social world of older people by excluding them from activities or social groups because of their age. These negative images may pervade the self-identity of the old. If older people accept the stereotype of age as a time of decline when they must relinquish normal activities they may then act in a way which makes the stereotype become true. By accepting the negative stereotypes of ageing the older person may not seek help for a problem which (s)he perceives as part of the ageing process but which, in fact, may be the early manifestation of disease. A feeling of tiredness may be viewed as part of normal ageing and not as a symptom of anaemia. Elderly people may not claim all the welfare benefits to which they are entitled because they perceive old age as a time of poverty.

Individuals may try to deny the appropriateness of the label 'old' because of its intense negative connotations. Older people may try to pass as younger by their clothing, mannerisms, or the company they keep. It may also be that older people, aware of bearing this stigma or what Goffman (1963) termed a 'spoilt identity', withdraw from social relationships or interaction which they are perfectly capable of sustaining.

The elderly as a 'worthy' group

Although attitudes towards elderly people are highly negative, there are a second set of images about old age. This relates to the old as a 'worthy' group and often results in them being treated in a patronizing way. Britain is characterized by a very negative evaluation of those who rely upon state welfare benefits for their income. However elderly people are an exception from this general set of beliefs. They are seen as a group 'deserving' of support in the form of pensions and benefits. A survey by the author demonstrated almost universal support for elderly people as a group entitled to support from the welfare system (Victor, 1985).

The image of older women

Ageism is not experienced equally by men and women for older women experience both ageism and sexism. They are discriminated against because they are both old and female. This double disadvantage is reflected in what has been termed the double standard of ageing (Sontag, 1978).

This double disadvantage experienced by older women has a long historical pedigree. Hippocrates considered that old age started for men between the ages of 55 and 60 whilst for women old age started a decade earlier. Similarly, Plato saw the prime of life as 30 years for a man and 20 years for a woman. More recently Neugarten, Moore and Lowe (1965) found that there was popular consensus in America that old age started between the ages of 65 and 75 years for men and 60–70 years for women. This discrepancy in the perceived onset of old age has no biological basis as life expectancy for a male is several years shorter than that of a female. Rather, this difference in the perceived onset of old age is socially defined and constructed. Old age for women starts earlier than for males and lasts for a much longer number of years.

Modern western industrial society defines women as growing older sooner than men. What brings about this difference? Growing older is less problematic for a man because masculinity is associated with qualities such as competence, autonomy and self-control. These valued attributes withstand the ageing process much better than the qualities for which females are desired: beauty, physical attractiveness and childbearing. As Sontag (1978, p. 73) wrote 'Society is much more permissive about ageing in men.... Men are allowed to age, without penalty, in several ways that women are not.' Later life is a time when men become grey-haired, distinguished, wise and experienced whilst women are typified as worn-out, menopausal, neurotic and unproductive.

Whilst this double standard of ageing is probably most clearly manifested in the area of sexuality, it is present in all areas of life. Older men are seen as attractive. This is because their value as lovers or husbands is defined more by what they do than how they look. For women the converse is true, with the result that older women are negatively evaluated. The term 'old maid' has extremely negative social connotations in ways which 'old bachelor' does not. For men it is socially acceptable to be both old and unmarried. If a woman is not married by a certain age she is greatly to be pitied. Society sanctions the marriage of men to women many years their junior; indeed this is often acclaimed as evidence of their continued sexual prowess. Older women who become involved with men only a few years younger than themselves are considered to be behaving in an outrageous fashion.

As well as having lost their physical attractiveness (and hence their usefulness as a sex object) older women are handicapped because they can no longer fulfil their reproductive role. The combination of sexism and ageism result in the depiction of older women as dependent helpless creatures. Seldom are they shown as self-sufficient independent and sexually attractive.

AGEING AND CULTURE

The images society has of old age and of the ageing process are represented in the various aspects of popular culture and the mass media. This is one of the most important ways that society transmits social norms and expectations.

Old age in literature

The attitude towards the old in literature is, at best, ambiguous. Even in cultures where old age was venerated, literary treatment of ageing has interwoven respect with resentment, conflict, satire and ridicule (de Beauvoir, 1972). It is possible to identify a number of major themes in the literary treatment of old age; the conquest of obstructionist older people by the young as in Shakespeare's *Romeo and Juliet* or much early Chinese literature; old age as pathos, the emptiness of old age and the use of old age as a revelation of the absurdity of life itself. Old age is generally portrayed as pathetic rather than as tragic for old age is seen as lacking the strength, dignity and purpose which is required for tragedy.

Another aspect of old age in literature is its relative invisibility. Various studies have demonstrated the exclusion of older people from works of fiction, especially those designed for children. Where older characters appear in literature they fulfil a supporting role rather than constituting the central theme of the work. Few literary treatments of the aged tackle the problems of ageing. Rather older characters are depicted as leading an insulated life style, affecting few people and being affected by few in return. However there is some evidence that this is changing with the publication of novels dealing with later life, especially as it is experienced by older women.

Humour and ageing

Another method of the communication of cultural norms and values is by humour. Older people, like members of ethnic minorities, are the butt of essentially negative jokes. Palmore's (1971) study of jokes about the aged revealed that over half portrayed a highly negative attitude towards the elderly. Indeed some 'jokes' demonstrated open hostility to older people. Themes such as loss of attractiveness and sexual decline dominate jokes about ageing whatever method of humour – jokes, birthday cards or cartoons – is being used. Additionally, jokes about older women are much more negative than those relating to older men. Television situation comedies essentially ridicule the distressing aspects of ageing such as incontinence or failing sight, and present the older person as ridiculous (although it should be added that most other characters in situation comedy are presented in the same way).

Ageing and the mass media

Of all the mass media television is, perhaps, the most powerful pervader of images and stereotypes. In Britain the University of the Third Age undertook a monitoring exercise to evaluate the presentation of the image of the elderly on television (University of the Third Age, 1984). All programmes transmitted in a 2-week period in the winter of 1983 were reviewed by a team of 14 monitors aged 33–73. For the purpose of this exercise elderly people were defined as those aged 60 or over. During the study period the elderly appeared in 62% of programmes transmitted by BBC1; 51% of BBC2; 57% of ITV and 63% of Channel Four. This relatively high profile of the elderly is accounted for by the inclusion of world leaders, almost all of whom are older males, in news and current affairs programmes, thereby overemphasizing the visibility of the elderly in the media.

If we exclude current affairs and documentary programmes, older people become conspicuous by their absence. Older people were particularly likely to be excluded from plays, serials, soap operas, adventure programmes, comedies and children's programmes. Where older people appear in fictional representations they were rarely the central character. Rather, they were background characters moving into and out of the limelight as the story necessitated.

The overall balance of evidence from this study was that British television depicted the elderly as reasonably fit and healthy. Within this broadly favourable conclusion there was still considerable selection bias in the way the elderly were depicted. There was a significant trend to play down the sexual aspects of later life, and to minimize the financial hardships of old age by exaggerating levels of income. There was also a difference in the characteristics of 'young' and 'old' elderly. The young elderly are seen as being much more active and less passive than older people. Additionally, despite their numerical dominance in the elderly population, older women were less likely to appear than males.

For older women media images are not appealing. They have to overcome, as we saw earlier, the double stereotype of ageism and sexism. The awareness of the sexist images portrayed by the media largely dates from the growth of the women's movement in the late 1960s. A variety of publications describe the essentially sexist way that women are portrayed by all aspects of the mass media. However this analysis has tended to concentrate upon younger women. Older women are essentially invisible and it is only fairly recently that the women's movement has awoken to the problems of their older sisters. When older women are depicted in the mass media it is generally to be exhorted to stay young and beautiful and to conceal their true age. Typically they are shown as weak and helpless. Thus the Women's Media Action Group describe a skin cream advertisement as follows: 'Nobody minds if your husband looks his age. Men are lucky. They often get better looking over the years. Unfortunately, the same can't be said for us women.' (Itzin, 1984)

The other aspects of the mass media are newspapers and magazines, radio, theatre and cinema. Radio and the cinema tend to be rather youth-orientated media which pay only fleeting attention to the old. Newspapers, especially the popular tabloids, are only interested in the old either as victims of crime or family neglect, as manifestations of the perceived decline in moral standards or as examples of the burden of old age. A survey by the author indicated that newspapers were not interested in normal ageing but only the more shocking and exceptional aspects of growing old in modern Britain. Women's magazines are aimed at the young or middle-aged and only pay attention to the necessity of preventing the onset of old age rather than to the more positive and rewarding aspects of later life. The 'empty-nest' stage of the life cycle is often portrayed by these publications as a time of crisis for women rather than as a time of opportunity. The apparently straightforward reporting of events may also be highly ageist. For example the ages of 'elderly' judges being reported when they err in their judgement but when younger judges err their age is excluded from the report.

There is some evidence that ageing is becoming a more viable subject for the mass media and that greater interest is being paid to the positive aspects of ageing. The major British television channels have started to produce special programmes for older viewers, probably in response to the increasing size of the 'ageing' market. However in the most general terms the old continue to be invisible within the mass media unless they are being portrayed in a very negative fashion as dependent and as a burden to the rest of society.

CONCLUSION

In this chapter we have considered images of ageing at two levels of analysis: the individual and the societal. At the individual level each of us has an image of ourselves. One aspect of this is our subjective age identity, or how old we think we are as distinct from our actual chronological age. As we move through the life course our subjective age identity changes in response to changes in our social environment. Empirical studies indicate that the adoption of the age identity of 'old' is prompted by changes in physical health status or social role such as retirement or bereavement which result in the person having to alter their lifestyle. However, other dimensions of self-image such as personality seemed to remain remarkably constant over the life course. A person who has been friendly and outgoing during their younger years will probably maintain these characteristics as they age. Thus we should not see later life as bringing about enormous changes in the self-image of people. Rather, old age should be seen as the continuation and culmination of characteristics displayed in younger life.

Older people (and of course other age groups) have an image of the way they feel the rest of society perceives them. Older people in Britain feel that they are well treated by the rest of society and cite provision of various services and benefits as evidence to support this view. Elderly people do not, however, comment that the levels at which these services are provided are inadequate and do not permit them to function as full members of society.

At a societal level we saw that there exist numerous highly negative stereotypes of old age. However, the personal attitudes of the old are very much more positive than the stereotypes held by other age groups and the representation of ageing that is often portrayed in the mass media. Such negative stereotypes are rooted in excessive fears of ageing based upon misinformation, or no information, combined with a social system which values ageing negatively. In the subsequent chapters of this book we will consider how accurate (or inaccurate) the commonly held stereotypes of old age actually are.

6

The demography of ageing

Much of the stimulus for the development of social gerontology as an academic discipline, and as an area of social concern, has come from the increase, over this century, in the number and proportion of persons classified as elderly. In this chapter we examine the demographic trends which have brought about the growth in the size of the elderly population. We then describe the demographic characteristics of the elderly population. Finally we consider the geographical distribution of the elderly population and the growth of retirement migration.

THE SIZE OF THE ELDERLY POPULATION

In Britain the elderly population is, by convention, that fraction of the total population eligible to receive the state retirement pension; over 60 years of age for women and over 65 years for men. At the 1991 100% decennial census, the elderly population of Great Britain comprised 9 820 130 persons or 18.1% of the total resident population.

Estimating the percentage of older people in the British population at earlier times in our history is the province of the historical demographer or sociologist. This is a difficult task as, for periods before the start of the compulsory 100% decennial census in 1831, the only information available are parish records and other highly localized datasets.

The percentage of the population of England over 60 years of age remained remarkable stable, at about 7–10%, from the 16th century up until the early 20th century (Table 6.1). The percentage of the male and female population aged over 60 remained approximately equal up to the 1930s. However, since this time a marked imbalance in the sex structure of the elderly population has developed.

Table 6.1 Proportion of elderly in the English population – % population aged 60+
(Laslett, 1981, Table 1 and Central Statistical Office, 1992, Table 2.5)

	Male	*Female*
1541–96	8	9
1601–46	8	9
1651–96	9	10
1701–46	7	10
1751–96	7	9
1801–46	7	7
1851–71	7	7
1901	7	8
1911	7	9
1921	9	10
1931	11	12
1951	14	18
1961	14	20
1971	16	22
1981	17	22
1991*	18	23

* estimated

The increase in the numbers of the British population defined as elderly started in the early part of this century. Between 1901 and 1991 there were marked increases in the numbers of people aged 60 from 2 883 000 to 11 904 000 (see Table 6.2).

Table 6.2 United Kingdom: the growth of the elderly population 1901–91 (in 000s)
(Central Statistical Office, 1992, Table 23; source: Askham *et al.* 1992, Table A)

Age	*1901*	*1931*	*1951*	*1971*	*1991*
60–64	1064	1897	2422	2935	2876
65–69	743	1455	2068	2800	2760
70–74	535	1005	1620	2393	2267
74–79	313	581	1049	1707	1850
80–84	157	263	506	967	1261
85+	61	113	224	601	890

Expressed in percentage terms, Table 6.3 illustrates the very dramatic increases in the size of the population aged 65+ experienced between 1901 and 1931.

Table 6.3 United Kingdom: percentage change in the elderly population 1901–91

	1901–1931	*1931–1951*	*1951–1971*	*1971–1991*
65–74	+92	+50	+41	−3
75–84	+80	+84	+72	+16
85+	+85	+98	+268	+48
All 65+	+89	+60	+55	+7

Current projections, based upon forward projection of current patterns of mortality and fertility, indicate only a slight increase in the population aged 65+ by the year 2001 (see Tables 6.4 and 6.5). The growth of the very old, i.e. those aged over 85, will continue well into the next century.

Table 6.4 United Kingdom: projections of the elderly population 1991–2031 – all figures in thousands (Central Statistical Office, 1992, Table 25)

	1991	*2001*	*2011*	*2021*	*2031*
65–74	5028	4801	5236	6121	6928
75–84	3111	3244	3193	3559	4151
85+	892	1171	1337	1351	1538
All 65+	9031	9225	9766	11031	12617

It is the projected rise in the proportion of the over-85s that has aroused much interest from politicians and government policy makers. This growth in the numbers of the very elderly is seen as having dire consequences for the British economy, living standards and welfare state provision. It is important to put these proportional increases in the size of various sectors of the elderly population into perspective by looking at the actual numbers involved.

Table 6.5 United Kingdom: projected percentage change per decade in the elderly population 1991–2031

	1991	*2001*	*2011*	*2021*	*2031*
65–74	− 4	− 9	+17	+17	+13
75–84	+ 4	− 2	+11	+11	+17
85+	+31	+14	+ 1	+ 1	+14
All 65+	+ 2	+ 6	+ 6	+13	+14

Table 6.4 shows the actual numbers in the three main age divisions of the elderly population of United Kingdom from 1991 until the year 2031. Although the percentage increase in the number of people aged 85 years and over is large, the actual numbers remain fairly small. The percentage increase predicted is, however, modest compared with that observed between 1931 and 1951. If these projections are accurate then there will be an extra 279 000 people in the United Kingdom aged 85 and over in the year 2001 compared with 1991. The numerical size of this increase hardly seems to merit the panic which it has aroused amongst those responsible for health and social policies. All the negative attributes ascribed to an individual older person have been transferred to ageing populations. These are characterized as lacking in energy, enthusiasm, innovation and artistic and intellectual achievement.

The increase in the elderly population in Britain over the last 50 years is not something which has taken the government (or demographers) by surprise. In 1954 the Phillips Committee estimated that the numbers of pensioners would increase from 6.9 million in 1954 to 9.5 million by 1979. This estimate was very accurate: the actual number of pensioners was 9.46 million in 1979. Thus the current numbers of the very elderly are completely in line with population predictions. Protestations by governments of all political persuasions that they have been taken by surprise by the increase in the numbers of older people are not, therefore, very convincing.

The increase in the proportion of the population defined as elderly during the 20th century is not unique to Great Britain. Rather, it is characteristic of most advanced industrial societies, as Table 6.6 shows. In France the fraction of the total population aged over 60 has increased

Table 6.6 Percentage of the population aged 65 and over in various countries (Laslett, 1981, Table 7)

	1900	*1985*
Australia	4.3	10.2
Austria	5.0	14.3
Canada	5.1*	15.1
France	8.2	13.0
Germany	4.9	14.8
Great Britain	4.7	11.0
Italy	6.2	12.1
Netherlands	6.0**	17.2
Sweden	8.4	11.9
USA	4.1	10.4

* 1901
** 1899

since 1900 from 8% to 13% whilst in the United States the increase was from 4% to 10% during the same period.

WHAT HAS BROUGHT ABOUT THESE DEMOGRAPHIC CHANGES?

The age structure of any population is the result of the complex inter-relationship between three factors; fertility, mortality and migration. The increase in the proportion of the population classified as elderly in the countries of the industrialized west is largely attributable to changes in fertility and mortality rates, especially infant mortality.

Fertility

The fertility rate is usually defined as the number of births per 1000 females aged 15–44 years. This is a crucial element in determining the age structure of a population. A decrease in fertility, by definition, reduces the numbers in the younger age groups and consequently increases the per-centage in the older age groups. If fewer people are being born then it follows that the older age groups will form an increased fraction of the total population.

Fertility rates in Britain started to decline in the late 19th century in response to a variety of factors including decreases in infant mortality and increased education about methods of birth control. Since 1900 the fertility rate has decreased from 26.7 per 1000 to 15.9 per 1000. Changes in fertility rates are reflected in family size. People born in 1871 would have had, when they became parents, an average of 4.8 children. Of these chil-dren 2.7 would have survived until age 45. When the generation born in 1921 became parents the average number of children was 2.0 and 1.6 sur-vived to age 45 (Grimley-Evans, 1981). Fertility has continued to decline in the late 20th century and average family size is now at, or below, replacement level, with an average of 1.9 children.

Although fertility rates overall have declined, there are still substantial yearly variations in the numbers of births. This annual difference in total births has been as large as 300 000. These peaks and troughs in the number of births also exert an influence upon the age distribution of the population by the creation of 'baby booms' or 'birth bulges'. The largest 'birth bulge' experienced in Britain occurred between 1918 and 1920. This post-First World War baby boom was larger than that which occurred after the Second World War although it was not maintained for as many years. The result of the post-1918 birth bulge was that in mid-1981 there were 50% more people aged 61 years than aged 63 years (666 000 and 420 000) respectively (Craig, 1983).

Mortality

The crude mortality rate describes the number of deaths per 1000 total population. In combination with these decreases in fertility there has been a halving of crude mortality rates over the last century and a half. Between 1841 and 1845 the death rate for males in England and Wales was 22.1 per 1000 compared with 12.3 in 1976–80. For females the death rates at each of these times were 20.6 and 11.6 respectively.

The crude death rate is related to the age structure of the population. So the changes outlined above may simply reflect changes in population structure rather than in mortality. A better way of looking at overall changes in mortality is to examine age-specific rates (see Table 6.7).

Table 6.7 England and Wales death rate (deaths per thousand) by age and sex 1841–45, 1976–80 and 1990 (Office of Population Censuses and Surveys, 1985a, Table 2 and Central Statistical Office, 1992, Table 2.22)

	1841–45		1976–80		1990**	
Age	Males	Females	Males	Females	Males	Females
1–4			0.6	0.5	2.2*	1.7*
5–9	8.8	8.5	0.3	0.2	0.2	0.1
10–14	4.8	5.1	0.3	0.2	0.2	0.2
15–19	6.7	7.6	0.9	0.3	0.7	0.3
20–24	8.9	8.6	0.9	0.4	0.9	0.3
25–34	9.3	9.9	0.9	0.6	1.0	0.5
35–44	12.2	12.1	2.0	1.5	1.8	1.1
45–54	17.2	15.1	6.7	4.1	4.8	3.0
55–64	30.3	27.2	18.9	9.9	14.8	8.8
65–74	65.5	59.1	48.8	25.3	39.5	22.4
75–84	143.7	131.8	112.4	70.8	94.3	58.9
85+	305.1	288.6	237.0	192.8	187.8	156.7
All ages	22.1	20.6	12.3	11.6	11.2	11.1

* aged 0–4
** United Kingdom

The major changes in mortality have occurred in infancy and early childhood. In the 1840s death rates per 1000 children aged 5–9 were 8.8 (males) and 8.5 (females). For the period 1976–80 the rate per 1000 for the same age and sex groups had decreased to 0.32 and 0.22 respectively.

Decreases in mortality during this period have been much less dramatic for older age groups. Death rates for males aged 75–84 in the 1840s were 143 per 1000 compared to 112 in the late 1970s and 94 per 1000 in 1990. Female death rates in this age group show more change, decreasing from 131.8 per 1000 in 1841–45 to 70.8 per 1000 in 1976–80 and 58.9 per 1000 in 1990. This failure of male death rates to decrease during this period is probably related to the high prevalence of cigarette smoking amongst this cohort of males, with its attendant increase in death rates from cancers, respiratory diseases and heart disease.

This table also shows that there were substantial decreases in mortality for women in the 20–44 years age groups. This improvement reflects the substantial decrease in maternal mortality rates and improvements in public health which took place during this period.

Over the same period there has also been a massive decrease in the numbers of children dying within the first year of life. This is known as the infant mortality rate and is usually expressed as a rate per 1000 live births. In the period 1841–45 the infant mortality rate was 148 per 1000 compared with 13 per 1000 in 1976–80. This decrease in infant and early childhood mortality resulted from the decreased potency of childhood diseases such as measles and diphtheria, and other communicable diseases such as smallpox, cholera and typhoid, resultant from improvements in public health measures and the changed natural history of these diseases. Indeed McKeown (1979) argues that the majority of the decrease in mortality over the last 150 years can be attributed to the control of infectious diseases.

These changes in death rates have influenced life expectancy. Life expectancy at birth in England between 1530 and 1800 was between 40 and 45 years, although there were variations between different social groups. In particular females had a shorter life expectancy than males because of high maternal mortality. As late as 1901–1910 life expectancy for a newborn male was still only about 48 years (see Table 6.8). By 1981 this had increased by almost 22 years to 69.8 years. For women life expectancy at birth increased by 20 years from 51.6 to 76.2 years.

Table 6.8 United Kingdom: expectation of life at various ages in 1901 and 1983 (Social Trends, 1985, Table 7.1)

Age	1901		1983	
	Males	*Females*	*Males*	*Females*
Birth	48.0	51.6	69.8	76.2
20	42.7	45.2	51.2	57.4
40	26.8	29.1	32.0	38.0
60	13.4	14.9	15.6	20.6

If, however, we look at life expectancy at age 60 this has increased very little over the last century. In 1901 a 60-year-old male could expect to live another 13 years compared with 15 years in 1983. For females the increase over the same period was from 15 to 20 years. Thus most of the increase in life expectancy over the century results from improvements in mortality during infancy and early childhood. There has been little over-all increase in the actual human life span. Rather, it is the number of people who manage to live to old age which has increased.

One of the most interesting demographic changes over the last 150 years has been the imbalance in the fraction of males and females surviv-ing to old age. As we saw earlier, ancient populations were characterized by a balance between the sexes in later life or possibly a slight excess of males. As late as the 1930s the population of Britain was characterized by approximately equal proportions of elderly men and women. In 1901 females lived, on average, only 2 years longer than men. However now females live, on average, 7 years longer than males.

This male–female difference in life expectancy is now accepted by many as being one of the 'objective facts' of ageing. Many see this differ-ence in life expectancy between the sexes as being a manifestation of a nat-ural biological difference between the sexes. In chapter one we saw that biological experiments have suggested that there is no biological difference in the cellular basis of ageing between men and women. Consequently it looks as if this difference in life expectancy is an artifact brought about by differences between the sexes in either lifestyle or environment. Data from America suggest that the increased differential in life expectancy between the sexes is due the high prevalence of smoking and its related diseases amongst males. The generation of women now experiencing old age has very low rates of smoking. This, therefore, seems to be a plausible explana-tion for this differential. Women took up smoking in large numbers during and after the Second World War. Indeed women are still continuing to smoke whilst males are giving up the habit. It is interesting to speculate about how these changed patterns of smoking behaviour will influence the life expectancy and health in later life of future generations.

The expectation of life for children in Britain is very similar to that of other western industrial countries (Table 6.9).

At birth, a British male can expect to live to the age of 70 compared with 72 years for his counterpart born in Scandinavia. Similar differences are characteristic of females. There are variations in life expectancy within the United Kingdom. Expectation of life is longer in England and Wales, for both males and females, than in either Scotland or Northern Ireland. A Scottish male would expect to live 2 years less than his coun-terpart born in England and Wales whilst a male born in Northern Ireland has a life expectancy 2.5 years shorter. Similar differences are characteristic of the female population.

There is also a marked difference in life expectancy at birth between the developed and undeveloped parts of the world. Table 6.10 shows that

Table 6.9 Expectation of life at birth for various countries (Office of Population Censuses and Surveys, 1985a, Table 2)

	Males	*Females*
Australia	68.5	75.4
Canada	70.5	78.2
France	69.9	77.7
Norway	72.4	78.8
Sweden	72.5	79.0
United States	69.4	77.3
West Germany	69.2	76.0
England and Wales	70.2	76.3
Scotland	68.2	74.4
Northern Ireland	67.5	74.1
Belgium	68.9	75.5
Netherlands	72.0	78.7
Switzerland	72.0	78.9

at birth life expectancy in Africa and South Asia is less than 60 years. This reflects the continued high infant mortality rates in the Third World from infectious diseases. However there is less difference in life expectancy at age 60 between the different parts of the world.

Table 6.10 Life expectancy in various parts of the world 1975–80 (Hoover and Siegel, 1986, Table 5)

	At birth	*At age 60*
Africa	48.6	14.1
East Asia	67.6	16.9
South Asia	50.6	14.3
North America	73.0	18.8
Latin America	62.5	16.1
Europe	72.0	18.3
USSR	69.9	18.2
Oceania	65.6	16.6

Migration

Migration is the third main influence upon the demographic profile. Large outflows of young people can bring about the ageing of a population whilst the immigration of the young will have the opposite effect. In Britain migration, either into or out of the country, has had only a very marginal impact upon the national demographic profile. However migration, especially the emigration of the young in search of employment, has been an important influence upon the demographic profile of many areas within Britain.

THE STRUCTURE OF THE ELDERLY POPULATION

At the 1981 census 9 000 000 people in Britain were defined as being of pensionable age. In the next sections we shall examine some of the more detailed demographic characteristics of this group and consider the extent to which this profile varies from historical characteristics of the elderly population.

PLACE OF USUAL RESIDENCE

The pensionable population is usually divided into two groups; those resident in private households and those in non-private households. This latter group describes those living permanently in institutions of various types such as hospitals or residential homes. Approximately 5% of those of pensionable age were resident in non-private households, mainly resi-dential homes. Contrary to popular belief, there has been little change in the percentage of the elderly population living in institutions over the course of this century. In 1911 about 5% of the population aged over 60 was resident in some form of institution, usually the workhouse. How-ever it is important to remember that although the term 'communal establishment' is used to refer to both types of living arrangement the reality of the living conditions has clearly changed.

The percentage of the elderly population classified as resident in an institution increases with age from 1% of those aged under 75 to 50% of those aged over 90. There is a marked variation with gender in the pro-portion of elderly classified as living in non-private households. At all ages after 75 years, a higher percentage of females than males live in resi-dential homes. Although comparatively few elderly, in any age group, were permanently resident in a hospital or psychiatric hospital, this frac-tion also increases with age. Only in the very oldest age group does the fraction of females enumerated as resident in a hospital exceed that for males.

It is difficult to make cross-national comparisons in the proportion of elderly living outside private households, because of the varying defini-tions of the term 'institution'. Table 6.11 indicates that the fraction of people aged 65 and over living in institutions varies throughout Europe. Britain has the lowest fraction, 5%, of its elderly population (those over the age of 65) living in institutions whereas the Netherlands with 10% has the highest. These variations reflect both differences in the demo-graphic structures of the nations of Europe and the social policy responses to the perceived problems of old age.

Table 6.11 Proportion of elderly (65+) living in institutions in various countries (Wall, 1986, Table 1)

Country	% in institutions
Belgium	5
France	6
Great Britain	5
Eire	8
Netherlands	10
Denmark	6
Norway	7
Sweden	6

HOUSEHOLD STRUCTURE

The vast majority of the elderly population is, therefore, resident within private households in the community. For those elderly living in private households 30% were living alone and 43% were living in a household which contained at least one other pensioner, usually their spouse. Only a minority of elderly, less than 10%, lived in households with two or more younger people.

It is the type of household in which older people live which has attracted considerable attention. As we have already noted the romantic view of the past presents pre-industrial society as a society in which the extended family was the basic building block of the social fabric. Protagonists of this viewpoint argue that the nuclear family has replaced the extended family with a resultant increase in the neglect of the old.

It is quite clear that there have been changes in the types of household in which older people live. This has been the most marked change in the nature of the elderly population over this century. In pre-industrial England probably less 10% of the elderly population lived alone. Wall (1984) suggests that 7% of males over 65 and 15% of females lived alone in Britain in the period 1684–1796. In 1981 the respective fractions were 17% and 45%. These changes in the household composition of the elderly reflect wider social changes in household and family formation patterns, especially in the years since 1945. Indeed Wall (1984) observes that during the 20 years from 1961–81 the percentage of elderly living alone increased as much as during the previous 200 years.

Commensurate with this growth of households headed by lone elderly people there has been some decrease in co-residence between the elderly and other generations. However these two trends represent the culmination of very complex social changes and do not imply neglect of the old.

The type of household in which elderly people live shows substantial variation with age; the fraction living alone increases with age whilst the fraction living with a spouse decreases (Table 6.12). Only at the very oldest age groups does the proportion living with non-elderly people, usually daughters or sons, increase substantially. At all ages females are most likely to be living alone whilst males are most likely to be living with a spouse. This reflects the tendency for females to marry males several years older than themselves, combined with their superior longevity.

Table 6.12 Great Britain: the household composition of the elderly population – % living in different types of household (Askham *et al.*, 1992, Table 23)

	60–64		65–69		70–74		75–79		80	
	M	F	M	F	M	F	M	F	M	F
Lives alone	13	22	15	29	20	43	25	58	34	65
With spouse	60	56	67	54	64	40	61	26	50	17
Other	27	22	19	17	17	17	13	16	16	19

The household structures in which older people live are usually assumed to be straightforward and unproblematic. Many studies divide the elderly into three categories; those living alone, those living with other elderly and 'others'. As Table 6.12 indicates, a substantial minority of elderly live in households with younger people. These household structures can be quite complicated, ranging from two-generation structures, which may mean an older person living with an unmarried offspring or with a young couple, to households containing three or more generations. The extent of this complexity is indicated by the 25-category typology of household structures developed by Evandrou *et al.* (1985) to describe the sample of elderly included in the 1980 General Household Survey.

The percentage of older people living alone varies within Europe (Table 6.13). Eire, which remains perhaps one of the more 'traditional' of

Table 6.13 Proportion of elderly (60+) living alone in various countries (Wall, 1986, Table 6)

Country	Males	Females	All
Belgium	17	32	26
France	16	43	32
Great Britain	20	45	35
Eire	14	22	18
West Germany	16	53	39
Denmark	NA	NA	35
Norway	NA	NA	35

European societies, has the lowest fraction of older people living alone; West Germany has the largest fraction of the elderly living by themselves. Consistently throughout Europe females are much more likely to be living alone than males.

SEX STRUCTURE

67% of those of pensionable age are female, reflecting their earlier retirement age and greater longevity (Table 6.14). This domination of the elderly population by females is a feature of fairly recent origin. Significantly more women are classed as very old, 85 years or over, than men. At all ages there is a marked imbalance between the sexes. The number of females per 100 males increases markedly with age. For those over 85 there are 298 females per 100 males.

Table 6.14 United Kingdom: sex structure of the pensionable population 1991 – thousands in each age group (Central Statistical Office, 1992, Table 25)

Age	*Males*	*Females*	*Sex ratio*[**]
60–64	1386	1490	108
65–69	1278	1482	116
70–74	980	1288	131
75–79	720	1130	157
80–84	422	839	199
85+	224	668	298

[**] Sex ratio = females per 100 males

CIVIL STATUS

Civil status refers to the legal classification of the population as married, widowed, divorced or never married. The civil status of the pensionable also shows a variation with age and sex. At all ages men are more likely to be married than women (Table 6.15).

This reflects, as noted earlier, the tendency for women to marry men older than themselves. For both sexes the proportion classified as widowed increases markedly with age as does the fraction of females classified as single. This latter characteristic of the elderly population is a cohort effect reflecting the lack of marriage opportunities for many now elderly women because of the high mortality of men in the First World War. Only a very small fraction of the now elderly population are classed as divorced. It may be expected that, in future generations of elderly, the fraction who are defined as divorced will increase markedly.

The demography of ageing

Table 6.15 Great Britain: civil status of the elderly population (%) (Askham *et al.*, 1992, Table 2.2)

	60–64		65–69		70–74		75–79		80–84	
	M	F	M	F	M	F	M	F	M	F
Single	8	6	7	6	6	6	3	9	5	11
Married	82	69	80	60	73	44	69	28	56	18
Widowed	5	20	10	29	17	47	28	62	37	70
Divorced	5	5	3	5	3	3	1	1	2	2

Widowhood is now a feature which is associated mainly with later life, both for males and females. This represents a change from earlier times in history when higher mortality rates in the earlier phases of the life-cycle meant that widowhood was a feature of almost every phase of the lifecycle. Probably as many as a third of all women would have been widowed before the age of 55 in the 19th century. Whilst it is now uncommon for a man to be widowed before old age it would have been an accepted feature of everyday life in previous centuries.

Table 6.15 indicates that the experience of widowhood in later life varies between males and females. By the age of 70 almost a half of women have been widowed compared with less than 10% of males. Even in the oldest age group, the over-80s, 56% of males are married compared with only 18% of females. Thus women in later life have to experience a longer period of widowhood than males. Amongst ever-married women widows constitute a majority of the population by the age of 72 in England and Wales, compared with 86 for men (Wall, 1986). These trends are evident throughout Europe and North America.

THE SPATIAL DISTRIBUTION OF THE ELDERLY

Within Great Britain the elderly population is not equally distributed throughout the country. Rather, it illustrates a distinctive geographical pattern. The main concentrations of the elderly population have developed in non-industrial coastal areas of the south-east and in rural areas such as mid-Wales and Norfolk. Conversely the areas with fewest elderly are the suburban or semi-rural areas around London, the West Midlands and the larger cities such as Bristol, Leicester, Cardiff and Hull. In particular the major concentrations of elderly are to be found in the resort towns of the south coast, in Devon and Cornwall and in some rural areas.

This distinctive spatial distribution of the elderly population has developed over this century. In 1921 above average concentrations of the elderly were found in a belt running across the country from the south-west to Norfolk with two additional clusters in mid-Wales and Suffolk. By 1981 the pattern had altered to one in which the elderly had shifted to dominate the coastal peripheries.

In order to explain these changes in the geography of the elderly we must first consider changes in the distribution of the total population during the same period. In very broad terms population growth since 1921 has been concentrated, both relatively and absolutely, in the south-east. In addition there has been a marked drift away from urban inner city areas. Within this broad pattern the present geographical distribution of the elderly population has been brought about by the inter-relationship between three major factors; the growth of retirement migration, ageing *'in situ'* and the out-migration of younger age groups.

RETIREMENT MIGRATION

Migration at, or about, retirement age has been an important influence upon the current distribution of the elderly within Great Britain. Retirement migration is not, however, a recent phenomenon. The Romans constructed retirement communities for military officers who had retired from active duty. In medieval England the craft guilds constructed villages for retired members (Karn, 1977).

Retirement migration is not confined to Britain. Rather it is a common feature of North America, western Europe and Australasia. However it is probably most developed in North America. In America retirement resorts have existed for the last 100 years, largely concentrated in the 'sunshine' states of Florida, Arizona and California. Initially the retirement function of these resorts developed in an unplanned way as older people moved to warmer climates. Towns such as Palm Springs developed into popular retirement areas in a way similar to British seaside resorts such as Worthing. More recently planned retirement communities such as Moosehaven in California have been developed. These planned retirement communities are age-segregated in that people below a specified age are not allowed to purchase (or rent) a property in the community. Typically these communities are self-sufficient, including shops, recreational facilities and medical facilities, and are separated (or partially separated) from the larger community. Within Europe the resorts of the Mediterranean in France and Spain and the Algarve in Portugal have expanded their role as retirement towns although there has been little of the planned retirement community development of North America. However there are plans to develop such communities within Britain along the south coast retirement area.

Retirement migration in Britain on any significant scale is a very recent phenomenon. The earliest developments of any significance took place during the period 1919–1939 when the retirement role of the south coast resorts near to London such as Bexhill, Worthing, Seaford and Margate first expanded. The development of retirement areas during these years was closely allied to the second home movement and was confined to a very narrow and wealthy segment of the elderly population. These areas were attractive to elderly people because they experience the most favourable climatic conditions in Britain as well as being near to London and well away from extensive industrial development. Additionally property prices in these areas were comparatively cheap. During this period there was little or no such development in the rural areas of East Anglia or the West Country. Since the war the retirement role of the south coast resorts has been consolidated whilst newer centres have developed in north Wales, East Anglia and Devon and Cornwall.

Whilst retirement migration has largely been confined to the more affluent elderly some urban Local Authorities, most notably the now abolished Greater London Council (GLC), have constructed bungalows in south coast areas for their tenants to retire to. Also when new towns such as Basildon and Harlow were built older people were encouraged to move out the new towns when their young family members were moved. However this policy ignored the subsequent migratory behaviour of the younger families. More recently as the practice of retirement migration has started to filter down the social scale particular areas and resorts have been favoured by different groups. Thus although Frinton and Clacton in Essex are adjacent they cater for very different types of retirement migrant.

The desirability of the south and south-west as places to live is not confined to the old. Rather in expressing this spatial preference they are mirroring the views of the general population. A survey of British school leavers indicated that the preferred areas to live were the south and south-west.

The majority of retirement migrants originate from the conurbations and particularly from London and the south-eastern area (Karn, 1977; Warnes and Law, 1984). This is probably because this is the most affluent area of the country and retirement migration is closely associated with affluence in old age. Secondary source areas are clearly identified with the cities of the Midlands and north. Whilst it is relatively easy to establish the location of the major retirement areas it is much more difficult to estimate the actual numbers and proportion of people moving at, or around, retirement age.

The characteristics of retirement migrants

Those who move at retirement are distinguished from non-movers along four main dimensions; the frequency and distance of residential mobility during their working life; dislike or perceived unsuitability of pre-retirement house; the frequency of contact with children; age at retirement (Law and Warnes, 1980). Those opting for a change of residential location at, or about, time of retirement were generally younger and from higher socio-economic groups than non-migrants. This reflects a marked difference in the affluence and income of these two groups. Additionally retirement migrants were differentiated from non-migrants by a higher degree of non-local moves in earlier phases of the lifecycle and a higher level of dissatisfaction with their dwelling. Looser ties with their children and other family members was also an important factor distinguishing between retirement migrants and non-migrants.

The specific reasons given for moving at retirement are highly diverse. In Karn's study migration was precipitated by health reasons, the desire for a better climate (hence the dominance of the south and west), the desire for a change or to be near family or friends. In addition a move to an area with cheaper house prices was seen as a way of 'liberating' some of the capital older people had locked up in their houses.

Much public concern has been voiced about retirement migration and the perceived problems resulting from it such as a loss of social contacts for the elderly and the strain upon local services. Again Karn's study indicates that most moves have been successful, especially for the fit elderly. However she did indicate that those who became disabled seemed to face greater problems because of the strain upon social and medical support services in the major retirement areas.

AGEING *IN SITU*

Part of the distinctive geography of the elderly in Britain is accounted for by ageing *in situ*. Great attention has been paid to the way that population movements bring about changes in the geography of the elderly. However it is often forgotten that residential stability also influences the pattern. Probably only 10% of the British population move in any year and the great majority of the population remains in the same house for many years. Often families remain in the same house that they originally set up home in. Thus concentrations of elderly build up as 'estates' age with their population. Examples of this are to be found on large public housing estates which were originally populated with young families; 30 years later such estates may be dominated by the elderly as their families have grown up and moved away from the area.

OUT-MIGRATION

The final influence upon the geography of ageing is out-migration by younger age groups. If large numbers of young people leave a district in order to find employment this will result in the elderly representing an increased fraction of the areas population. This factor almost certainly explains the high proportions of elderly in many of the remoter rural areas of mid-Wales and Scotland and in the older industrial areas of south Wales and the north-east. This out-migration by the young has obvious social policy implications because it brings about a massive dislocation in the social networks of the older people who remain behind.

CONCLUSION

In this chapter we have seen that the proportion of the population defined as elderly has increased over the last century. It has been these demographic changes which have done much to prompt the perception of the elderly as a 'social problem' and stimulated research into the problems of an ageing population.

This increase in the fraction of the population defined as elderly has arisen in response to the decreases in mortality, especially infant mortality, and fertility rates over this period. Future projections suggest that the total fraction defined as elderly will decrease towards the turn of the century but this will disguise a large increase in the fraction classified as very elderly, i.e. those aged over 75 years of age. Thus once again the spectre of the increasing burden of the elderly has been invoked. However although large in proportionate terms the actual increases in the numbers of the very old is not so dramatic.

Perhaps of more importance is the influence which changes in family size and the participation of women in the labour market over the past century will have upon the availability of family members, especially women, to care for the elderly. Eversley (1982) indicates that an elderly couple born at the turn of the century would have had about 42 female relatives of various generations alive during their old age. For a person born in the 1920s it is predicted that they would have only a quarter of this number of female relatives, most of whom would be employed. Whilst much has been made of the impending disaster brought about by the comparatively small numerical increase in the very elderly population, little attention has been given to the potentially more significant decrease in the numbers of family members available to care for the elderly.

The composition of the elderly population demonstrates several interesting features. Most striking is the marked imbalance in the numbers of men and women surviving to old age. Thus any discussion of old age and ageing is very largely concerned with women rather than men. Far from this being a demonstration of the biological superiority of females it seems to be a reflection of the differences between the sexes in terms of smoking patterns and the resultant health effects. It remains to be seen whether the widespread adoption of smoking by women during and after the Second World War will reduce the difference in life expectancy.

The age-related increase in the fraction of women classed as never married is a cohort effect reflecting the lack of marriage opportunities in the years after the First World War. Divorce is comparatively rare amongst the older age groups. However it is interesting to speculate about the how increased prevalence of divorce amongst the young will influence their experience of old age.

It is a popular belief that the old are condemned to spend their final years living in an institution of some type. However we have seen that, even in the very oldest age groups, only a minority of the elderly are resident in non-private households. In Britain this fraction has shown comparatively little change over the last century. However there has been a substantial change in the types of household in which those elderly resident in the community live. The elderly, like younger age groups, express a marked preference for living in their own household rather than living either with other elderly people or with members of younger generations. This reflects a general societal trend for individuals to establish single households rather than living in larger groups. This trend reflects a desire for autonomy and independence amongst those of all age groups rather than being a demonstration of lack of interest between members of different generations.

Whilst most elderly people either live by themselves or with their spouse the elderly are also resident in a great variety of different types of household. These diverse groups tend to be various forms of 'extended' household and involve a variety of generations living together. Thus it is important to remember that, even in something as mundane as household composition, the elderly population is characterized by a considerable diversity of experience.

We have also shown that a distinctive geography of the elderly now characterizes Britain and that retirement migration has had an important effect upon the current pattern. In Britain most of the retirement migration has been to age-integrated communities. Within Europe there have not yet been established age-segregated communities of older people. This may indicate a difference between these locations in the importance attached to the concept of disengagement and separation in later life. Within Britain retirement migration is largely confined to the more affluent elderly. The most attractive locations for such moves being the most climatically favourable areas of the south coast. In recent years there has been a trend for older people from Britain to move to Spain and other countries with a more favourable climate.

However retirement migration is not seen universally as being a 'good thing'. Areas characterized by a large inflow of older people continue to express doubts about their ability to provide services for what is perceived as a 'burden' to the local health and social services. Similarly areas characterized by a significant out-migration of the young also express fears about their ability to cope with the perceived demands for services. The full implications of these demographic changes have not, however, been identified.

7
Housing and the elderly

Housing is an important dimension of lifestyle and quality of life for all sectors of the population. For older people, however, housing is more than mere shelter for it may exacerbate (or minimize) many of the social, physical or financial aspects of ageing. In this chapter we will look at various aspects of the relationship between housing and older people. Initially we describe the characteristics of the housing used by older people. This involves considering the quality of the housing inhabited by older people, their distribution within the housing market and other aspects of their housing including heating and difficulties experienced because of the physical design of the house. The second part of the chapter examines policies related to the housing of older people. This includes the analysis of the impact of general housing policy upon older people as well as the consideration of policy concerned only with older people. This section is dominated by a discussion of sheltered housing as this has been the dominant focus of housing policy for older people. The chapter concludes with a review of recent initiatives in housing for older people, especially the development of private sheltered housing and community alarm systems.

HOUSE TENURE

The housing market in Britain is divided into three sectors; owner occupation, i.e. dwellings which are either owned outright or are being purchased on a mortgage; dwellings rented from the local authority or a housing association (i.e. the public sector); and accommodation rented from a private landlord. This latter category is subdivided into those rented dwellings rented unfurnished and those rented furnished. This distinction is made because of legal differences in the security of tenure attached to these different forms of rented accommodation.

The tenure patterns of elderly people reflect choices about housing made some considerable time in the past when the housing market had a different configuration than the current one. In particular the private rented sector was considerably more important than it is today. Thus we find that the elderly are less likely to be home owners than the rest of the population and more likely to be resident in rented dwellings. This under-representation of home ownership amongst the elderly is presumably because they made decisions about their housing before the institution of Government policies, most notably tax relief on mortgages, designed to encourage the large-scale growth of home ownership.

There are variations in the main forms of housing tenure amongst the elderly population (Table 7.1).

Table 7.1 Great Britain: housing tenure of the elderly (%) 1988 (Askham *et al.*, 1992, Table 3.1a)

	65–69	70–74	75–79	80+
Owner outright/with mortgage	52	45	48	47
Rented	9	8	3	3
– local authority	31	38	32	32
– housing association	2	3	5	5
Other	7	6	13	13

With increased age the percentage of elderly who are home owners decreases slightly as does the percentage renting from a local authority whilst the percentage renting privately increases. In very general terms those members of the population who rent from a private landlord are usually considered as the most 'deprived' in terms of housing because of the problems about security of tenure which characterize this sector of the housing market.

The housing tenure arrangement of older people varies over time. During the period 1979–1988 there has been a significant increase in home ownership amongst older people (see Table 7.2). This is projected

Table 7.2 Great Britain: housing tenure trends 1979–88 (%) (Askham *et al.*, 1992, Table 3.5)

	1979			1988		
	60–69	70–79	80+	60–69	70–79	80+
Owned	47	45	46	62	52	50
Local authority rented	37	37	39	29	36	32
Rented from housing association	1	2	1	2	3	5
Other rented	15	16	14	7	9	13

to increase further during future decades. The capital asset represented by housing has prompted interest in the degree to which older home owners will be able to realize the asset and pay for part, or all, or their care needs.

HOUSING QUALITY

Traditionally housing quality in Britain is assessed by access to two standard amenities; a fixed bath or shower and a toilet. Data about the provision of toilet facilities is subdivided into facilities inside and those outside the dwelling. Access to these facilities is differentiated between those households who have sole use of the amenity and those who have to share it with one or more other household.

Table 7.3 shows that there were considerable improvements in housing quality as measured by this index during the decade 1971–81. These improvements continued during the 1980s so that at the 1991 census only 1.6% of pensioner households lacked or had shared access of bath/shower and/or inside WC.

Table 7.3 Great Britain: lack of access to housing amenities in 1971 and 1981 (%) (Office of Population Censuses and Surveys, 1984, Census Guide Number 1, Table 4)

	1971		*1981*	
	All	*Elderly*	*All*	*Elderly*
Lack of bath	10.0	14.3	1.9	4.1
Lack of WC	11.5	16.8	2.7	5.0

The quality of the houses in which elderly live is related to factors other than simply age. Older people from the lowest social classes or who are disabled experience housing standards considerably below those which characterize the rest of the elderly population (Victor, Jones and Vetter 1984; Victor and Evandrou, 1986).

There are marked geographical variations in the access of the elderly to housing amenities. This spatial distribution generally reflects the pattern of housing quality for younger age groups. The elderly living in the older industrial areas of the country such as south Wales and the north-east are more likely to experience lower housing standards than those resident in the south and east of the country. Within the most deprived areas of the country the older people are more likely to experience poor housing than other age groups.

Three main reasons seem to explain the poor quality of housing in which many older people live. The first and most obvious reason is that older people tend to live in older houses which were constructed to lower quality specifications. One third of households whose head was aged 65 years or over lived in houses built before 1919 compared to 17% where the household head was aged between 25 and 44 years of age (Department of the Environment, 1979). Typically, houses built before 1919 were constructed to a standard which is far inferior, in terms of amenity provision, to those which have been built more recently. For example it is unlikely that pre-1919 houses in England and Wales, unless they were constructed for a high status group, would have been provided with a bathroom and inside toilet.

Secondly, more old people live in the private rented sector than do younger people. This segment of the housing market tends to contain more lower quality accommodation than other sectors often because landlords have not, for a variety of reasons, improved the property. In addition many of these types of dwelling are occupied by multiple households making the sharing of facilities essential.

Thirdly, there are the problems of elderly home owners. For many older people their home becomes a liability rather than an asset with increasing age. Older people are much more likely to own an older house which is often in need of extensive modernization or repairs to bring it up to acceptable modern standards. The Cullingworth Committee (Ministry of Housing and Local Government, 1969a) identified the problems of elderly home owners as: physical inability to cope with maintenance, accommodation that was too large; and the financial and physical problems of upkeep or undertaking improvements where the older person had only a very limited income and deteriorating health. Grants are available to allow older people to improve their properties by installing bathrooms and inside toilets and generally bringing the house up to modern standards. However as these grants cover only part of the cost these have been little used by the elderly, probably because they lack the financial resources to pay the required supplement. This will be discussed further in the section on housing policy.

DWELLING OCCUPANCY RATES

Another aspect of housing quality is overcrowding. In Britain this is usually recorded by two indices, persons per room and the 'bedroom' standard, although neither has any statutory meaning. The first index used is the calculation of the number of persons per room (p.p.r.). This computation naturally includes only those rooms which are used for living and sleeping. It does not include areas such as the kitchen or bathroom. A density of 1.5 p.p.r. is usually taken to indicate overcrowding. Alternatively the National Housing and Dwelling Survey defined the 'bedroom standard' as a measure of overcrowding. This index is based upon accepted norms of bedroom occupancy such as one for every child of a different sex over 10 years of age and one for each married couple. For each household the number of bedrooms required to meet the standard is calculated and this is subtracted for the number they actually have. The resulting index gives a numerical measure of overcrowding. Although both these measures present a numerical index of dwelling occupancy rates they are based upon subjective decisions, such as the what is the right age for children to stop sharing a bedroom.

Overcrowding is not, however, a housing problem typical of the elderly. Indeed rather the reverse is true, with older households usually typified by the under-occupation of dwellings as recorded by these two indices. The National Housing and Dwelling survey (Department of the Environment, 1979) reported that 5% of households headed by an elderly person were living in dwellings defined as overcrowded. Similarly the 1980 General Household Survey (Office of Population Censuses and Surveys, 1982) indicated that 67% of individuals and 80% of couples over 60 had at least one bedroom more than they required according to the bedroom standard. However these standards are entirely subjective. Thus Age Concern argue that the appropriate standard for older couples is one bedroom per person rather than one per couple.

HEATING

In addition to the standard housing quality characteristics several other aspects of dwelling quality are of particular importance to older people. Of paramount importance is the type and adequacy of heating within a dwelling given the increased risk of hypothermia amongst older people.

Data from the 1988 General Household Survey indicate that 73% of those aged 65–69 had central heating compared with 65% of those aged 80 and over (Askham *et al.*, 1992). However this does not indicate how many actually use the heating.

Unlike other groups of poor people the elderly are less likely to have fuel debts or be disconnected. This is not a reflection of their relative affluence. Rather it reflects the way that the old limit their fuel consumption to avoid receiving a bill they cannot pay. Thus we have the paradox that older people spend a much higher fraction of their income on heating than the rest of the population but achieve a much lower level of heating.

ACCESS

Older people may be further disadvantaged by problems of access both to their dwelling and within it. The presence of internal steps or stairs, or of steps leading up to the dwelling may make an elderly person less mobile and less able to get out. A survey of the elderly in Wales revealed that 55% of those aged 70 years and over had external stairs and 72% had steps inside their house (Victor, Jones and Vetter, 1983). The presence of these barriers to mobility did not decrease with age and there were few examples of aids and adaptations to make the external and internal access to the house easier. Additionally, Victor, Holtermann and Vetter (1986) have indicated that difficulties of internal and external dwelling access was one important reason why an augmented home care scheme failed to improve the outcome for older people discharged from hospitals in the Rhondda area of Wales.

LENGTH OF RESIDENCE

Older people are, not surprisingly, characterized by a long length of residence in their dwelling. In Wales a survey of the over-70s revealed that three-quarters had lived in their present dwelling for more than 5 years and this proportion increased with age (Victor, Jones and Vetter, 1983). These findings are probably typical of Britain as a whole.

EMERGENCY SUMMONS

Various surveys have looked at the means by which older people could summon help in an emergency. In Wales less than a half of those aged 70 and over have any method of calling for help in an emergency. Where such help was available, telephones were the most commonly quoted source of help rather than specially provided alarms or window cards. There was an important relationship between age and the availability of emergency help. The very oldest age groups were much less likely to have some method of emergency contact available to them than the younger elderly.

   This aspect of housing for the elderly has been the subject of extensive recent debate. In particular a number of local authorities and charities have been developing community alarm systems for older people living in their own homes. We shall consider this topic further in a later section of this chapter.

SATISFACTION WITH HOUSING

Despite the low standards of housing relative to other members of the population, surveys have consistently reported that the elderly express a high degree of satisfaction with their housing. In Wales only 5% felt that their housing was unsuitable and this did not alter with the age. Where such unsuitability was reported this usually related to the size of the dwelling or garden rather than the provision of amenities. However, Age Concern (1974) reported that at least 15% of residential moves made by the elderly were because of problems with their housing such as maintenance and upkeep. Emergency admission to residential homes is also associated with poor housing.

HOUSING POLICY FOR OLDER PEOPLE

Although housing constitutes only one element of the wider living environment of the elderly, it is a factor which is of considerable importance given that, even in very old age, the majority of people are resident in the community in their own homes. In Britain recognition of the importance of housing to the overall welfare of the elderly can be traced back to the construction of almshouses in the Middle Ages. More recently the Government Green Paper *A Happier Old Age* stated that 'aside from his spouse, housing is probably the single most important element in the life of an older person' (Department of Health and Social Security, 1978). However good housing is not seen by policy makers and planners merely as being important in its own right, rather it is viewed as an alternative to the now much discredited institutional sector. Any form of disability may be exacerbated by the lack of an inside toilet, awkward stairs or inadequate heating. The broad objective of housing policy for the elderly has been to enhance their ability to live independent and useful lives within the community.

Housing policy for the elderly is the product of the interaction between general statements of housing policy and those directed specifically at the elderly. General housing policy obviously has an effect upon the elderly. However in its formulation the interests of the aged have to be weighed up against those of other groups such as young families or the single mobile seeking housing. Rarely have general statements of housing policy contained detailed assessments of their impact upon the elderly (or indeed any other part of the population). The elderly have been affected by schemes for urban renewal, housing improvements, the initiation of minimal standards, rent controls and legislation dealing with security of tenure. It is difficult to ascertain with any certainty what, if any, the impact these policies has been upon the housing status of the elderly. However we do know that the elderly have been particularly badly affected by slum clearance schemes which broke up many established inner city communities and decanted the residents to the periphery of many of our cities.

One of the major problems of elderly home owners was that of repairs. The failure to undertake repairs, for whatever reason by the elderly, leads to an inevitable decline in the quality of the housing stock. These may be sub-divided into those required to keep the house weatherproof, those required to maintain security, those required to modernize the house and routine minor repairs.

One of the major barriers to the elderly undertaking house repairs is lack of money. Thus the elderly living in accommodation lacking certain amenities are eligible to receive improvement grants. Currently the elderly receive 33% of all such grants. However the take-up of these grants is limited because they do not cover 100% of the cost of the work. Many elderly who would like to take advantage of these incentives are unable to pay their contribution towards the work. Although there are some elderly who would not want the upheaval of having their houses modernized several workers have reported that many elderly would be happy to apply for improvement/repair grants if they covered the total cost of the work required and/or applicants were not subjected to a 'means test' (Welsh Office, 1983).

The focus of successive governments' housing policies for the elderly has been the provision of specialist accommodation. Rather less attention has been given to developing policies which enable the elderly to remain in the dwellings which they have often occupied for many years. One innovative policy response to the problems of home ownership amongst the elderly has been the 'Staying Put' scheme developed by the Anchor Housing Trust (Wheeler, 1982) which was piloted in seven areas of the country. This scheme has a twin emphasis upon both housing assistance, offering assistance with repairs, improvements and adaptations, and helping the older person to remain independent in the community. This scheme offers a contrast with past policy for the elderly which has stressed that housing for the elderly needs to be purpose-built, a preoccupation which has obscured other potential types of housing policy response to the difficulties of older people. There has been little in the way of a policy response to the problems of older people resident in substandard private rented housing, with the exception of legislation concerned with the setting of appropriate rents.

Another approach to the problems of elderly home owners has been the 'Care and Repair' approach pioneered in the Ferndale area of the Rhondda Valley in Wales. This subsidized repair project sought to improve the houses of older people to standards acceptable to the elderly themselves, rather than attempting to bring it up to some 'notional national minimum'. Although this concept does little for the problems of the elderly in private rented dwellings, area-based subsidized repair teams could do much to improve the quality of the nation's housing stock.

SHELTERED HOUSING

Approximately 5% of the retired population live in sheltered housing. This is usually defined as purpose-built housing provided with a resident warden, an alarm system and occupied only by older people. Such grouped dwelling schemes have been the major focus of the housing policy for the elderly pursued by governments of all political persuasions. The construction of sheltered housing schemes was initially undertaken by local authorities. Additionally voluntary agencies and charities such as the Anchor Housing Association and the Abbeyfield Extra Care Association have also been active in the construction of such dwellings.

Recently there has been a boom in the construction of sheltered dwellings for sale, especially in the more affluent southern and eastern parts of the country. These developments provide warden services and communal facilities just as in the public sector. They also stress the companionship and security which they can provide. Thus this type of development is based upon the assumption that old age is inevitably a time of dependence. Such developments are not cheap to purchase. A one-bedroom flat in Godalming, Surrey would cost around £45 000 plus service charges.

THE ROLE OF SHELTERED HOUSING

The first aspect of sheltered housing to be considered is, what role does it play in the maintenance of older people in the community? Examination of policy documents relating to specialist housing for older people indicates that this concept has evolved in a rather pragmatic fashion. This pragmatism and changing objectives is not, however, confined to the field of specialist housing but is characteristic of many social and medical policies for older people. However the evolution of sheltered housing policy has resulted in considerable ambiguity about both its physical form and role and relationships with other services. The role of sheltered housing in relation to other aspects of policy for the elderly, especially the institutional sector, has never really been clarified. Consequently some writers see sheltered housing as an alternative to residential care whilst others argue that it is a half-way stage on a continuum of care ranging from normal housing to institutional care. There have, as we shall see below, also been considerable debates about the physical form this type of housing should take.

Despite the underlying ambiguity it is possible to identify three main roles that have been suggested for sheltered housing. The first view conceptualizes sheltered housing as a response to the poor housing conditions of the elderly that we described earlier. Thus this is a view of sheltered housing which excludes wider social policy objectives and is therefore simply seen a narrowly focused housing-centred approach. A more wide-ranging view envisages sheltered housing as a means of preventing admission to residential care. This is a concept which expresses both housing and social policy aims and objectives. Finally there is a highly socially orientated approach which sees specialized housing as a way of responding to the perceived loneliness and social isolation of old age. The respective importance of these factors has varied at different times during the development of sheltered housing.

THE DEVELOPMENT OF SHELTERED HOUSING

The history of the development of sheltered housing may be divided into several sections. The first relates to the innovative period when the concept was first developed. Following this was a period of widespread expansion when sheltered housing was seen as the complete answer to the perceived problems of old age. Subsequently the relevance of specialized housing as a major policy objective was questioned and there was a period of retrenchment. Finally the policy has been resurrected but is now only proposed as being appropriate to specific groups of older people. These periods in the development of sheltered housing are identified in the subsequent sections.

Two of the three distinguishing characteristics of sheltered housing, a grouped congregation of elderly and the presence of a person acting as warden, are displayed by the almshouses built in medieval England. According to Butler, Oldman and Greve (1983) the earliest reference to an almshouse is the St Cross Hospital which was founded in Winchester in 1136. However, little attention was given to the housing problems of the old until the beginning of this century. In 1909 the Majority Report of the Poor Law Commission (His Majesty's Stationery Office, 1909) commented favourably on special housing schemes for the elderly which had been developed in such areas as the Woolwich district of London. These schemes were usually designed to meet housing rather than social needs.

The generally accepted prototype sheltered housing scheme is credited to Sturminster Newton Council in Devon. However, Butler, Oldman and Greve (1983) suggests that it is possible that the first two schemes providing a warden and an alarm system were operating before the outbreak of the Second World War in 1939.

The origin of the term 'sheltered dwelling' or 'housing' is difficult to establish. One of the earliest references to the term is to be found in the 1944 Housing Manual which referred to the locating of special grouped schemes for the elderly in sheltered sites to assist in keeping warm. However the term is now generally taken to mean sheltering from the storms and troubles of life rather than from climatic ones.

In the immediate post-Second World War era the main thrust of housing policy was towards housing families and reconstructing war-damaged property. There was no acknowledgement by the government of the day that there should be a housing policy specifically concerned with the elderly. Without the support of central government the construction of sheltered housing units was slow and development almost totally confined to specific local authorities in the west country area. The growth of development in the south-west of England resulted from local council-lors and officials visiting sheltered housing schemes in neighbouring areas and deciding to emulate them in their own locality.

This essentially piecemeal and localized pattern of development was encouraged by a lack of clarity about the responsibility for funding of such developments. In the first instance finance was provided entirely by the local housing authority. Social services were not required to contrib-ute to the construction and financing of these schemes. Almost from its inception sheltered housing was characterized by an ambiguous relation-ship between housing and social service departments in its construction, funding and running. Inevitably this resulted in a tension between the housing and the welfare aspects of sheltered housing developments.

It is difficult to be precise about the numbers of sheltered dwellings constructed and inhabited at different points in time because of the spars-ity of official records relating to these topics. However Butler, Oldman and Greve (1983) suggest that by 1950 approximately 10 000 elderly people in England lived in some 7000 sheltered dwelling units (see Table 7.4).

Table 7.4 Growth of sheltered housing for elderly people (Williams, 1992, Table 2.4)

	Units (000s)	*Occupants (000s)*
1950	7	10
1960	21	28
1970	97	130
1981	299	400
1988	400	520

Opinion about the most appropriate way of caring for the elderly started to change in the 1950s with the start of the movement towards care in the community rather than in institutions. Sheltered or special housing for the elderly was seen as one method of responding to the policy objective. Thus as part of the newly conceived policy of community care a stream of circulars and discussion documents was issued by central government encouraging local authorities to construct specialized dwellings for older people which included three characteristic features: a communal room, a warden and a an alarm system connecting residents to the warden.

At this stage in the development of sheltered housing the government envisaged it as being one aspect in a continuum of care for the elderly which ranged from independence to institutional living. Thus the 1958 design document *Flatlets for Old People* stated that 'What is needed now is accommodation which is halfway between a self-contained dwelling and hostels providing care'. In this manifestation sheltered housing is expressing policy objectives which are more wide-ranging than a simple concentration upon improving housing standards.

Three factors underpinned this new emphasis upon the construction sheltered dwelling. Firstly, residential care was increasingly being viewed as the last resort and a very expensive way of delivering care to an increasing fraction of older people. Secondly, policy makers were becoming aware of the desire of older people to remain independent in their own homes for as long as possible rather than move into an institution. Thirdly, there was an implicit assumption on the part of policy makers that older people would move to the community services that would allow them to retain their independence rather than vice versa and that this would enable the more efficient provision of care in the community.

Whilst there was some comment in these policy developments, however obscurely presented, about the role of sheltered housing, there were few explicit statements about the type of person sheltered housing was intended for or the precise policy objectives sheltered housing was attempting to fulfil. Rather, these directives contained the implicit assumptions that this type of housing was best suited to the older and frailer members of the community without identifying the characteristics of this group in any detail. There was no debate about whether those elderly deemed suitable for residential accommodation could be catered for in sheltered housing and vice versa. Rather, there was an implicit assumptions that these two groups were one and the same.

The more positive attitude of the government towards sheltered housing is reflected in the increase in the numbers living in such dwellings during the late 1950s. According to Butler, Oldman and Greve (1983) by 1960 there were 21 000 units, accommodating 28 000 elderly people. Of this total the majority had been constructed by local authorities and 14% by the voluntary sector.

The government was very active in providing advice about the design and location of sheltered housing. However, it did not develop guidelines about the amount of sheltered housing which local authorities should provide. The oft quoted norm for provision of 50 dwellings per 1000 persons aged 65 and over was suggested by Peter Townsend, in his book *The Last Refuge* (1964) where he advocated the replacement of institutional care for the elderly by sheltered accommodation. He based this norm upon three factors; the fraction of elderly living alone; the proportion without any family support and the fraction of the elderly population classified as severely disabled. The proposed norm did not take into account other factors such as the quality of housing currently used by the elderly or the availability of other forms of care and services.

In 1969 probably the most influential circular on sheltered dwellings was published by the government. In *Housing Standards and Cost: Accommodation Specially Designed for Old People,* Circular 82/69, the theme of providing dwellings which would enable the old to live independently for as long as possible was reiterated (Ministry of Housing and Local Government, 1969b). Again there was the implicit assumption that sheltered housing would be occupied by the older and frailer members of the elderly community without the articulation of any specific criteria to define this group. The circular specified minimum design standards. An optimum scheme size was suggested as 30 residents. This was considered to be a workload which a single warden could manage. Larger schemes were not favoured because of fears about creating a ghetto of older people.

Much of the advice contained in this circular has been realized. The average size of local authority schemes was 27.32 units and 24 units for schemes constructed by Housing Associations. The average size of scheme constructed has increased with time. In 1962 the average local authority scheme consisted of 23 units. By 1977 the average scheme size had increased to 31 units. Housing Association schemes have usually been smaller in size than those constructed by local authorities. In 1962 the average scheme consisted of 17 units, by 1977 this had increased to 30 units, only slightly smaller than the local authority average.

Circular 82/69 was also important because it established the concept of 'category 1' and 'category 2' schemes. This division of sheltered housing into two distinct categories arose in response to the view that it was both unnecessary and undesirable to provide services and facilities for all residents of all sheltered housing schemes. Two distinct types of sheltered housing client were envisaged. Category 1 schemes were designed to accommodate the more active elderly and were not to be provided with the whole plethora of facilities. Category 2 dwellings, in contrast, were thought of as being suitable for less active lone pensioners and would be provided with a full range of facilities such as common rooms and laundries etc. Category 1 schemes were a response to the housing and social contact 'problems' of the elderly whilst category 2 schemes were seen as the alternative to institutional care. Thus the continuum of care between 'normal' housing and the institutional sector was further sub-divided. Although never explicitly stated, it was assumed that the older person would move through these different stages as (s)he experienced the ageing process. Although the notion of category 1 and 2 types of sheltered housing schemes has been very popular, the definitions have never been operationalized. Consequently the distinctions between these two types of housing have largely been ignored.

Another idea about sheltered housing which was popular in the 1960s was the linking of such developments with existing local authority residential homes, allowing the easy movement of residents between sectors. Whilst this seemed a sound idea in principle it was never really favoured by those building and designing schemes and gradually fell into disfavour. Additionally there were often practical problems in building sheltered housing units in close proximity to existing residential homes. However recently multipurpose projects such as Queens Park Court in Billericay, Essex have gone a long way to overcoming these problems.

By 1970 there were about 100 000 sheltered housing units. In the public sector expansion continued up until the 1980s by which time there where approximately 281 000 units housing around 400 000 people (see Tables 7.4 and 7.5). With the advent of cash limits and stricter control over public spending since the election of the Conservative government in 1979 there has been relatively little expansion of public-sector sheltered housing since this date. However the voluntary sector continues to grow, as do private sector developments.

Table 7.5 Provision of specialized dwellings for elderly people 1986 (Williams, 1992)

	Sheltered dwellings
Local authority	281 000
Housing association	92 000
Private	16 000
Other	3 000
Total	392 000

Whilst the government has been active in trying to guide the architectural shape of sheltered housing development and the construction of these types of dwellings it has, as noted earlier, been reticent about establishing norms of provision. This failure to define the minimum level of provision results from the failure to decide upon the level of dependence (or independence) that sheltered housing was considered appropriate to cater for.

Given the lack of guidelines local authorities have been free to construct as much (or as little) sheltered housing as they liked. This has lead to marked geographical variations in levels of provision in different parts of the country. In Wales there are 555 Local Authority sheltered housing schemes consisting of a total of 13 685 units. A further 88 schemes and 2663 units are provided by the voluntary sector, giving a total level of provision of 37.3 units per 1000 population aged 65 years and over. This overall figure masks substantial variations in levels of provision within

Wales ranging from 140.9 units per 1000 in the Delyn district to 8.9 units per 1000 in Dwyfor (Fisk, 1986).

THE MANAGEMENT OF SHELTERED HOUSING

Sheltered housing is characterized by two fundamental ambiguities. The first relates to the relationship between the housing and welfare aspects of such schemes and their relationships with other aspects of the care of the elderly. Secondly there is the issue of the dependence and independence of residents. These tensions are reflected in the practical management of such units. Two concepts seem to dominate allocation policies for sheltered housing; need and independence. Typically allocation is made upon a basis of need although the meaning of this term is rarely defined. Additionally, however, there is also the criteria of independence. For acceptance into a scheme the potential resident must demonstrate that they are both 'in need' and basically capable of independent living. The basic contradiction between these two characteristics seems to have escaped many of those involved in the allocation process. Other criteria by which places are allocated relate to age, length of residence in the area, and tenure. Few local authorities formally exclude home owners from sheltered housing. However the operation of points systems for eligibility seems to formally exclude most home owners. This is one factor which has probably stimulated the development of sheltered housing complexes in the private sector.

In examining allocation procedures and criteria two models may be identified. The first conceptualizes sheltered housing simply as part of the total public housing stock. This is essentially a housing management view of sheltered housing. The alternative view sees sheltered housing as a radical alternative to residential care and, by implication, part of the resources available to the social services part of local government. It is impossible to understand the allocation and management process in an area without a knowledge of what model of sheltered housing they are operating with. It is certain that these procedures vary substantially both between authorities and within authorities which practise decentralized decision-making practices.

THE REALITIES OF SHELTERED HOUSING

Various aspects of sheltered housing have been studied. By examining these studies we can establish how the reality of sheltered housing provision accords with the numerous statements of policy. This analysis also highlights some of the issues concerning the development of this type of provision for older people.

The role of the warden

The provision of a resident warden is one of the distinguishing characteristics of sheltered housing. Indeed some would argue that the warden is the central feature of sheltered housing. However the role of the warden is characterized by the tensions and ambiguities which characterize sheltered housing in general. Two models of the role of the warden may be distinguished. The first perspective conceives of the warden as an organizer and facilitator of care. The second view envisages a more active caring role for the warden as an integral part of the complex interdependent multi-service system of providing care to the elderly in the community. Typically it is the housing authorities who hold the first view whilst social services departments envisage the warden as a care-giver.

Several surveys have looked at the characteristics and duties of the people employed as wardens in sheltered housing schemes (Phillipson and Strang, 1985; Butler, Oldman and Greve, 1983). Very little variation in results has been observed either between different areas of the country or between local authority and voluntary sponsored schemes. Wardens are predominantly female, middle-aged and middle-class. Few have any formal qualifications, although many have previous work experience in dealing with the elderly in either the voluntary or statutory sectors.

The prevalent ambiguity about the role of the warden was reflected in the very vague job descriptions most worked to. Few wardens had received any formal training for the job although the vast majority would have liked training. Staff turnover was, however, very low. In spite of the key role wardens are theoretically supposed to play in contacting other components of the community care few had any regular liaison with the main service-providing agencies. Where contacts were established they were usually with a particular home help or district nurse; rarely were such relationships established with more senior members of these organizations. The wardens had a poor sense of occupational identity, complaining of their isolation from others doing the same job and the lack of support from line management.

Wardens themselves define their main duties in terms of routine surveillance and 'good neighbourliness'. However examination of the types of task they actually perform for residents indicates that they are providing social and medical services to patients far in excess of the original notion of the warden as a 'good neighbour'. Thus the wardens are operating as providers rather than facilitators of care.

The residents of sheltered dwellings

As we have seen, there has been a consistent theme running through policy statements about sheltered housing that it was aimed at the less able, but still independent, elderly. How far has sheltered housing been successful in reaching the population considered most appropriate for this type of housing? Table 7.6 presents a summary of the major studies that have looked at the characteristics of public-sector sheltered housing residents.

Table 7.6 Demographic characteristics of the residents of sheltered housing schemes

Study	Average age	% over 75	% female	% living alone
Wales (1)	71.9	NA	NA	NA
Devon (2)	73.7	NA	75	63
West Midland (2)	74.6	NA	75	63
Scotland (3)	75.1	50	73	77
Liverpool (4)	75.0	53	84	79
W. London (5)	78.0	NA	NA	NA
Hull (6)	77.0	61	NA	NA
National (7)	NA	53	73	70
All elderly (GHS, 1980)		36	59	39

Key:
1. Fisk, 1986
2. Heuman and Boldy, 1982
3. Wirz, McGinn, Wilson, 1981
4. Middleton, 1981
5. Bowling and Bleatham, 1982
6. Cunnison and Page, 1985
7. Butler, Oldmann and Greave, 1983

This indicates that, compared with the elderly living in other types of housing, sheltered housing residents are older, and contain a much higher fraction of women and those living alone. All the schemes included in this summary have an average age of residents of over 70 years of age; at least 70% of residents were female and at least 60% of residents lived alone. The residents of sheltered housing schemes are not, therefore, typical of the elderly population as a whole.

Table 7.7 Dependency characteristics of residents of sheltered housing schemes (N.B. studies where data was unavailable are excluded)

Study	% unable to			
	Go outside	Manage stairs	Shop	Cook
W. Midlands (2)	NA	16	NA	3
Scotland (3)	13	17	43	NA
Hull (6)	NA	NA	25	NA
National (7)	NA	NA	16	3
All elderly (GHS, 1980)	12	8	14	7

Key: as Table 7.6

Throughout the policy documents there is an implicit assumption that sheltered housing tenants will constitute some of the frailer members of the elderly population. It is not easy to ascertain the dependency characteristics of sheltered housing residents and make comparisons with the general population of elderly because of the great variation in measures of disability used in the various studies. Table 7.7 does, however, try to make some rudimentary comparisons between studies of sheltered housing residents and the elderly resident in the community.

This table indicates that the residents of sheltered housing demonstrate a high degree of independence and are not significantly more disabled than their contemporaries living in ordinary housing when the increased age of sheltered housing residents is taken into account. This similarity in the characteristics of older people living in ordinary and sheltered dwellings seems to refute the idea that the sheltered housing population is coming rapidly to resemble that characteristic of residential and nursing homes. Rather than these two types of living environment being suitable for the same populations they are if fact catering for two very distinctive client groups.

Where do sheltered housing residents come from?

Another issue concerning sheltered housing has been from which sectors of the housing market such tenants are drawn. Confining our remarks to public/voluntary provision, at least 45% of residents are drawn from local authority housing (Fisk, 1986; Wirz, McGinn and Wilson, 1981; Middleton, 1981). A further 30% are drawn from the private rented sector with only a minority of residents having previously been owner occupiers. Half of all sheltered housing tenants had previously occupied a 2- or 3-bedroomed dwelling (Butler, Oldman and Greve, 1983). By the older person moving into such dwellings a house has been made available for family use. This should perhaps be borne in mind when policy makers are calculating the cost of constructing sheltered dwellings, the potential increase in the housing stock being offset against the construction costs of sheltered housing. Thus it seems that in many areas sheltered housing schemes have been used by the local authority as a means of releasing a large house for occupation by a family as much as for any wider social reasons such as preventing admission to an institution.

Residents' use of the warden and other facilities

As well as providing good quality, if small, housing sheltered housing is characterized by the provision of a range of facilities including wardens, communal rooms and alarm systems. Some schemes also provide guest rooms and laundry facilities. How much use do residents make of these facilities? Studies have consistently reported that in schemes where a resident warden is provided residents remain in daily contact either via the intercom system or in person. Typically tenants reported that the warden had helped them when they were ill, assisted with shopping or contacted relatives. We shall see in later sections that communal rooms and alarm systems are used rarely by residents. Thus we might question whether the provision of these facilities is really necessary.

Provision of community service

Two competing views have been expressed about the use of domiciliary services by sheltered housing residents. The first states that because of the presence of the warden they will be less likely to receive domiciliary support services such as home help or meals on wheels. Alternatively Middleton (1981) argued that because they represent a visible concentration of elderly, which makes needs more obvious and provision of services easier, they will receive a disproportionate amount of help from the statutory services.

The evidence presented in Table 7.8 clearly supports the hypothesis that sheltered housing residents receive services in excess of that characteristic of the general population of elderly.

Table 7.8 Receipt of services by sheltered housing residents (%)

Study	Home help	Meals on wheels
Wales (1)	19.8	5.7
Devon (2)	23.6	NA
West Midlands (2)	26.2	NA
Scotland (3)	34.0	10.0
Liverpool (4)	24.3	NA
W. London (5)	32.0	18.0
Hull (6)	43.0	5.0
National (7)	34.0	6.0
All elderly (GHS, 1980)	9.0	2.0

Key: as Table 7.6

At least 20% of residents had a home help compared with the national average of 9%. These high levels of service use are not, however, explained by the age and disability characteristics of sheltered housing residents. It would seem that they are being made a high priority for service receipt. This may reflect their highly visible concentration or the activity of the warden as an advocate in obtaining services for scheme residents.

Sheltered housing: a response to loneliness?

One of the implicit assumptions of sheltered housing is that it helps to overcome the social isolation and loneliness which is seen by many, policy makers and public alike, as being one of the most fundamental problems of old age. To date the empirical evidence suggests that these schemes have had only a marginal impact upon tenants' perceptions of loneliness and that many look outside the physical confines of the scheme to family and previous friends for much of their social interaction.

A feature of most sheltered housing schemes is the provision of communal rooms such as a common room, laundry and guest rooms. Only two-thirds of residents seem to make use of these facilities and then often only on a sporadic basis. It seems that the provision of these facilities has not stimulated the social interaction the planners had in mind when they were conceived (Middleton, 1983).

Why move to sheltered housing?

The reasons why people moved into a sheltered housing development seem to be very complex and difficult to disentangle. However three sets of factors, health, inadequate housing and the desire to be near friends/relatives, seem to explain the decision (Fisk, 1986; Wirz, McGinn and Wilson, 1981; Middleton, 1981). The major reason for such moves relates to problems associated with the previous dwelling such as the house being too large or in need of modernization or repairs. In any case we might speculate as to how much pressure was brought to bear upon older people occupying large houses in the public sector to move to a sheltered flat thereby releasing a house for family occupation. Factors relating to health were also of considerable importance in the decision. The final sets of reasons given related to the desire to be nearer relatives. However family factors were usually of less importance than the other two variables. Few mentions were made of sheltered housing being considered as an alternative to residential care.

The role of alarm systems

Central to the development of sheltered housing has been the assumption of the importance of the alarm system. However recently studies have questioned its role and importance (Butler, Oldman and Greve, 1983). One study reported that the majority of tenants, over 80%, had not used the alarm in the year before interview. Another study demonstrated that only 23% of elderly who experienced an 'emergency' used the alarm system to call help (Feeney, Galer and Gallagher, 1974).

It is difficult to define objectively emergency calls and 'trivial' incidents. Fisk (1984) reports that trivial calls and false alarms constitute a substantial fraction of calls made via alarm systems. In some circumstances it could be convincingly argued that provision of alarm systems fosters dependence rather than independence. The wider availability of telephones amongst older people may prove to be a more satisfactory way of summoning help in an emergency than a specific alarm system.

A recent development in housing for the elderly has been the development of community alarm systems. Fisk (1986) observes that the rise of these systems has been rapid since the establishment of the first scheme in Christchurch in 1975. However, he also notes that there has been a failure on the part of those developing the systems to specify exactly what the objectives of this type of scheme are. One motivation for these developments has been the desire to save money by replacing a resident warden. Additionally by developing these types of schemes local authorities can give the impression of developing new services for caring for the elderly at home without spending large amounts of money. Certainly the limited role which alarm systems seem to play in the sheltered housing environment suggests that their expansion to the wider community would be of only limited utility. Indeed the widespread provision of alarm pendants to individual older people can only help to foster the image of old age as a time of dependence and reliance upon others, rather than stressing autonomy and choice. However this must be balanced against the fears of individual elders living alone for whom an alarm, even if it is not used, may provide a 'lifeline' for continued independence.

NEW DEVELOPMENTS IN SHELTERED HOUSING

As noted earlier, construction of public sector sheltered housing has slowed considerably since 1979. This decrease in construction rates partly reflects a dissatisfaction with sheltered housing as a solution to the 'problems' of the elderly. However of more importance in restraining construction has been the severe limitations imposed upon the capital expenditure of local authorities by a central government committed to restricting public expenditure.

The most spectacular area of growth has been in the construction of sheltered housing for sale. McCarthy and Stone, the leaders in this component of the house construction business, build an average of 3000 units per annum. Baker and Perry (1986) estimate that there are 17 636 units in this sector of the housing market worth at least £500 000 000. Of the currently constructed units only 11% were built before 1980. Such is the perceived importance of this sector of the housing market that the number of starts and completions of private sheltered housing are now included in the Local Authority Housing Statistics published by the Department of the Environment. Baker and Perry (1984) estimate that the potential market for private sheltered housing in Great Britain could be 400 000 units. However, as Table 7.5 indicates, private developments do not provide as many units as the public sector.

The growth of the sheltered housing market is unevenly distributed throughout Great Britain. Of the units constructed by 1985 48% were in the counties of Devon, Hampshire, Kent, London, Surrey and Sussex. Units under construction demonstrate a similar pattern of concentration in the more affluent areas of the south and west of the country. This concentration is largely explained by the high property prices and levels of home ownership in these areas. Many elderly home owners have moved to sheltered housing as a means of releasing some of the capital 'tied up' in their home, as well as for reasons relating to the size of the dwelling and garden.

What has brought about the growth in this sector of the housing market and how closely does it resemble public sector developments? These are difficult questions to answer unequivocally. Like public sector developments, private sheltered housing usually provides a warden, an alarm system and a variety of communal facilities. How extensively these facilities are used remains a factor of debate. Residents have to pay for these services and it remains to be seen whether there are problems in the future with older people being unable to pay service charges that seem to rise at rates considerably in excess of inflation.

The cost of sheltered housing is generally high. Rarely is it possible to enter the market below £30 000 and in many areas a one-bedroom flat will cost considerably more than this. There are financial drawbacks to entering this sector of the housing market as some developers require residents to sell back the property to them at the original price. Other developers set excessive charges for re-selling the property and insist upon managing the sale without allowing the elderly person (or their children) to sell on the open market.

The residents of private sheltered housing are drawn from the opposite end of the social class distribution from those in public-sector provision. Generally private-sector residents are less old, less disabled and less likely to be living alone than their public-sector contemporaries (Williams, 1990). As with the public sector housing-related issues prompt most of the moves to private developments. However the detailed reasons are very different for in the private sector the elderly person is often using the move to release capital 'tied up' in their house by 'trading down' in the housing market. The wardens or 'housekeepers' employed in private sheltered housing are similar in character to those employed in the public sector.

CONCLUSION

Housing is a key element in the physical environment of both old and young. Using empirical data we have demonstrated that older people tend to occupy worse housing than younger age groups. Using the indicators of tenure and provision of amenities the elderly experience markedly lower standards of accommodation than other sub-groups of the population. Thus we have the paradox that the oldest and frailest members of the community experience the worst housing conditions. Additionally, as we shall see later, the elderly often lack the financial resources to improve the standards of housing.

As well as deprivation in terms of standard amenities the elderly are often disadvantaged by the physical design of their dwelling. Features such as internal steps and stairs may create substantial problems for older people. Additionally problems of access to the house such as stairs leading up from the street may handicap an older person by restricting their mobility.

Housing policy for older people has concentrated almost exclusively upon improving 'standards' with little attention being paid to the provision of small adaptations like ramps or handrails which could significantly decrease many of the barriers currently experienced by older people.

Although older people have affected by general housing improvement initiatives the impact of these policies has probably been minimal. Central government has shown little innovation in developing improvement schemes for older home owners. It is significant to note that initiatives such as 'Staying Put' and 'Care and Repair' have come from the voluntary or local authority sector rather than national government. However it seems to be in no-one's best interest to let the housing stock deteriorate, excluding any thoughts about the potential of housing improvements to improve the quality of life of older people. Elderly home owners are, on average, willing to improve their property. All that is lacking is the money. Thus it would seem appropriate to award this group 100% grants for the improvement of their property. However this issue, like many other 'welfare issues', illustrates the debate about whether benefits should be universal or means-tested.

The government response to the housing problems of the elderly has been to construct sheltered housing units. These are purpose-built schemes that segregate the elderly from the wider community. Thus this type of policy response seems to consider that the housing problems of older people can best be solved by detaching them from the rest of the community and is thus based upon an acceptance of the highly questionable theory of disengagement.

Although specialist housing has formed the basis of the policy response to housing in later life these policies are characterized by fundamental ambiguities in both aims and objectives. Thus there has been a

fundamental conflict between the housing and social welfare components of sheltered housing. A central theme of this type of housing relates
to the desire to foster the continued independence of residents. However
the idea that the objective of complete independence can be maintained
in sheltered housing is probably false. Thus Middleton (1981) argues that
the mere fact of moving to such a scheme and accepting the surveillance
of the warden mitigates against continued independent living. The high
usage rates of statutory services, which are not explained by the characteristics of the residents, would also seem to suggest that sheltered housing promotes assisted independence rather than total independence.
However it could be argued that it is the provision of information which
promotes the high service use of sheltered housing residents. A research
project involving information to older people in 'ordinary' housing
would test this hypothesis.

Given the expense of constructing purpose-built dwellings which do
not achieve the desired objective of maintaining the independence of the
elderly, perhaps the efficacy of this policy requires questioning. Perhaps a
more cost-effective response to the housing problems of the elderly
would be to concentrate upon improving and modifying their existing
dwellings. This would certainly prevent the documented problems of the
elderly losing contact with the wider community when moved into these
types of schemes (Clayton, 1978; Hillhouse, 1983; Fennell, 1985).

The growth in privately constructed sheltered dwellings also brings some
problems which will require attention in the future. Many of these relate to
the financial aspects of such developments, especially the imposition of
high service charges and restrictions on the resale of the property.

That many older people are disadvantaged in terms of most aspects of
the house they reside in is not to be doubted. Consequently what is
required are more innovative policy responses that are sensitive to the
needs of the older person rather than reflecting the attitudes of younger
people. Thus in developing future initiatives extensive account should be
taken of the needs and aspirations of the elderly themselves. In housing,
as in other aspects of life, too often the elderly have been perceived as
passive recipients of care. Also policy makers must understand that
housing is not an aspect of lifestyle that can be divorced from other issues
like provision of services or income maintenance. Thus there is a need to
integrate housing policy within the overall framework of social policy.

The housing needs of older people are probably little different from
those of the younger members of the community. Like the rest of us they
require warmth, security and convenience in their dwelling and housing
which fosters rather than hinders their independence and integration
within the community. Thus future policies should aim to achieve these
objectives by a radical programme based on the needs and wishes of the
elderly.

8

Work and retirement

The work ethic is an important organizing principle in modern society. In this chapter we provide a brief summary of the role and functions of work in industrial western society. This is then followed by an examination of the status of the older worker within the labour market. Subsequently we discuss the emergence of retirement and early retirement and consider the way that older people adjust to retirement.

WORK

The view that retirement results in a fundamental crisis of identity for the individual is very prevalent. However this perspective assumes that work is both central to the life of the individual and that it is the major characteristic defining personal identity. To look at the relevance of this stereotype and to understand the impact of retirement, for the individual and the wider society, we must first look at the role work plays in modern industrial society. The role of work has varied both between societies and historically. Amongst the Greeks, work was thought fit only for slaves. For the first Christians, work was seen as a penance. During the Renaissance, work, especially creative pursuits, was seen as a joy in itself. The advent of the Protestant revolution brought about a new attitude towards work with it being viewed as a religious devotion. In particular the followers of John Calvin saw work and labour as a way of gaining God's favour. Though work is no longer perceived as a sign of salvation in most Western industrial societies, society is still imbued with a strong Protestant work ethic.

Sociologists have identified four main functions that work performs in the lives of individuals. These are; the provision of a wage, the regulation of time, the provision of social status and the provision of social relationships. To fully understand the impact and meaning of retirement we must examine its effects upon each of these functions.

The first, and perhaps most obvious, function of a job in an industrial society is to provide an income or financial reward to the employee. This the individual can then use to maintain his/herself and to purchase all the goods and services s/he requires.

A second function of work is as a regulatory activity. The undertaking of gainful employment normally requires the individual to be at a certain place, either a factory, office or some other place of work, for specific days and times. In Britain this is usually 5 days a week for 8 hours a day. The amount of time spent at work has been decreasing over this century. Before the Second World War the working week consisted of 48 hours or more. However despite the decrease in the length of the working week a large fraction of an individual's time is still spent in work. Thus work provides an important organizing framework around which people organize many other aspects of their lives such as leisure, hobbies or social relationships.

Work provides a sense of identity for the individual and also serves as a status-organizing concept. In Britain the concept of social class is usually organized and measured with respect to the individual's occupation. Thus a job is an important component contributing to the social standing of the individual in the community. Those without work, either because of unemployment or retirement, are usually accorded a lower social status than those currently in employment.

Finally work also serves as a basis for social relationships. It is a major source of social contacts and a primary reference point.

In any particular occupation there are a variety of sources of satisfaction and dissatisfaction which will affect the meaning of retirement for the individual. These sources of satisfaction and dissatisfaction are rooted in such diverse factors as the financial rewards of the job, relationships with other workers and the amount of control exercised by the worker over her/his working environment. Not surprisingly given their lack of autonomy, working-class employees are less attached to their job and shown higher levels of dissatisfaction than those from higher status occupations. This might suggest that retirement would be easier for working-class employees as there would be less to miss. It also seems that levels of satisfaction, for all types of employees, are lower in large corporations than in smaller firms.

THE OLDER WORKER

Older people have, over the course of this century, gradually withdrawn from participation in the labour market as the practice of retirement has gained widespread acceptance. In 1931 50% of males over 65 were in the labour force. This had decreased to 7% in 1986 (Laczko and Phillipson, 1991). The widespread acceptance of retirement at specific ages has had important consequences for older workers remaining within the labour force.

Older workers, that is those in the years immediately preceding mandatory retirement age, often suffer discrimination in the labour market because of several commonly held beliefs or stereotypes (Harris and Cole, 1980). Firstly, it is often argued that older workers cannot meet production requirements and are too slow. However empirical evidence suggests that they are more productive than younger workers (Harris and Cole, 1980). Secondly, it is argued that they cannot meet the physical demands of jobs. Whilst this may be true for some very specialized heavy jobs it is not appropriate for the majority of jobs, especially with the advent of labour-saving machinery and devices. Thirdly, older workers are often accused of excessive absenteeism through sickness and poor health, although data do not support this (Harris and Cole, 1980). Older workers are finally thought to be difficult to retrain and set in their ways and characterized by old and outdated skills.

In Britain, older workers, aged between 55 and retirement age, are over-represented amongst jobs at the extremes of the occupational distribution. We find that older workers are very heavily concentrated in low-paid unskilled jobs such as caretaking and cleaning, agriculture and self-employment. Part-time employment is also very prevalent amongst this age group. However it is something of a paradox that there are concentrations of older workers in the highest paid and most responsible jobs, such as those within business, commerce and the legal profession.

Given the widespread prejudices about the capabilities of older workers it is hardly surprising to find that unemployment is also high amongst this age group, especially in a time of economic recession. However changes in the methods of defining unemployment often make it difficult to define precisely the unemployment levels amongst older workers. In addition it is argued that in times of recession and high unemployment the transition from work to retirement becomes increasingly complex and it becomes more difficult to categorize older people in terms of their attachment to the labour force.

Older workers may be thought of in terms of two groups: those in the years prior to statutory retirement and those who opt to continue to work after normal retirement age. Some people do opt to continue working rather than taking retirement at the earliest age. A survey by Parker (1980) revealed that two-thirds of those who opt to defer retirement are women. Workers who delay retirement are usually employed on a part-time basis and cite money reasons combined with liking their job or a wish to avoid boredom as the main reasons for delayed retirement. This group of workers probably experience considerable discrimination in the labour market and are probably finding it increasingly difficult to maintain employment given the current high levels of unemployment.

RETIREMENT

Retirement is usually defined as the formal withdrawal from the labour market and gainful economic activity at a specified age. In Britain this is more usually associated with eligibility for the state retirement pension. Currently men are eligible for the state retirement pension at 65 years of age and women at 60 years. However a recent ruling by the European Court has deemed that it is illegal to discriminate between men and women in terms of the age of retirement. Whilst there is agreement that retirement pension ages should be equal for both men and women the details of this policy change have not been worked out.

There are wide variations within Europe in the age of statutory retirement (Table 8.1). In the Scandinavian countries 67 years is the age of retirement compared with 60 years in Italy. Only the United Kingdom, Italy, Belgium and Switzerland have a different retirement age for men and women.

Table 8.1 Retirement age for men and women in Europe (*Observer* 5/4/86)

	Males	*Females*
Eire	65	65
Switzerland	65	62
Belgium	65	60
United Kingdom	65	60
France	60	60
Italy	60	55
Norway	67	67
Denmark	67	67
Netherlands	67	67
Sweden	65	65
Spain	65	65
West Germany	65	65

Two major approaches towards retirement may be distinguished. The first involves retirement at a fixed age whilst the second offers a more flexible timetable for the transition from work to retirement. There has been a long debate about the relative merits of fixed-age and flexible retirement. Fixed-age retirement is usually justified by the reference to several arguments which are outlined below (Palmore, 1978).

Proponents of fixed retirement argue that it creates employment opportunities for the young. This approach argues that without compulsory retirement the work force would become 'clogged up' with older workers. There would be fewer opportunities for new people to join the labour market and younger people would be confined to unemployment.

This argument is, of course, predicated upon the assumption that the number of jobs within the labour market is finite. This is an assumption of questionable validity. Additionally this is an essentially ageist perspective upon the rights of different age groups to employment. This argument suggests that in a choice between young and old it is the old who should suffer exclusion from employment. However this is not an issue which has been openly debated within society.

Related to this is the idea that without mandatory retirement young people would be denied promotional opportunities. The obvious counter to this would be to abolish seniority and tenure above a fixed age and let older workers compete for their own jobs upon a basis of ability rather than seniority.

Fixed-age retirement is often justified because older workers are seen as less desirable than the young, being perceived as less efficient, less well educated, with declining physical and mental capacities. However all the evidence suggests that older workers are more reliable than younger workers and just as capable in timed tasks. In addition older workers often have skills lacked by the young. Thus by forcing them to retire at a fixed age it could equally well be argued that we are decreasing the over-all efficiency of the economy.

Retirement is often justified because pensions, both state and occupational, provide income opportunities not available to the young. This again is an essentially ageist position because pensions rarely match earnings from employment. By making retirement mandatory we are forcing large groups of people into lower living standards just because of their age. Again there has been little formal debate about whether it is socially desirable to force large sectors of the population to accept a decrease in their living standards simply upon the basis of age.

It is argued by its proponents that mandatory retirement makes planning easier for workers and employers by having a fixed age at which retirement must take place. However people change jobs or retire early through ill health and companies can adjust to these circumstances. Flexible retirement with a statutory period of notice from the employee would seem to be a viable solution especially with the increasing availability of computerized record keeping.

In Britain, as we shall see below, fixed-age retirement has become the norm. The economic difficulties of the late 20th century have forced many countries to rethink their retirement policies. Thus in Britain the idea of a flexible 'decade of retirement' with workers gradually withdrawing from the labour market over a period of years seems to be increasing in popularity. The increased popularity of early retirement and partial retirement, combined with the effects of economic recession, are forcing a more flexible approach towards the transition from work to retirement. Given the widespread popularity of retirement and the increasing availability of

computer systems it seems likely that the opportunities for phased retirement will increase during the next decades.

The growth of retirement

The expectation of retirement is now the norm for most members of the
labour force. However this is a social expectation or norm of fairly recent
origin. In Britain in 1986 17% of males and 3% of females aged over 65
were classified as being economically active by the census. This contrasts
with 1951 when 48% of males aged 65–69 and 20% of those over 70 were
classed as being economically active. Similar decreases in the fraction of
older women participating in the labour market have been documented
over the same period.

The percentage of older people remaining in the labour market varies
between countries. In the USA 20% of older men and 10% of older
women continue in the labour market. In Japan some 50% of retired
males are in employment. However in all western industrial countries
the post-war trend has been for a decrease in the fraction of older
workers participating in paid employment.

The emergence of retirement

As we have noted the emergence of retirement from the labour market at
a specified age is a characteristic of fairly recent origin. Retirement was
almost unheard of in Victorian Britain. Older people expected to continue
working until they were physically incapable of doing so any longer.
People were seen as being old when they ceased to be financially or
physically independent. Old age was therefore seen as a flexible concept
which varied between individuals. One result of the growth of retirement
has been the twinning of the onset of old age with retirement with the
resultant expectation that old age starts at a definite chronological age
(Thane, 1983).

The growth and institutionalization of fixed-age retirement has been a
20th century phenomenon and has developed in response to both positive and negative factors. On the positive side retirement would have not
emerged without the growth of pensions provision, both by the state and
private employers. In a more negative sense retirement has grown in
acceptance because of changes in the labour market, especially economic
recession and the decrease in demand for labour and specific types of
skills. The emergence of retirement is linked with the growth of pensions
in a way which is complex and difficult to disentangle. In addition the
growth of retirement and pensions policy are inter-related with changes
in the labour market such as changes in general demand and in demand
for particular types of skill. In this context retirement policy has been

used as a method of controlling the labour market in times of over-supply.

In Britain the first occupational group for whom a fixed retirement age was introduced were civil servants. Pensions were made available to civil servants aged 65 and over from 1859 onwards. However it is important to remember that at this time there was no state financial provision for old age. The Northcote–Trevelyn report of 1857 on the efficiency of the civil service first promoted the idea of retirement. The authors of this report argued that the efficiency of the civil service would be enhanced by the removal of older workers by providing them with pensions. So from its inception retirement has been seen as a way of improving the economic efficiency of firms and organizations rather than as a reflection of concern for the well-being of the work force. The selection of 65 years as the age at which retirement was appropriate was based upon impressionistic notions rather than empirical data. It was generally felt that people became old and unfit for work during their early sixties. In addition the Friendly Societies found that this was often the age at which retirement became desirable from a medical point of view.

The Northcote report also considered the merits of the competing strategy of flexible rather than fixed-age retirement. This would have permitted retirement at an age at which civil servants were ruled to be medically unsuitable for regular and efficient working. However this strategy was rejected because it was considered to be administratively cumbersome. Consequently the subsequent development of retirement in Britain has been orientated towards fixed-age rather than flexible retirement.

Fixed-age retirement was slow to develop in the last century. However by the time of the 1891 census there was a separate category for those offi-cially retired from the labour market. The decennial census of that year was the first to enumerate the retired as a separate category and found that 35% of males over the age of 65 could be so defined. Initially the growth of retirement was almost exclusively confined to occupations under the control of local or central government. In 1890 policemen received a pension after 25 years service whilst in 1892 elementary school teachers were awarded a pension at 60. Two years later pensions were awarded to all non-manual public employees. During the last decade of the century private companies such as the railways started to pay pen-sions, but again only to non-manual workers. Thus from its inception pensions policy has discriminated between manual and non-manual workers. There has also been a trend for occupational pensions to be con-centrated amongst those employed by the public sector rather than those in private employment.

The idea of pensions payable at a specified chronological age was first suggested by Daniel Defoe in 1690. He thought that all people over the age of 50 should receive a pension. However it was not until the late 19th century that popular opinion began to favour the provision of both state and occupational pensions. Agitation for the provision of state pensions came from philanthropic, religious and labour sources. A series of reports from social commentators such as Charles Booth in London and Seebohm Rowntree in York produced ample evidence of the poverty and hardship which characterized Victorian old age. This stimulated the agitation for old age pensions. However there was still a core of *laissez faire* proponents who opposed pensions and any other form of state intervention. Thus Geoffrey Drage wrote in 1895 that 'intemperance, want of thrift, and, most of all, want of backbone, are in the majority of cases the cause of destitution in old age'. Despite this view late Victorian England was characterized by a more sophisticated understanding of poverty and its causes. Increasingly it was recognized that even the most thrifty and temperate of working people experienced poverty in old age because their working wages had not been adequate to allow them to save for it.

The first national state pensions policy was suggested by Canon Blackley in 1878 and Charles Booth produced the first costed plan for a state funded pensions scheme in 1891. It was not until 1908 that a non-contributory means-tested old age pension was introduced by the Liberal government of Lloyd George. All those over the age of 70 were entitled to apply for this pension, which amounted to 5/- (25 pence) a week. In order to receive this pension the older person had to pass a means test to ensure that they had an income of less than £21 a year. Receipt of the pension was also restricted to those of British nationality who had resided in the country for at least 20 years. However a moral test also had to be passed before the pension was paid out. Bornat, Phillipson and Ward (1985, p. 25) state that 'To receive the pension a person had to be sober and law-abiding and not someone who habitually failed to work'.

Almost as soon as this pension was introduced there were demands for the retirement age to be decreased to 65 years but it was not until 1925 that the pension age was lowered. At this time there was no discrimination between males and females in terms of retirement age. The reduction of the retirement age for females to 60 in 1940 followed an extensive campaign by the National Spinsters Association. This group argued that single women deserved pensions at 55 because they were usually employed in lower paid occupations than men and therefore had to work much harder simply to exist. In addition it was also argued that women declined physically at an earlier age than men because not only did they participate in the labour market but they had a home to maintain as well. These retirement ages have subsequently remained fixed and show little sign of changing in the near future.

What brought about the growth of pensions?

The development and growth of occupational and state provided pensions was a prerequisite for the growth of retirement. So the next question is what brought about the growth of pensions? Several interlinked pressures for pensions and retirement may be discerned. Firstly, there was a genuine concern amongst social reformers for the problems of poverty in old age. Secondly, there was the development of a more sophisticated theory of the causes of poverty than simple idleness or fecklessness. Most of the social surveys carried out at this time identified old age as a cause of poverty. The elderly came to be seen as a special group that had particular social needs requiring specifically formulated social policies to deal with them. Hence the pressure for universal state-financed pensions to alleviate the problems of poverty in old age. Thirdly, there was substantial agitation from organized labour for the provision of state pensions. This was a concession which governments felt that they could justifiably meet in order to reduce labour unrest at a time of considerable social tension.

However the increased social consensus for the concept of pensions and retirement was not wholly philanthropic. There were also wider labour market concerns. Firstly, there was the widespread discrimination against older workers in the labour market. In late 19th century Britain older workers were threatened by changes in work practices and the obsolescence of their skills. This was reflected in the high rates of unemployment amongst older workers. Secondly, this was a time of economic depression and great international economic competition with the other nations of Europe, particularly Germany. Older workers were caught in a situation of shrinking job opportunities and a decrease in demand for their particular skills. Pensions, both occupational and state-financed, were seen as a legitimate way of excluding older workers from the job market and thereby decreasing the demand for employment. Thane (1978) considers that the spread of pensions is best explained by growing demands for increased productivity and efficiency. Thus we have already seen that the introduction of the first British pension scheme in the civil service was justified upon the grounds of economic efficiency.

Changes in the labour market and retirement

The growth of retirement has also arisen in response to changes in the characteristics of the labour market. In times of high unemployment older workers are at risk. During the great depression of the 1930s it was argued that older workers should retire in order to give opportunities to the young and to reduce the scale of unemployment. This concept of the old retiring to make way for the young was advanced from all sides of the political spectrum. In 1919 a Trades Union Congress report argued that increasing the pension would induce 'those above the age of 65 to take a well earned rest from their work to allow the younger men, who are waiting for a job, to come into their place' (Trades Union Congress, 1919, p. 195 quoted in Phillipson, 1982).

Decreased opportunities for employment were, therefore, an important set of pressures leading to the institutionalization of fixed age retirement. In addition there were increased demands for efficiency and the elderly were perceived, rightly or wrongly, as being inefficient. Thus older workers were threatened by the obsolescence of their skills. However it is important to remember that labour market policies change over time and the elderly can fulfil the role as a reserve army of labour to be called upon in times of economic growth. During the full employment of the 1950s there was considerable enthusiasm for employing older workers because of labour shortage and pessimistic fears about demographic balance between productive and unproductive workers.

Thus there is a consistent linkage between labour market policies, retirement and pensions policy. In its earliest phase retirement was advocated as way of shedding unwanted labour from a saturated job market. However in times of labour shortage the opposite case is advanced. The immediate post-war period in Britain was characterized by the reversal of the trend towards retirement by encouraging older workers to stay in the job market and delay the time at which they would become dependent and non-productive. Beveridge was one of the first for a considerable number of years to question the inevitability of excluding older workers from employment and he felt that older people should be encouraged to defer claiming their pension and carry on working. However the period of full employment was short-lived and the exhortations to older people to delay their retirement ceased in the early 1960s.

EARLY RETIREMENT

In Britain the position of older workers in the labour market has deteriorated considerably since the early 1970s. A world economic recession combined with a deterioration in Britain's position with regard to other capitalist economies have produced continuing high levels of unemployment. In addition the growth and introduction of new technology threatens the skills of older workers. In this combination of circumstances retirement is accepted as the norm and the growth of early retirement, i.e. retirement before the statutory age, has developed as a socially sanctioned activity.

As a method of reducing unemployment, especially amongst younger people, early retirement commands almost universal approval. Thus we find that early retirement has developed for two major sets of reasons.

First, early retirement has been justified upon social grounds. For example trade unions have consistently argued that retirement at the age of 65 years discriminates against manual workers, who are often in poorer health than those in non-manual occupations. The second major impetus behind the development of early retirement is wider labour market concerns. These include the use of early retirement to disguise long-term unemployment amongst older males, release jobs for younger people and reduce the labour force without recourse to redundancies. Early retirement schemes have thus been used to remove from the labour force the workers perceived as least productive, such as the long-term sick.

We have already observed the decrease in economic activity rates of people aged over 65. The last 20 years have seen a remarkable decrease in economic activity amongst those within ten years of formal retirement age as early retirement has gained in both popularity and social respectability. As Table 8.2 shows, the percentage of males aged 55–59 classified as economically active has decreased from 93% in 1971 to 80% in 1986. In addition to this the fraction of older economically active males classed as unemployed has increased substantially. Thus in 1973 6% of economically active males aged 60–64 were unemployed. Ten years later this fraction had almost doubled to 11%.

Table 8.2 Great Britain: economic activity rates 1971–86 (%) (Laczko and Phillipson, 1971, Tables 2.1, 2.3)

	35–59		60–64		65+	
	M	F	M	F	M	F
1971	93	51	82	28	16	6
1981	89	53	69	22	10	4
1986	80	52	53	19	7	3

Opportunities for early retirement are not equally distributed throughout the labour market. Traditionally retirement ages in certain sectors of the public service have been fixed below the age of 65. Members of the fire, police and prison services have a retirement age of 55 whilst the civil service retirement age is fixed at 60 for both sexes. Some private firms such as banks and large corporations such as ICI also specify retirement at 60. Thus the Department of Health and Social Security estimates that 40% of all male workers in occupational pension schemes or approximately 25% of all male workers can retire on a full occupational pension before the age of 65 years. Opportunities for early withdrawal from the labour market are greatest amongst those engaged in professional and non-manual occupations.

The growth of early retirement represents an extension and maintenance of the trends which first stimulated the retirement such as concerns about the efficiency of older workers and continued high levels of
unemployment. Indeed early retirement may be seen as a response to
unemployment. To these influences we should also add:

1.   the decline in unskilled and semi-skilled jobs;
2.   the entry of women into the labour market;
3.   the growth of provision for early retirement;
4.   the growth of early retirement as a positive alternative to full-time
     employment;
5.   the development of policies for early retirement;
6.   the growth of attractive leisure opportunities;
7.   the move towards 'second' careers.

Policies for early retirement

Policies for early retirement may be divided into two types; labour
market policies and social policies for the older worker. In Britain there is
no facility for the early receipt of the state retirement pension. Public
policy for early retirement in Britain has largely concentrated upon the
labour market aspects, unlike some other European countries such as
Sweden which have provided partial pensions for those who retire early
or withdraw gradually from full-time employment and which express
concern with the social goals of early retirement.

The most positive mechanism by which older workers in Britain
have been encouraged to leave the labour market has been the Job
Release Scheme (JRS). This was introduced in January 1977 and allows
men aged 64 and women aged 59 to leave work early and receive an
allowance providing that their employer replaces them with someone
from the unemployment register. This is a highly restricted early
retirement scheme when compared with some of the policies developed in the rest of Western Europe. Despite its limitations, since the
scheme came into operation some 250 000 people have retired early.
The majority of those taking advantage of this route to early retirement have been males and it seems as if this scheme has helped to
create wider opportunities for early retirement amongst workers from
manual occupation groups. Bushell (1984) has shown that approximately three-quarters of entrants to job release schemes in 1978 and
1984 were from manual occupations.

The existence of the JRS does not account for the increase in early
retirement in Britain. At most it probably accounts for no more than one-
third of the increase in the early retired. What it has done, however, is to
establish and legitimize the concept of early retirement.

Workers who are unemployed register with the Jobcentre in order to safeguard their national insurance contributions to the state retirement pensions and other forms of benefits. Recently the 1983 budget removed this requirement for men aged 60–64. This move on the part of the government had the advantage of artificially deflating the number classified as unemployed at a time of considerable social unease about the high extent of unemployment in Britain. This requirement has substantially reduced the number of older males who now register as unemployed by up to 85 000 (Sinfield, 1979). This, it might be argued, gives a more accurate count of the unemployed as it has removed all those who were registering to protect pension credits and who had no real intention of obtaining another job. However this administrative procedure does serve to disguise the true picture of unemployment amongst older workers.

This fairly meagre policy response of the government towards early retirement is partly compensated for by the private sector. Most occupational pensions have early retirement clauses. However these are usually concentrated amongst the better paid white collar workers and thus help to preserve inequality between different sectors of the working population.

Early retirement: voluntary withdrawal from the labour market?

To appreciate the social dimensions and meanings of early retirement it is necessary to determine whether withdrawal from the labour market was voluntary or involuntary. There is a very strong feeling within society that in times of high youth unemployment older workers are morally obliged to retire to make opportunities for the young. This was articulated by the House of Commons Social Services Committee (1982, p. 17) who stated that 'the strongest pressure [for early retirement] comes from the high rates of youth unemployment leading to individual and collective belief that older workers should retire to make way for younger ones'.

In addition it is well established that to maximize management control when a company is being run down, pressure, often of a very direct kind, is brought to bear upon certain individuals to retire early. Thus individual decisions about whether to take early retirement are currently being made against a background of extreme economic insecurity. A simple division into voluntary and involuntary retirement is probably highly arbitrary. A survey by McGoldrick and Cooper (1980) reported that, whilst most respondents felt that their decision to retire early had been made voluntarily, labour market considerations had played a significant role in the decision-making process.

Table 8.3 describes the reasons given for early retirement amongst a sample of males included in the General Household Survey.

Table 8.3 Great Britain: reasons for early retirement – males aged 60–64 (%)
(Laczko, 1986)

	Non-manual	*Manual*
Health	7	8
Voluntarily retired	66	61
Compulsorily retired	15	5
Redundancy	5	24
Other	8	1

This implies that the majority of males from both manual and non-manual occupation groups choose to retire early. However these data apply only to males who entered early retirement from paid employment. It excludes those who were sick or unemployed before early retirement. Thus these results probably under-estimate the extent of 'compulsory' early retirement. Even so this table suggests that at least a third of the early retired did not make the decision to retire voluntarily. For workers from manual occupations, redundancy was a major reason for early withdrawal from the labour market.

Despite the exclusion of those who were sick before entering early retirement, health does not seem to have been a major reason for leaving the labour market. However these data probably under-estimate the degree to which health issues and concerns were involved. Laczko (1986) demonstrates that, compared with the employed and unemployed, the early retired demonstrate a higher level of ill health. Additionally there are variations in health status within the early retired population. Consistently, those from manual occupations exhibit higher levels of ill health than their colleagues who retired from non-manual employment.

Considerable evidence, therefore, exists to suggest that a substantial fraction of workers are being excluded from the labour market with a substantial degree of compulsion. However many would argue that this is fully justified because it is better than the alternative outcome, increased unemployment amongst the young. This essentially ageist stance is justified upon the grounds that the early retired are financially well provided for, especially in comparison with the young unemployed.

The notion that all the early retired are financially secure is far from the truth. The acceptance of early retirement, unless covered by a clause in an occupational pension, may well result in a lower pension than if the employee had continued working until 'normal' retirement age. Laczko (1986) demonstrates that a fifth of those who retired early from manual occupations had incomes at or below the supplementary benefit level, a tradition index of poverty. Additionally a third of such workers were defined as living on the margins of poverty. Conversely few of those who had retired early from non-manual occupations were defined as having a low income. These differences in the experience of poverty in early retirement, as in retirement (Chapter 9), stem from variations in the receipt of occupational pensions between manual and non-manual former employees. Over 80% of non-manual early retired receive an occupational pension compared with 65% of the manual early retired (Laczko, 1986). Additionally the early retired non-manual group receive a weekly pension which is on average double that received by the manual early retired.

ATTITUDES TOWARDS RETIREMENT

As we have seen, older workers have increasingly withdrawn from the labour market and retirement at a fixed age (or even earlier) has become the norm. Indeed most working people now expect and want to retire at a specific age. Parker (1980) in his study of older workers reported that 59% of males and 53% of females were looking forward to retirement; only 8% and 15% respectively were unhappy at the prospect of retiring. This contrasts with Townsend's study in the East End of London when as recently as the 1960s he considered that many 'viewed approaching retirement with uneasiness and ill-concealed fear' (Townsend, 1964, p. 158).

Data from Britain indicate that only a small minority of the retired, 10%, expressed the desire for a job although almost a third would have liked to have stayed on at their job if it had been possible (Age Concern, 1974). Of these very few had actually tried to find employment, probably because they felt that they would be discriminated against and that they might lose other financial benefits such as pensions. The two main reasons for wanting a job were financial and social.

As well as expecting to retire the vast majority of workers, 96%, expect to be worse off financially when they retire (Parker, 1980). Thus interviews with the retired generally indicate that the majority of problems experienced relate to money rather than other aspects of retirement and many retired people express a desire for more advice about the financial aspects of retirement.

General attitudes towards retirement are obviously not uniform. They vary with age, occupation and sex. Those with higher levels of income, occupation or education have the most favourable attitude towards retirement, probably because they are the best insulated from the negative effects of dramatic decreases in income. British research has shown that the most favourable attitudes towards retirement, as recorded by agreement with the statement 'I was very happy to retire' came from the newly retired, perhaps because of the novelty of their new situation (Age Concern, 1974). A substantial minority, roughly a third, did not agree with this statement and were obviously dissatisfied with their new way of life. When questioned about the source of their dissatisfaction, responses related to time hanging heavy, loss of income or loss of social contacts. It seems that few dissatisfied retired people missed the job itself.

RETIREMENT AS A SOCIAL PROCESS

Retirement is a many faceted social process. However we know relatively little about the transition from employed to retired and how responses to this important social transition vary between social groups.

Phillipson (1982) distinguishes three different attitudes towards the entry into retirement. The first of these is termed stable withdrawal. This occurs where the individual accepts the likelihood of retirement and undertakes to confront the subsequent changes in lifestyle and behaviour which may result. Such individuals may feel that they have accomplished all that is possible in the world of work and that they 'deserve' their retirement. In contrast an unstable withdrawal from the labour market may be characterized by the exclusion of the older worker from the labour force by objective pressures such as redundancy. In this type of situation unemployment and retirement may merge leaving the individual with both declining material resources and a declining perception of her/his own worth. However the largest group seem to be those who make few advance plans for their retirement and are content to let things just happen.

Sociologists define certain events such as weddings or starting work as rites of passage. These are events which alter the status of the individual in the eyes of society and bring about changes in social role. Retirement is, therefore, very clearly an important rite of passage. For most workers the formal entry into retirement is usually marked by some form of ceremony, the precise nature of this being dependent upon the status of the worker involved. A retirement 'celebration' may range from a few drinks with the girls at lunchtime to, for a world-famous academic, a conference arranged in her honour. Whatever the precise form the ceremony takes, these events tend to focus upon past achievements rather than upon future expectations and hopes as is typical of a wedding or school-leaving ceremony.

Retirement is a complex phenomenon and it is far too simplistic to divide people into the retired and the non-retired. Rather it is a complex social process which may be divided into a series of phases (Atchley, 1976a). These phases constitute an ideal type and not every experience of retirement will experience them all. However these phases do serve to stress the variety of experience covered by the term retirement. These kinds of phase are not unique to retirement but are typical of all major role transitions.

1. **Pre-retirement** during which expectations about retirement are formed. However we have already seen that relatively few workers

formally prepare for retirement despite the considerable expansion of pre-retirement courses and education.

2. **Honeymoon**. Immediately following retirement a honeymoon period may follow. This is reflected in people trying to do all those things they never had time for in work such as travelling or visiting relatives and particularly grandchildren (or great grandchildren).
3. **Disenchantment**. This may set in if the individual fails to develop a satisfying and stable routine. Retirement, which may last as long as 20 years, is after all more than an extended holiday.
4. **Reorientation**. In this phase the individual takes stock of the choices available in retirement and starts to develop a satisfying routine.
5. **Stability**. This identifies the stage when the individual can deal with retirement and its changes.
6. **Termination**. A stage may be reached where retirement is no longer of importance. For some this is reflected in a return to employment. More commonly this stage is manifested as the onset of disability or poor health and the adoption of a dependent rather than retirement role.

Adaptation to retirement

Identification of the factors which characterize a successful retirement would obviously be useful in designing pre-retirement education courses and literature. However attempting to isolate those aspects of retirement which bring satisfaction and dissatisfaction is rather difficult. Most research seems to have focused upon the negative aspects of retirement as if expressing a subconscious expectation by the researcher that retirement ought to be an unsatisfactory experience. However it may be that retirement remains unsatisfactory because of the conditions which accompany it such as low income or poor health, rather than retirement *per se*. We have seen already that both in Britain and America only a minority of the elderly want to work and then only for financial reasons. The aspects of work that were missed related to income and interaction rather than the work itself. Studies of retirement often carry the inbuilt assumption that the loss of the work role creates a void in the social world of the individual that must be filled by various substitutes. Thus it seems possible that the problems of retirement arise because of the lack of suitable alternatives to the activity and social interaction provided by work.

One aspect of retirement that has received attention is the consideration of feelings of usefulness amongst the retired. We have seen that ours is a society which values usefulness and contributions from its participating members. There seems to be little good evidence that the retired extensively feel that they are not contributing. Some studies have demonstrated an increase in feelings of uselessness following retirement. However only about a fifth of the change was attributable to retirement itself, the rest related to other profound changes in circumstances such as loss of a spouse or the onset of a disabling illness which occurred at the same time as retirement. Many of the negative expectations of retirement identified by Townsend (1964) related to the association of retirement with ill health and a decrease in physical activity.

Another important area of retirement is that of status. One of the major dimensions of social stratification in Britain is social class, which is strongly allied to occupational status. There is a tendency amongst many social researchers to perceive the retired population as a homogeneous mass isolated from the major status-giving trait, employment. However amongst the retired themselves there is a very strong tendency to cling to identification with their former occupation. Thus a retired person may describe his/herself as a retired teacher (or what ever his/her former job had been) rather than just as retired.

However one aspect of status that is important is income. This will be discussed in more detail later. Suffice it to say here that for many, retirement is a time of extreme financial hardship. Some workers may experience a drop of 50% or more in their income upon entering retirement (Townsend 1964). The financial background of the retired person has a very strong influence upon the successful (or otherwise) adaptation to retirement.

Disengagement theory would indicate that retirement is a start of a more general process of withdrawal from social contacts. Given the importance of work in providing social contacts retirement could be seen as being highly disruptive to the social network of the individual. Amongst certain groups, especially those in more working-class occupations, retirement certainly reduces contacts with colleagues or work-based social organizations such as unions. However this should not be over-stressed and most research indicates that retirement does not bring about any significant change in social or community activity levels.

Thus patterns of social interaction created during the working life are maintained. This means that the experience of retirement may be very different for those from different occupational groups. During their working life manual workers may have had little opportunity to develop community activities in contrast with those from non-manual occupational groups. At retirement the full consequences of this different lifestyle may manifest itself.

Retirement also has its positive aspects. Satisfaction with the experience of retirement is most usually expressed in terms of the enjoyment of leisure and the freedom to organize one's time without the constraints associated with work (Age Concern, 1974). This view of retirement as 'liberation' is expressed in a survey of the early retired which reported that, given the same circumstances, the vast majority would retire early again. These kinds of views are expressed in comments from retired people about being given a new lease of life, of being released from the rat race or the dictates of the clock. Other positive benefits were greater freedom to plan holidays and to engage in favourite pastimes and leisure pursuits.

As we have seen retirement has been a central focus of much research in social gerontology. However, the majority of these studies have been based upon cross-sectional data. Consequently it is difficult to distinguish between the causes and the consequences of retirement. Palmore *et al.* (1985) have used longitudinal data from seven major studies of retirement in America undertaken during the period 1961–81. These data suggest that retirement seemed to have little effect upon social activity levels or attitudes. The authors distinguish between those retiring voluntarily and those who are forced to retire. The least advantaged group seemed to those who retired because of poor health. The involuntary retirer and early retirers also seemed to have a less satisfactory retirement. This implies that the efficacy of the current trend towards early retirement is open to question.

WOMEN AND RETIREMENT

Retirement is traditionally seen as a male problem. For women, even those employed in the labour market, family roles have been seen as the main source of identity. There is a very pervasive attitude that perceives employed women, even those engaged in a 'career job', as working for 'pin money' rather than for any more fundamental reasons. As yet there are very few data available about the impact of retirement on women. The data that are available remain ambiguous; some evidence indicates that retirement was less problematic for women (Palmore *et al.*, 1979) whilst other work indicated that women adjusted less well to retirement (Atchley, 1976b).

The impact upon women of their husband's or partner's retirement has not yet been thoroughly investigated. Thus our comments are, at best, speculative. For the full-time housewife it is possible that the retirement of a spouse may bring some relief to the loneliness and isolation which often accompanies this lifestyle. The retirement of a spouse from a dangerous occupation such as mining or fishing may reduce pressure upon a couple's relationship. However the impending retirement of a spouse may put considerable pressure upon a couple's relationship if there has been a traditional division of labour between the couple: here the male may be seen as encroaching upon the female's territory. Additionally females with well developed social networks outside the home may feel that these are threatened by the approaching retirement of a spouse.

CONCLUSION

In modern western societies work is one of the central factors influencing the life and development of the individual. As well as providing an income work also provides social status and opportunities for social interaction. The meaning and impact of retirement is affected by changes in each of these dimensions.

Two approaches to retirement may be distinguished, fixed-age and flexible retirement. However we have seen that, as the 20th century has progressed, older workers have been progressively excluded from the world of work. Retirement, and increasingly early retirement, have become institutionalized at a fixed age. The stimuli for this major change have been the twin developments of pensions and a perceived need to rid the labour market of excess workers in times of high unemployment. Thus retirement has often been used as a method of labour-market control by artificially reducing unemployment and providing opportunities to the young. Retirement has developed very largely from the needs of the wider society rather than expressing the concern felt by society for the old or being an expression of the desires of older people.

The experience of retirement for the individual is shaped by many factors. In Britain a characteristic feature of retirement is the variation in the types of pension and benefits received by the retired. These are usually related to previous occupation. This provides one example of the way in which inequalities in the world of work are carried over into retirement which will be explored further in Chapter 9.

It used to be thought that retirement was a major personal and social crisis for all those who experienced it. However it is now obvious that this is far from the truth. Retirement is now accepted by most workers and is enjoyed by a great many. The transition is sometimes difficult but most workers seem to adapt. Expansion of pre-retirement preparation would probably go a considerable way to overcoming those problems which the retired do report facing. However the provision of such preparation is very unequally distributed throughout Britain and is unlikely that it will be expanded to any considerable degree in the current economic climate.

Retirement at a fixed age has been justified because of the complexity of the administration required to implement a more flexible approach to the transition from work to retirement. The latter approach could lessen the abruptness of the change and allow the elderly a degree of choice in the age and duration of their withdrawal from the labour market, something which is largely lacking from current retirement practices.

9

Standards of living

As we have seen later life is characterized by retirement and withdrawal from the labour market. This renders the elderly dependent upon pensions and other benefits, rather than earnings, for their income. In this chapter we examine current arrangements for financial provision in old age. We then consider the living standards of the elderly.

FINANCIAL PROVISION FOR LATER LIFE

The growth of retirement as a socially defined state has, as we noted earlier, been facilitated and paralleled by the growth of pensions. In Britain there are two main categories of pension, the state-provided sector and those paid by a former employer (subsequently referred to as occupational pensions). These two systems for financial support have developed separately.

STATE PENSION PROVISION

The basic outline of arrangements for social welfare provision in Britain stems from the 1942 Beveridge Report on social insurance. This report identified old age, unemployment, industrial injury and widowhood as the main 'causes' of poverty. To combat this Beveridge proposed a two-tier system of social support for old age and the other main causes of poverty. The first component of income support consisted of a series of benefits paid for out of general taxation. Eligibility for these benefits was defined by contributions made via the compulsory system of National Insurance. The state retirement pension is the National Insurance benefit which relates to the elderly. The second arm of Beveridge's welfare state provision was a means-tested set of additional benefits known as National Assistance (now termed Income Support).

Within the state sector, the provision of financial support to the retired is divided between the retirement pension and the means-tested supplementary pension. Eligibility for the State retirement pension, commonly referred to as 'the old age pension', is based upon the contributions an individual has made via the compulsory system of National Insurance. The retirement pension is paid to men at age 65 and women at age 60 provided that they have left the workforce. Non-working married women are awarded the pension upon the basis of the contributions made by their husband. Both men and women may opt to delay taking their pension for up to 5 years. Those who defer receiving their pension receive a small additional payment. The pension is paid at two rates, one for a single person and one for a married couple. A small supplement is paid to those aged 80 and over. In 1981–88 9 900 000 people in Great Britain were receiving the state retirement pension and income support at an annual cost of £21 100 000 000.

The state retirement pension was initially devised to provide a minimum acceptable income in old age. It was never intended to provide an income which equalled that which the person had received during their working life. Charles Booth, an early advocate of a pension for old age, felt that it should be paid at a level which was sufficient to maintain a home in later life, supplemented by savings and was small enough to deter scroungers. From its inception the state retirement pension has been inadequate for anything but the very lowest standard of living.

The level at which the state retirement pension is paid is set annually by Parliament. Since 1980 increases in the pension have been linked to increases in wages. Previously the pension was linked to the increases in wages or prices, whichever was the larger. According to Walker (1986) the result of this change in the method of setting the pension has been a 12% cut in the value of the pension.

It is meaningless to compare the actual monetary value of the pension over time because of inflation. A better way of looking at the 'value' of the pension is to compare it with average male manual worker's wages. Table 9.1 shows that the value of the pension has increased in value only slightly since its inception.

Table 9.1 United Kingdom: retirement pension as a percentage of male earnings 1948–85 (Falkingham and Johnson, 1992, Table 4.5)

	% Male manual earnings	*% Male earnings*
1948	19.1	
1955	18.4	
1961	19.1	
1971	19.5	17.5
1981	22.9	19.8
1985	22.5	19.2

Government legislation has attempted to supplement the basic state retirement pension in order to improve the living standards of older people. The 1966 National Insurance Act created a graduated pensions scheme. This scheme tried to link pensions after retirement with previous earnings. Higher pensions were payable to those who had opted to pay higher contributions whilst they were working. However if employers provided a better scheme than the state then the employee was free to contract out of the state scheme.

Unfortunately this scheme had a flawed design. It was written and costed in cash terms with no allowance for inflation, even though this was a period of high inflation rates. Consequently the scheme had to be abandoned because of the low monetary value of the payments involved. This scheme was replaced in 1978 when the Social Security Act of 1975 came into force. This introduced the State Earnings Related Pension Scheme (SERPS). This scheme had a number of attractive features. It was to be based upon contributions made during the 'best 20 years' of an employee's working career, rather than the last 20 or 40 years. This recognized the disadvantaged position of most women in occupation pension schemes where interrupted work histories, because of family commitments, resulted in low pensions. Again those employees covered by an occupational pension could contract out of the scheme. The major disadvantage of the scheme was that it was earnings-related, thus the lowest paid receive the lowest pension. Therefore SERPS preserved income differentials in later life rather than attempting to reduce inequality. In its original form the scheme would also have discriminated against part-time workers.

As a pension scheme, SERPS had many attractive points. However it has now been modified and is much less generous. In 1993 there was a wide ranging review of welfare which involved looking at state provision for 'old age'. Firstly, opponents of SERPS and now universal state pensions have consistently adopted the essentially ageist attitude that the elderly are increasingly a 'burden' which we cannot afford to maintain at a reasonable level of living without threatening the living standards of the rest of society. This view stems from the desire to reduce public expenditure. As the largest single item in the public expenditure budget is social security, of which the elderly are the main consumer group, any attempt to decrease government spending has implications for the living standards of the elderly.

Critics of SERPS and the provision of a state pension constantly stress the increase in numbers of the elderly over the next two decades. Chapter 6 demonstrated that, although there will be a large percentage increase in the numbers of over-85s, the actual numerical increase will be small. Jefferys (1983) has, however, observed that this obsession with the rising numbers and burden of the over-80s has been used as a moral 'panic' to divert attention away from the increasing numbers of unemployed and other pressing social issues.

The second line of attack upon SERPs and universal pension provision has been expressed by many actuaries as well as politicians. This suggests that the promises contained in SERPS as originally formulated are more generous than we can afford and considerably more than pensioners need. This is a more insidious argument which is based upon the premise that the elderly are now relatively affluent. To provide SERPS as originally planned would have meant that the state was 'over-providing' for old age.

The basis of this line of attack is that pensioners' share of total disposable income increased from 7% in 1951 to 15% in 1984/85 (Fiegehen, 1986). This increase is almost entirely due to increases in the numbers of pensioners and not to massive increases in their living standards. As we saw earlier the value of the retirement pension, expressed as a fraction of the average male wage, has remained remarkably constant since 1945. The main reason that the elderly are seen as being better off is because of the vast increase in the numbers of the unemployed and the substantial reduction in the value of benefits paid to this group. The main improvement in the position of the elderly is with regard to other 'poor' groups rather than the rest of society. There is little evidence to support the notion of the 'woopie' (well-off older person) (Falkingham and Victor, 1991).

MEANS-TESTED BENEFITS

The second major element of state pensions provision for later life are the means-tested benefits. Eligibility for Income Support is dependent upon the claimant demonstrating that their income is below a pre-defined level (this is commonly known as undergoing a 'means test') and that they have few capital assets such as savings in a bank deposit account or building society. This group of benefits is the direct successor to the old Poor Laws and, as such, are perceived in a very negative light by many people in Britain.

In his original report Beveridge saw the means-tested system of National Assistance (as it was then called) as a safety net to cover those who were not fully covered by the National Insurance scheme. It was thought that as the new insurance-based scheme increased its coverage of the population National Assistance could be phased out. In reality the opposite has happened. The number of claims made for supplementary benefit and the numbers of people dependent on it has increased steadily since its inception.

OCCUPATIONAL PENSIONS

Occupational pensions are also an important means of income main-tenance in later life. Indeed this a method of income support for later life which the 1979 and 1983 Conservative administrations have been keen to encourage by providing generous incentives. Unlike the state system these are not paid universally. The very first pensions paid in Britain were occupationally-based rather than state-provided. In their initial manifestation these types of pension were used as a method of attracting and retaining staff in occupations for which a lengthy training was required. However they were also a means of 'ridding' the workplace of older workers who were seen as being inefficient.

Occupational pensions are arrangements run either by individual employers or groups of employers to provide a supplement to the basic state pension. These pensions are usually based upon the length of time the individual has worked for the employer and are related to the level of final earnings. Under most arrangements the individual receives a fraction of the salary received at the time of retirement. This type of scheme preserves inequalities in living standards characteristic of the working life into old age.

As yet occupational pension schemes do not cover all of the working population (see Table 9.2). In the public sector most full-time employees are part of an occupational pension scheme. However in the private sector only approximately 50% of males and 30% of females are covered (Groves, 1986). Thus we find that 60% of males and 35% of women were members of an occupational pension scheme in 1985 (see Table 9.2). The coverage of these schemes amongst part-time workers is very much lower. Future generations of elderly are going to be strongly differentiated between those who only have recourse to the state pension and those who have an additional pension from a previous employer.

Table 9.2 Great Britain: membership of occupational pension schemes – % of total work force (excluding unemployed) 1956–87 (Falkingham and Johnson, 1992, Table 4.4)

	Men	*Women*	*All*
1956	43	21	35
1967	66	28	53
1971	62	28	49
1979	62	35	50
1987	60	35	49

However occupational pension schemes, as developed in Britain, are also characterized by some fundamental limitations. Perhaps the most significant criticism is that there are not 'occupational' schemes in the true sense of the term. The current system is for a series of employer-based schemes rather than a system based upon specific occupations. A shop assistant who changes her job from Woolworths to Marks and Spencer has not changed her occupation but she has changed her job. This means that she will have changed her pension scheme membership because there as yet no single scheme for shop assistants. Consequently she will become an early leaver from one pension scheme and a new entrant to another. With the exception of the public sector, occupational pensions penalize those who change jobs frequently.

EUROPEAN PENSION PROVISION

It is a typically myopic British view that our system for pension provision (or any other aspect of health, welfare and education) is the best in Europe. However the reality is a long way from this statement. Economists suggest that, because work expenses are no longer payable, a retirement income of 65–80% of working income would be adequate to maintain former living standards. Within Europe only West Germany and Sweden provide a retirement income of this level (Table 9.3). In comparison with the rest of Europe income levels for British pensioners are a long way below those of their European cousins.

Table 9.3 Pensions for men as a percentage of earnings in the year before retirement – a comparison of European countries (Nusberg, 1981, Table 11.1)

	Single elderly	*Couple*
Austria	54	45
Canada	39	57
France	46	55
West Germany	50	50
Italy	67	67
Netherlands	38	54
Norway	41	55
Sweden	59	76
Switzerland	36	53
United Kingdom	26	39
United States	38	57

Total weekly income

In considering income the first factor to consider is average gross total weekly income based upon household information. Gross weekly income relates to the total income accruing from earnings, unearned income and pensions and benefits. No deductions for income tax (where appropriate) have been made. Similarly it does not give any information about housing costs or other items of expenditure. Neither does it take into account income received from family or other 'in kind' sources of income. Table 9.4 shows that income decreases with age and is always lower for households headed by women.

Table 9.4 Great Britain: income of elderly people 1988 (Askham *et al.*, 1992, Table 4.6)

Age	Average gross weekly income (£)		Average net weekly income (£)	
	M	*F*	*M*	*F*
60–64	157	59	127	155
65–69	125	58	112	56
70–74	107	53	57	52
75+	92	59	85	57

In addition there are marked variations in income between social classes. Those elderly who had been employed in unskilled or semi-skilled manual occupations (Victor, 1985) had a median weekly income of only half of that accruing to those from professional occupations. This relationship between class and income is independent of age, sex and disability of the elderly (Victor and Evandrou, 1986).

POVERTY AND OLD AGE

Another way of looking at overall living standards is to record the incidence of poverty amongst older people. Poverty may be measured in a variety of ways. One commonly used approach in Britain has been to relate income to the level of income support. The rates for this benefit are set annually by Parliament and have come to be viewed as society's minimum acceptable income.

In 1980 23% of pensioners in the GHS sample had incomes at, or below, the supplementary pension rate. A further 33% were living on the margins of poverty i.e. within 40% of the scale rate. According to the General Household Survey 56% of the elderly were defined as living in, or on the margins of, poverty. Using only the receipt of income support as their indicator, Arber and Ginn (1991b) report that 17% of women and men aged 65+ were in poverty in 1989.

Some groups of elderly are more vulnerable to poverty in old age than others. Particularly at risk are those over 80 years of age, women, the disabled and those who had held semi-skilled and unskilled jobs during their working life (Victor, 1986). In modern Britain the oldest, and most vulnerable groups are the most likely to be living on very low levels of income. This is illustrated by Table 9.5 which shows the age-related increasing percentage of people in the bottom 25% of the income distribution.

Table 9.5 Elderly people in the top and bottom income quartiles (% in each category) 1988 (Askham *et al.*, 1992, Table 4.3)

| | 60–64 | | 65–69 | | 70–74 | | 75–79 | | 80+ | |
	M	F	M	F	M	F	M	F	M	F
Top 25%	20	15	14	11	7	8	11	7	8	7
Bottom 25%	22	26	27	30	38	36	40	44	43	33

The relationship of poverty with old age is not a new finding. Rather poverty has always been a large feature of the experience of old age in Britain. As early as 1895 there was a Royal Commission which investigated the problems of the aged poor. Since then a whole variety of social surveys and reports have documented the relationship between old age and low income. Despite the institution of State pensions the fraction of older people classified as poor seems to have changed little and the same groups, the very old, women, the disabled and those who held manual jobs during their working life are still most at risk of experiencing poverty in later life. Perhaps this reflects the institutionalization of a cultural norm which expects old age to be a time of hardship and deprivation. Consequently policy makers do not feel that it is a realistic or desirable goal to increase the monetary value of pensions paid to the elderly.

SOURCES OF INCOME

Table 9.6 shows the source of pensioners' incomes 1951–86. Reliance upon state benefit has increased during this period and this is the principal source of income for older people.

Table 9.6 Great Britain: source of pensioners' total gross incomes 1951–86 (%) (Falkingham and Johnson, 1992, Table 3.2)

	1951	1961	1984	1986
All state benefits	42	48	55	59
Occupational pensions	15	16	15	20
Earnings	27	22	17	7
Savings	15	15	13	14

Table 9.6 suggests that one clue to the high prevalence of poverty amongst the elderly is their heavy reliance upon state benefits for the

majority of their income. The 1980 GHS revealed that 53% of the elderly had no income other than that provided by the state, either retirement or supplementary pension (Victor, 1986). Thus low levels of state benefits will inevitably be reflected in a high incidence of poverty amongst older people.

The percentage of income received from state benefit is highest amongst the very elderly, women, the disabled and those who held manual jobs during their working life (see Table 9.7). Victor and Evandrou (1986) report that 5% of the income of elderly in classes 4 and 5 is derived from either occupational pensions or savings. For those elderly who held professional or managerial jobs during their working life, 47% of their income was derived from non-state sources.

Table 9.7 Great Britain: sources of pensioners income by age and sex 1988 (%) (Askham *et al.*, 1992, Table 4.6)

| | 60–64 | | 65–69 | | 70–74 | | 75+ | |
	M	F	M	F	M	F	M	F
State benefits	23	55	57	71	65	79	71	82
Savings	8	17	7	13	7	11	7	9
Occupational pension	20	12	25	10	23	6	19	8
Employment	44	12	8	3	3	2	1	–
Other	5	4	3	3	2	2	2	1

For pensions in the top quintile (20%) of the income distribution, 25% of their income was derived from state benefit compared with 90% for their contemporaries in the bottom 20% (Table 9.8).

Table 9.8 Sources of pensioners income by income quintile 1986 (%) (Falkingham and Johnson, 1992, Table 3.4)

	Bottom 20%	Top 20%
Social security	90	25
Occupational pension	3	31
Savings	6	31
Employment	1	13

Income support

Pensioners have consistently had to turn to the Income Support system to increase their disposable income. In 1984/85 1 529 000 of the retired population were receiving a supplementary pension at an annual cost of £792 000 000. The elderly have always been the major client group of the Income Support system. In 1948 70% of those receiving National Assistance were retirement pensioners. However the percentage had decreased to 57% in 1984/85 (Department of Health and Social Security, 1985). We should not interpret this decrease as reflecting a massive increase in the living standards of the elderly. Rather, it is a reflection of the enormous increase in the number of long-term unemployed now reliant on means-tested benefit.

Income support is not paid automatically but after the potential claimant has been means-tested. Consequently not all of those eligible for the benefit, at any age, are claiming it. The percentage of those eligible for a means-tested benefit that are actually in receipt of the benefit is termed the take-up rate. There are two distinct aspects of the benefits take-up problem. Beltram (1984) distinguishes between primary and secondary take-up rates. Primary take-up relates to those eligible for a benefit who are not claiming it; i.e. non-claimers. An example of this would be pensioners who, although eligible to receive Income Support, fail to claim it. Secondary take-up relates to those who are already in receipt of a benefit, such as supplementary benefit, but who are not receiving their complete entitlement; i.e. under-claimers. An example of under-claiming would be pensioners who are receiving their basic Supplementary Benefit but not the extra weekly additions (known officially as additional requirements) for heating to which they are entitled.

The non-claiming of benefits by the elderly is a significant problem. It was estimated in 1991 that 20% of pensioners eligible for a mean-tested benefit were not claiming. No data are available on the under-claiming of benefits by the elderly (or any other claimant group). However as benefits-take-up campaigns generate a large number of successful claims from existing clients of the welfare system it seems probably that under-claiming is a significant problem.

The low take-up of means-tested benefits by pensioners (and other groups) is usually explained with reference to three factors; lack of information, difficulties using the service and stigma. As Hill (1982, p. 135) wrote 'the general case against means-tested benefits is that they confuse, deter and stigmatize those who need help'. This tripartite explanation has been expanded in recent years to encompass factors such as perceived need and utility. The relative importance of these reasons for low take-up between different claimant groups has not yet been thoroughly established although Victor (1985) has undertaken a preliminary analysis.

The first perspective suggests that low take-up results from lack of information by potential claimants. At its most fundamental this argument suggests that eligible claimants cannot proceed to make a claim if they are unaware of a benefit's existence. Taylor-Gooby (1979, p. 17) considered that 'survey evidence indicates that simply not knowing what one is entitled to claim is the biggest single obstacle to claiming'. However this perspective is rather more sophisticated than just involving knowledge about benefits for it also encompasses knowledge about eligibility or the method of claiming. A survey by the Ministry of Pensions and National Insurance (1966) suggested that 33% of pensioners entitled to National Assistance did not claim because of lack of information about the benefit and the method of claiming it. Similarly Broad (1977) also suggested that 41% of eligible elderly did not claim benefits because of misconceptions about entitlement or the applications procedure.

Recent work by Victor (1985) has shown that the elderly are much less informed about the existence of welfare benefits than other groups and less aware of where to go for help about a benefits problem. This suggests that lack of information, in the broadest sense, is a very real barrier preventing the elderly from claiming all the benefits to which they are entitled.

However it is difficult to assess just how influential lack of information is in explaining low take-up. Meacher (1972) concluded that 72% of all under-claiming resulted from inadequate information and Taylor-Gooby (1976) reports that two-thirds of his sample gave ignorance as their reason for not claiming rent rebates. However he also reports that two-thirds of these failed to claim when specifically told of the benefit and their entitlement. The evaluation of a take-up campaign promoted by the Greater London Council revealed that only about one-third of those informed by an advice worker of a specific entitlement to a benefit proceeded to make a claim (Victor, 1984). For the elderly only about 20% of those informed of a potential entitlement pursued the advice. A similar fraction was reported Kerr (1982). For older people, therefore, the simple provision of information about benefits will encourage about 20% of the elderly to make a claim for benefit. That so many do not make a claim, even when advised of a definite entitlement, indicates that there are many other factors influencing the decision to claim supplementary pension by the elderly.

The second explanation of low take-up invoked relates to the difficulties experienced by many claimants (or would be claimants) in using the social security service. This may relate to a number of factors but particularly emphasizes the perceived time and effort that has to be expended, for instance in numerous visits to the offices and the completion of complex forms, in order to make a benefits claim. This may, however, be less of a barrier to claiming by the elderly than for some other groups of claimants. Age Concern (1974, p. 82) observed 'Most elderly who apply for SB, whether the application is successful or not, feel that they have been well treated'. Additionally a survey by Briggs and Rees (1980) pointed to the high degree of satisfaction amongst elderly recipients of supplementary benefit. However it may be that such attitudes are not characteristic of elderly non-claimers of supplementary benefit.

Recent work supports the idea that the complexity of the claiming process and difficulties experienced in using the system seem to be less of a disincentive to the elderly than other groups (Victor, 1986). The elderly express a higher degree of satisfaction with the service provided by the DHSS and fewer suggest changes to the claiming system. This difference between the elderly and younger claimant groups, who are almost universally hostile to the practices of the DHSS, may result from the elderly receiving better treatment in their dealings with the DHSS, compared with other groups of claimants. Alternatively it may be that the elderly are much less critical of the procedures of the DHSS than younger subjects. As several other studies have reported similar findings (Briggs and Rees, 1980; Age Concern, 1974) it seems that the elderly probably incur fewer difficulties in their dealings with the DHSS than do other types of claimants and are generally treated more favourably, because they are perceived as a 'deserving' group, by the DHSS.

Stigma is the third paradigm which has traditionally formed an explanation of the low take-up of means-tested welfare benefits in Britain. Both Engels and Rowntree refer to the reluctance of the poor to seek help. Despite the historical pedigree of this explanation of low take-up, stigma itself has remained a rather ill-defined, nebulous concept. It has often been used as a general term to describe variously a sense of pride, personal failure, humiliation, an unwillingness to display private matters for public scrutiny, a desire to be seen as independent and a fear of the loss of personal dignity in claiming. At its most general this paradigm suggests that potential claimants are deterred by the negative associations that claiming involves. This is thought to be a particularly important deterrent to claiming for the elderly who vividly remember the savage pre-war household means test.

Some empirical evidence supports this assertion. The Ministry of Pensions and National Insurance (1966) study suggested that a third of elderly indicated pride/feelings of accepting charity as a reason for not claiming National Assistance.

Work by Victor (1986) does not provide much evidence to support the hypothesis that the elderly are deterred from claiming benefits because of feelings of pride or stigma. The difference between these studies may illustrate a cohort effect, with the recent generation of elders expecting a better standard of living than earlier cohorts. However this work suggested that the elderly were much less ready to claim because they did not feel a need for extra money. This could be interpreted as another reflection of the stigma thesis; the desire to be seen as a good manager. However it seems more likely that this low desire for extra money probably reflects the very low levels of perceived need amongst the elderly. Broad (1977) reported that 40% of elderly stated that they did not experience any difficulty in meeting their living expenses. Additionally Age Concern (1974) reported a high level of satisfaction with their living standard by the elderly. It seems likely that this low level of perceived need derives from the fact that many elderly set their living standards by the criteria of the 1930s rather than the 1980s. Alternatively, the low level of expressed need for more money could reflect the widespread acceptance by older people of the stereotype that old age is a time of poverty and low income. Consequently they feel that it is inappropriate for them to desire a higher standard of living, resulting in a failure to claim their complete benefit entitlement.

EXPENDITURE

Older people spend more of their income on housing, food and fuel, items considered essential to life, than the rest of the population and less upon 'luxury' items such as tobacco, alcoholic drink, transport and consumer durables (Table 9.9). This reflects the low incomes on which most elderly exist. For the majority of elderly their level of income leaves little for luxury items once the essentials of life have been paid for. Of particular concern to many is the large amount of their income which older people have to spend on fuel and heating. Given the increased importance of keeping warm in later life, because of the increased risk of hypothermia, it is frequently argued that older people should receive subsidized heating. An increase in the level at which the pension is paid would provide the elderly with a higher standard of living and increase their choice as to what they actually spend their income on, rather than

Table 9.9 United Kingdom: patterns of household expenditure 1983 (Family Expenditure Survey, 1983)

Percentage average weekly income spent on	*Retired*	*All households*
Housing	20.9	16.8
Fuel	9.3	6.5
Food	22.0	20.7
Alcohol	3.7	4.8
Tobacco	2.5	3.0
Household goods	5.6	7.2
Other goods	7.5	7.6
Transport	10.9	14.7
Services	12.0	11.3
Miscellaneous	0.1	0.4

having subsidized heating or housing costs. This again takes us back to the debate about whether all pensioners need or should have pension increases or whether these should be targeted at the most needy. However it is probable that those who feel they do need more cash would rather have it as of 'right' than be means-tested or receive charitable handouts.

OWNERSHIP OF CONSUMER DURABLES

Another aspect of living standards relates to the possession of consumer durable items, such as washing machines and refrigerators. These items are now considered by many as essential rather than luxuries. Older people are much less likely to live in a household which has access to these items compared with the rest of the population (Table 9.10). There is a clear relationship between age and access to these items. Consistently the very old are much less likely to report ownership of, or have access to, these items than either the 'young' elderly or the rest of the population. Access to these items is also related to class. Those elderly from professional and non-manual backgrounds are much more likely to own these items than those from working-class occupations (Victor and Evandrou, 1986). This relationship remains when variations in the types of household that older people live in are taken into account.

Table 9.10 Great Britain: ownership of consumer durables 1980 (Askham *et al.*, 1992, Table 3.10)

	65–69	70–74	75–79	80+
Car	60	47	34	24
Telephone	90	88	83	80
Washing machine	86	75	69	55
Fridge/freezer	74	69	56	46
Tumble-drier	32	24	21	17
Microwave	29	20	13	10
Dishwasher	7	5	4	2
Television	98	99	98	97
Video	34	20	13	10

SATISFACTION WITH LIVING STANDARDS

The elderly are not a group that complains about their generally low standard of living. A survey of the over-70s living in Wales indicated that only 3% were not satisfied with their current standard of living. In addition only 8% reported that they were dissatisfied with their current financial situation. They also seem to have a remarkable confidence in their future living standards (Abrams, 1980).

It is difficult to interpret precisely what these types of responses to interview questions actually mean. It could be that because the now elderly grew up in the depression years between the wars they now consider themselves fairly well off. Alternatively, it could be that they have accepted the stereotype which identifies old age as a time of poverty and hardship and therefore expect to be poor during their later life. Whatever the reason it is unacceptably ageist for the rest of society to accept without a qualm the low standards of living and poverty that many older members of the community experience.

TRANSPORT

Access to transport is essential in a society where services are often centrally organized and where contacts with others and in community activities assume access to some form of transport. The transport problems of older people stem from four major factors:

1. the increasing dominance of the transportation system by private car ownership;
2. the high cost of transport for low-income elderly;
3. physical limitations and design barriers which inhibit many older people from using transport;
4. the inadequate transport system in areas, both urban and rural, where older people live.

A major and increasingly important aspect of the transport system is the private car. The increasing dominance of this form of travel has resulted in many urban areas expanding beyond the fixed routes provided by public transport. Many homes and other destinations such as shopping centres are only accessible by car. Additionally the bulk of the public resources allocated to transport are devoted to the construction and improvement of roads rather than to public transport.

Older people are much less likely than other age groups to own a car (Table 9.10). Additionally the proportion of older people living in households without a car increases markedly with age so that three-quarters of people over 75 do not have access to a car. At all ages females are less likely to have access to a private car than males. This reflects both the low income of this group and the relatively small fraction of now elderly women who have a driving licence.

Amongst those elderly who own cars the amount of driving declines with age. Slower response rates and deteriorating sight contribute to the decrease. Driving therefore becomes more hazardous for the older person. These difficulties are often enhanced by the increasing complexity of the road system. Fast traffic speeds on motorways, increased traffic and congestion and road signs that must be read and interpreted very rapidly combine to make driving more difficult for the older person and may force some to give up entirely.

For those elderly living on fixed or low incomes there are increased problems with the costs of maintaining the car, its licensing and insurance. In Britain older drivers are subject to a medical examination before the licence is renewed. Insurance companies often discriminate against older drivers by cancelling policies, denying them coverage or raising their insurance rates to exorbitant levels. However, to be balanced against this, some companies are now actively recruiting older drivers because of their lower accident risk.

As they lack access to a car many older people are forced to rely upon public transport such as buses or trains for their transport needs. The elderly, particularly females, are high users of public transport. However the fraction using public transport decreases markedly after the age of 70.

The major reason for the decline in public transport use with age are the increased infirmity of the older person, the inconvenience of the transportation system and its high costs. High bus steps, rapidly closing doors, large flights of stairs, difficulties with carrying luggage and badly placed handrails constitute formidable barriers to the use of public transport by the elderly. Many older people also face considerable psychological barriers in using the public transportation network such as the fear of getting lost. Bus and train schedules are often confusing and difficult to use whilst information conveyed over public address systems at bus or train stations is usually inaudible to those without acute hearing.

Apart from public transport the other major form of transport for older people is walking, but this is a problem in a car-dominated society. The smooth flow of traffic takes priority over the needs of pedestrians. Traffic lights and road intersections are geared to the needs of the driver rather than the pedestrian. Traffic lights and pedestrian crossings often change too quickly for the older person to get across safely. All of these factors contribute to the increased rate of pedestrian accidents amongst older people.

CONCLUSION

The elderly are, as we have seen, mainly reliant upon a variety of pensions and benefits for their income. These can be divided into those provided by the state and those from previous employers. For the majority of old people the state is their main source of income in later life. Because these benefits are low the majority of elderly experience low living standards and poverty in the last years of their life. This has become an accepted social norm which few question. Poverty is seen to be part and parcel of 'normal' ageing when in fact it is a socially constructed phenomenon resulting from the low financial value of benefits paid to the elderly.

However it is important to remember that there are wide varieties of income within the elderly population and that these represent a continuation of the inequalities experienced within the labour market. Those who earned the least whilst in employment are least likely to have had access to an occupational pension scheme or to have been able to 'save' for their old age. Current pension arrangements do nothing to address these inequalities.

The current trend in Britain is to encourage individuals and private employers to take over the responsibility of providing pensions. Through the erosion of SERPS and by maintaining an inadequate basic retirement pension the state is trying to withdraw from the arena of pension provision. However it is doubtful if the private sector and individuals can undertake this role effectively and efficiently. The state, as a collective body acting for us all would seem to be the most efficient mechanism by which to transfer resources from the working population to the retired. Indeed until the emergence of the 'New Right' philosophy of recent Conservative administrations it had been accepted for most of this century that society has a collective responsibility to provide for the retired. In return the current generation of contributors assume that when their turn comes they will be supported by subsequent generations. This consensus has been eroded by a reassertion of the importance of individual responsibility and the importance of saving for one's old age. The fundamental weakness of this approach is that it does little to address the problems of those who were unable to do this because they were paid low wages whilst working or because they were disabled or unemployed.

It is fashionable in some quarters to portray the elderly as not contributing to the economy. If we overlook their past contribution it is obvious that the elderly contribute to the economy in the role of consumers. They are an important source of demand for the goods and services produced by the working population. Increasing the income levels of the elderly would therefore increase the demand for goods and services. By giving the elderly a realistic rather than a subsistence standard of living we would enable them to take a more active part in the life of the community rather than forcing them on to the sidelines. If the elderly cannot take part in the normal activities of the community such as entertaining friends to tea or buying presents for grandchildren at Christmas or birthdays because of low incomes we are artificially isolating them from the society in which they live. Reforms of the pension system should concentrate upon giving priority to establishing a realistic basic pension which would do away with the need for inefficient means-tested supplements and allow the elderly to enjoy the same standards of living as the rest of society.

A recent and popular new image has developed to describe the financial situation of older people – the development of the myth of the 'woopie' (well-off older person). This image stresses the affluence of later life. Clearly although there are some very well-off older people, these remain in the minority. For most older people later life is a time of financial hardship. Later life is characterized by the continuation of income differentials observed during working life. Continued emphasis upon private rather than public provision for old age will result in increased inequality of income amongst the older age groups.

10

Family and social networks

Ageing takes place within a social context. At each phase of the lifecycle the individual belongs to a variety of kinship and social groups all of which bring interactions and relationships with family, friends and neighbours. The extent to which an older person is enmeshed within a social network of kin, friends and neighbours will greatly effect her/his experience of ageing. In this chapter we examine the extent to which older people are part of kinship networks and the role of the family in the care of older people. Finally we look at the wider social networks of older people and the perceptions of isolation and loneliness of the elderly.

THE FAMILY

Although sociologists and others identify a variety of different family structures two major types, the nuclear and extended, dominate any discussion of the family. The nuclear family consists of a woman, a man and their children and is the typical family group portrayed in the media, advertising and popular culture. The linking together of several nuclear groups by an extension of parent–child relationships, such as a married couple, their married offspring and grandchildren living together, produces the second major family type, the extended family. This is sometimes also known as a three-generational family, although examples of up to five generations living together have been enumerated.

Sociological studies of the family have shown a rather narrow and pessimistic concentration upon the prediction of the demise of the family in modern industrial society. Gloomy forecasts of the disintegration of the family as a social institution have a long historical pedigree. Cicero, in his study of old age, lamented that families were not what they used to be, especially in the way that they cared for and respected their elders. Many social commentators have idealized the extended family and lamented the perceived move to nuclear families without recognizing that the family is a very flexible unit which demonstrates a pattern of almost continual adaptation to changing social and economic circumstances.

Pre-industrial times are often portrayed as the golden age of both the family and 'ageing', when older people were both respected and cared for by their own families. Two inter-related assumptions govern this stereotypic and rather idealist view. The first is that the extended family was the normal pattern of family organization. Secondly, this view assumes that because the elderly lived in the same dwelling as the rest of the family they were cared for by the family and remained respected members of the kin network.

This idealistic view of the past is highly simplistic and is not supported by the available evidence. Historical research suggests that there is no single type of household or family unit which typifies pre-industrial society. There is a marked diversity in the typical patterns of household formation ranging from simple nuclear families in Britain to the highly complex extended networks of Austria and Germany. The explanation for this diversity lies with the differing cultural and demographic characteristics of pre-industrial societies.

Laslett (1983) concludes that the nuclear family was probably the norm even in pre-industrial Britain. He suggests that only about 11% of households in pre-industrial Britain could be classified as extended family groups. Additionally probably only about 6% of the population lived in three-generational households. For the vast majority of the population, the two-generational nuclear family was the main type of household structure. The demographic conditions prevalent between the Middle Ages and the Industrial Revolution consisted of large families with children continuing to be born late in the mother's life. Thus child-bearing occupied a longer phase of the lifecycle than it does today. This, combined with the shorter life expectancy, meant that more elderly were likely to be living in family groups simply because not all their children had yet left home to marry. Additionally the comparative rarity of older people in pre-modern Britain makes it very unlikely that the extended family could in any way be considered the normal or typical type of family.

In addition there is little direct evidence to support the assumption that co-residence with younger relatives necessarily guaranteed that the elderly would be well cared for. It was fairly common practice in pre-industrial societies for older people and their children to draw up legal contracts and wills in which property was exchanged for care and maintenance in old age. This does not suggest a society dominated by a desire to venerate and serve the old. It could also equally well be argued that, because our ancestors had a much greater struggle just to survive, they would have little excess energy to spare upon the care of dependent older people.

With the advent of modernization and industrialization the thesis advanced is that the extended family declined and was replaced by the nuclear family. It is this shift from the extended to the nuclear family which many social commentators suggest has brought about many of the major social problems that characterize modern industrial society. The common perception of the modern family is that the elderly are generally neglected by younger family members who abdicate their social responsibilities on to the state. This contrasts to the rather more caring image which characterizes our stereotypical view of the role of the family in the care of the elderly at earlier points in our history.

We have already seen that the extended family was a comparative rarity in pre-industrial Britain. How then did industrialization affect family and household structures? In the early phases of industrialization it seems that extended families were more common in the new urban areas than the rural localities (Anderson, 1972); a complete reversal of the modernization thesis. It seems that this apparent contradiction is explained by the housing shortages in newly developing towns and the use of older relatives as 'baby-minders' whilst their mothers worked outside the home. Similar findings have been reported for parts of the New England region of America (Chudacoff and Haraven, 1978). Thus, at least in the short term, industrialization increased rather than decreased the probability of co-residence between generations.

Modernization and the development of state support systems for the elderly have resulted, it is argued, in a decline in family support of the elderly. The increase in the fraction of elderly living alone and the growth of institutions are two pieces of evidence which are cited as indicating the decline in family support. Proponents of these views see family as being overwhelmed by the increase in the numbers of the elderly. Alternatively some writers consider that families willing to care for their elderly as being excluded from the process by a bureaucratic centrally organized state system.

There is, however, little good empirical evidence to support the view that modernization stripped the family of many of its functions. Anderson (1977) examined changes in income maintenance provision for the elderly in 19th century Britain and its effects upon family relationships. Before 1908 the main form of support was the Poor Law. This resulted in the workhouse being used as a threat against many elderly by their families. The introduction of a pensions scheme, however limited, Anderson (1977) considers to have lessened intergenerational pressures by giving the elderly a degree of independence. This resulted in family relationships which functioned upon a basis of mutual interdependence rather than a one-sided dependency. In Britain, despite the development of a sophisticated welfare state, the family remains the preferred source of help in a crisis and modern communications systems allow for interaction between family members to take place despite wide geographical differences in location.

THE AVAILABILITY OF FAMILY

The extent to which an older person is enmeshed within a series of kinship relations will obviously have an important effect upon the experience of ageing. For the social researcher, however, identifying kinship networks can be rather difficult. In this analysis we will confine our attention to the major kinship relationships, spouse, children and siblings. Excluded from the analysis are the more distant kin relationships. However we must remember that such relationships may make an important contribution to the overall family network of older people.

We saw earlier that the percentage of older people living with their spouse decreases with age (Chapter 6). At all ages, however, males are more likely to be married than females. We also noted that for this cohort of elderly women a substantial minority, up to 13%, never married. Spouses are rarely the same age. The typical pattern in Britain is for the male to be 3 years older than his spouse. This, combined with the higher death rates for males, largely explains the great prevalence of widowhood amongst the elderly women.

Amongst the now elderly population who ever married, small families are the norm. A survey of the elderly in Clackmannan, Scotland revealed that 18% of males over 65 and 29% of females had no surviving children; 17% and 15% respectively had four or more children (Bond and Carstairs, 1982). At all ages males are more likely to have surviving children than females (Table 10.1). This again reflects the high proportion of never-married women in the current cohort of older people.

Table 10.1 Percentage of elderly with surviving children (Research Team for the Care of the Elderly)

	70–74		75–79		80–84		85+	
	M	F	M	F	M	F	M	F
Yes	79	78	78	75	87	70	79	71
No	21	22	22	25	13	30	21	29

Similarly Abrams (1978) reported that for those aged 65–74 the average family size was 2.3 children. Completed family size and numbers of surviving children are obviously key influences upon the extent to which the family can be a source of support to the elderly. Those elderly with either no surviving children or with small families have, all other things being equal, fewer opportunities for being involved in family networks than those elderly with large numbers of surviving children.

Siblings are also an important aspect of the family network. One-fifth of males and 24% of females interviewed in the Clackmannan survey had no surviving siblings (Bond and Carstairs, 1982). The percentage of elderly with surviving brothers and sisters decreases with age (Table 10.2). There seems to be little difference between the sexes in the number with surviving siblings.

Table 10.2 Percentage of elderly with surviving siblings (Research Team for the Care of the Elderly)

	70–74		75–79		80–84		85+	
	M	*F*	*M*	*F*	*M*	*F*	*M*	*F*
Yes	83	81	79	77	66	70	54	52
No	17	19	21	23	34	30	46	48

As we can see from the previous two tables not all elderly are part of an extensive kinship network. Data from the study by Bond and Carstairs (1982) show that there are a minority of elderly, 6% overall, (8% of women and 3% of men) who have no children or siblings. Further 3% of the elderly had never married, had no children and no siblings.

HOUSEHOLD STRUCTURE

Another important aspect of family contact and networks is household structure. We saw in Chapter 6 that most older people live either with their spouse or on their own. Consequently, of the elderly living in the community, 84% live in single-generation households (Evandrou *et al.*, 1985). This means that the elderly person either lives alone or with one or more other elderly person, usually either her/his spouse or sibling. Two-generation households are where the elderly person lives with one or more people from the generation below them, usually their children. Overall 13% of older people are resident in two-generational households. A three-generation household is usually defined as one where the older person is living with both children and grandchildren. This type of household structure is much rarer. Data from the 1980 GHS reported by Evandrou *et al.* (1985) indicate that 3% of the elderly live in three-generation households.

The type of household in which older people live has shown much change over this century. Table 10.3 shows that, in his survey of the elderly (men aged 65 and women aged 60), Sheldon (1948) reported that only 10% lived alone.

Table 10.3 Household structure of the elderly in 1945–88 (%)

	1945 (1)	1962 (2)	1976 (3)	1980 (4)	1988*(5)
Lives alone	10	22	30	34	32
With spouse	30	33	44	45	49
With others	60	44	27	22	19

Source: (1) Sheldon, 1948, Table 34
      (2) Shanas *et al.*, 1962, Table 18
      (3) Hunt, 1978
      (4) General Household Survey, 1980
      (5) Askham *et al.*, 1992, Table 2.3
* population aged 60+

This contrasts with 34% in 1980. Similarly co-residence between the generations has decreased from 60% to 22% over the same period. These changes in household residence patterns reflect the trend for young people to move away from the parental home to establish their own household upon marriage. In addition the provision of a state pension has provided many older people with the financial resources to maintain their own household in old age.

The percentage living in different types of household varies with the demographic characteristics of older people. At all ages females are more likely than males to be living alone or with others, usually in two- or three-generation households. This suggests that, as in pre-industrial times, widowhood is a factor which precipitates co-residence between older parent and adult child. However, as Table 10.4 shows, even in the very oldest age groups the majority of older people live in single-generation households (see also Table 10.5).

Table 10.4 Great Britain: household structure of the elderly by age and sex (%) one = one-generation; two = two-generation; three = three-generation; (General Household Survey, 1980, unpublished)

	65–69		70–74		75–79		80+	
	M	F	M	F	M	F	M	F
One	89	80	89	86	88	86	84	79
Two	9	17	9	12	10	11	14	17
Three	2	3	2	2	2	3	2	4

Table 10.5 Great Britain: household structure by age and sex (%) 1988 (Askham *et al.*, 1992, Table 2.3)

	60–64		65–69		70–74		75–79		80+	
	M	*F*	*M*	*F*	*M*	*F*	*M*	*F*	*M*	*F*
Lives alone	13	22	15	29	20	43	25	58	34	65
Lives with spouse	60	56	67	54	64	40	61	26	50	17
Lives with others and spouse	22	15	13	6	9	4	6	2	5	1
Lives with others not spouse	5	9	6	11	8	13	7	14	11	18

The relatively low fraction of elderly who live with their children does not necessarily indicate a pattern of neglect by the offspring. Rather, it reflects the huge preference expressed by the elderly (and all other adult age groups) for independent living. A survey by Shanas *et al.* (1968) revealed that for only 8% of older people was living with the family the preferred mode of living. The vast majority, 83%, preferred their own home and the much valued commodity of independence. Moving in with offspring can result in a loss of independence for the older person and the reversal of roles between parent and child. Similarly Townsend (1964), in his study of Bethnal Green in London, reported that only 10% of elderly with children were in favour of sharing a house with them.

CONTACT WITH FAMILY

A popular image of the elderly depicts the lonely widow neglected by her children, family, neighbours and friends. Like many other popular images of ageing this stereotype is far from the truth. However we should remember when discussing the family relationships of the elderly that not all of them, as we saw above, have any children or close family.

In considering the role of the family in the social network of the elderly the first factor to consider is the spatial proximity of parents and children. Overall it seems that levels of geographical mobility have been rather low in Britain, compared with Europe and North America. Consequently the majority of children still live close to their parents. Surveys from Denmark, Great Britain and America revealed that three-quarters of older people with living children had at least one child within 30 minutes' journey of them (Shanas *et al.*, 1968).

In addition, almost half of the elderly population have a brother or sister living within 30 minutes' journey (Bond and Carstairs, 1982). Furthermore the survey of Hunt (1978) indicated that 95% of all elderly felt that they had a close relative living nearby.

Both the structure of an old person's family, such as number of children, and their geographical proximity influence the frequency of contact between the old person and the family. It is not very surprising to find that the larger an old person's family is and the nearer they live to the older person the more likely there is to be physical contact between them such as visiting. However contact can be achieved by other methods such as telephone calls or letters. Thus geographical separation does not necessarily imply neglect or lack of contact between the older person and the family.

For those with children overall levels of interaction are generally high. Almost all old people with children see at least one of their children weekly and only 10% with children had not seen them within a month (Bond and Carstairs, 1982). Of those with children not living with them almost a quarter were being visited daily by their offspring. The frequency of this contact between offspring and parents is influenced by the number of surviving children, their proximity and sex. Contacts between parents and children are highest when the elderly person is widowed rather than still living as a married couple. Older people are more likely to receive weekly visits from children if the offspring are females rather than males.

Overall, three-quarters of older people express satisfaction with the level of contact between themselves and their children. The vast majority of those who wanted more contact with their children cited distance as the main reason for not seeing enough of them. The vast majority of older people do not seem to want more contact with their children reporting that they see sufficient of them already. Where older people appear neglected by their children there is often a very good reason for this (Isaacs, Livingstone and Neville, 1972).

Levels of interaction are high with other family members such as siblings and grandchildren. Of those with siblings 8% were in daily contact (17% if those living in the same household are included) and almost 60% were in contact at least once a month. The never-married are likely to see more of their siblings than either the married or the widowed. This is largely explained by the high proportion of never-married elderly who live with siblings. Again levels of satisfaction with the degree of contact with siblings is high. Less than a third of elderly express a desire to see more of their siblings. The reasons for lack of contact are usually distance or infirmity of either the elderly person or the sibling.

However, overall contact with family members does seem to decrease with age. Amongst the elderly in Wales less than 10% of males and females aged 70–74 had not seen a family member in the month before interview. At the age of 85 years and over this increases to 15% of males and 20% of females. It seems likely that this decrease in overall family contacts with age arises because of the death of siblings and other family members rather than suggesting a pattern of neglect with the increased age of the elderly person. Despite this decrease in overall contact levels it is obvious that the elderly do maintain quite close contact with their family even in very old age.

There are some important exceptions from this overall pattern of a high degree of interaction between the older person and the family. At all ages the never-married were much less likely to have family contacts than either the married or the widowed.

The elderly are generally very contented with the extent of their contact with family members. Three-quarters of elderly are satisfied with the amount of contact they have with the family, although this does decrease slightly with age. This seems to reflect the inability of older people, because of physical disability, to go and visit. Of the quarter who would have liked more contact 80% felt that the distance between them prohibited greater contact. Less than 5% felt that they were rejected by the family.

The pattern of contact between the older person and her/his family seems to be fairly constant. This is confirmed by the finding of Abrams (1980) that two-thirds of older people felt that they saw as much of the family as they had 5 years before; 13% felt that they saw more of their family than previously and 20% that they saw less of them. Again this latter finding is largely attributable to the death of siblings and other family members.

THE ROLE OF THE FAMILY

What role does the family play in the lives of older people? Obviously there are the emotional and companionship aspects of primary family ties. The family can provide the older person with a wide-ranging kin-based social network. In turn the older person helps to keep the family together. Links with more distant relatives, such as aunts or uncles, is often maintained by the older family members. Older members provide a focus for the family and family gatherings and play a key role in such events as weddings and christenings. The loss of the older person through death can often lead to the breaking up of an extended kin network.

In addition to fulfilling needs of a personal and emotional kind the family is also a source of assistance. Help may be provided during times of illness, money or gifts given in times of hardship. These flows of help between generations are highly dynamic. It is incorrect to portray the elderly as being the 'receivers' and the young as the 'providers'. Rather, we must look at the contributions of both young and old within the family.

THE CONTRIBUTION OF OLDER PEOPLE

Gerontologists have tended to concentrate upon studying the role played by younger family members in caring for the elderly. There has been relatively little study of aid given by the old to the young. The former is the view which still informs much research in this area, especially that which is sponsored by the government. Consequently the 1980 and 1985 General Household Survey included an extensive series of questions about the role played by the family in the care of the elderly. However no consideration was given to the contributions made by the elderly to the family by such services as babysitting. However we must recognize that flows of help between the older person and the family are not uni-directional and that there is a considerable degree of reciprocity between the generations (Finch 1989). It is also important to remember that these relationships are highly fluid.

One of the most positive aspects of ageing is grandparenthood. Consequently this is one area of family life where the elderly can make a very positive contribution. A survey by Peter Townsend (1966) indicated that women in Britain became grandmothers at 54 and great-grandmothers at 72. Men were, on average, 3 years older when they achieved this status. Shanas *et al.* (1968) indicates that 90% of all elderly who had children have grandchildren; 23% also have great-grandchildren.

Contact levels with grandchildren are generally high. Abrams (1978) reports of those elderly with grandchildren one half had been in contact with them in the month before interview. Despite this generally high level of contact, 46% of elderly would have liked to have seen more of their grandchildren. The usual reasons for reduced contact were either the distance that they lived from the grandchild or their own infirmity.

Increased life expectancy, coupled with shorter periods of child-rearing, have exposed many people to the role of grandparenthood at a much earlier age. However it is an aspect of later life which has not been yet been extensively researched in Britain. Cunningham-Bowley (1986) has indicated that for many people grandparenthood is no longer associated with old age and later life. The respondents interviewed in Aberdeen rather felt that grandparenthood kept them young rather than made them feel old. It seems that grandparenthood has become an integral part of middle age. Cunningham-Bowley's work indicates that grandparenthood is seen by many as a rather symbolic role which links past, present and future (see also Thompson, Itzin and Abendstern, 1990). There is a gender difference in the way that grandparents define their role (Thomas, 1976). Women view the role as a source of biological renewal whereas males are much more concerned with the instrumental aspects of grandparenting.

Grandparenthood is a role which is seen as being open to most elderly people and is one which is almost universally welcomed. However we must remember that it is usually a secondary role. Thus the individual may be a wife in her major role with grandmother as a secondary back-up role. It seems unlikely that for any single grandparent the role will remain constant over time. Rather the role will develop in response to changes in both grandparent and grandchild.

A survey of the family life of older people in the East End of London revealed that two-thirds of older women with grandchildren performed some regular service for them such as fetching them from school, giving them meals, looking after then while their parents were at work or looking after them in the evening (Townsend, 1964). Grandfathers were much less active in this role than grandmothers with only a fifth performing a regular child-care function. American survey data also indicated that grandparents played an important role in the care of grandchildren, particularly in times of financial hardship, illness or when the child was attending school (college).

American data confirm that gender has an important influence upon the role of the grandparent (Hagestrand, 1985). She reported that grandfathers concentrated upon influencing matters relating to jobs and finance whereas grandmothers influenced the grandchild in interpersonal spheres as well. She also suggests that the grandparent role is essentially biased towards the matrilineal and that the grandfather's role is inherently less salient. Certainly Neugarten and Weinstein (1964) support this by their reports that grandmothers, but never grandfathers, act as surrogate parents.

What then forms the basis of 'normal' grandparenthood? The answer to this question is highly dependent upon the cultural context. An anthropological study by Apple (1956) looked at variations in the grandparenthood role between cultures. She found that in societies where grandparents remained the major power in the household, either in economic or status terms (or both), the relationship between grandparent and grandchild is highly formalized and often very unfriendly. In societies where grandparents retain little household power relationships are more egalitarian, indulgent and friendly. Other American research, which probably reflects the situation in Britain, indicates that most grandparents engaged in indulgent relationships with their grandchildren without assuming direct responsibility for the care and control of the child. Only in cases of serious family breakdown or orphaning do grandparents take over full responsibility for the child.

Neugarten and Weinstein (1964) investigated the diversity of the grandparent role in the United States. Their research identified five major styles of grandparenthood.

1. **Formal style.** Here the grandparent follows what is often portrayed as the appropriate role for the grandparent, giving presents and babysitting but not taking over the role of the parent.

2. **The fun-seeker.** Here the relationship between grandparent and grandchild is characterized by informality and playfulness, the older adult becoming almost a playmate for the child. This role is more often associated with grandfathers than grandmothers.
3. **The distant figure.** Here the grandparent emerges for holidays and special occasions but is otherwise out of contact. Contact is fleeting but usually benevolent.
4. **The surrogate parent.** This is most often the role played by a grandmother caring for a child while the mother works.
5. **The authoritarian.** This is a role usually taken by the grandfather who is the centre of the family. He is usually patriarchal, authoritarian and seen as the dispenser of family wisdom.

The research in America indicated that the most common style of grandparenting was the 'formal style' with remaining grandparents equally divided between the 'fun-seeker' and 'distant' roles. Grandparents following the surrogate parent or authoritarian model were rare.

Women seem to view the grandparent role rather more positively than men. They often experience anticipatory socialization for the role by knitting clothes for the new family member and providing helpful advice to the new mother or mother-to-be. Consequently they often perceive themselves as grandmothers well ahead of the birth of the child. However some younger grandmothers do experience anxiety in adopting the role as they may perceive it as threat to their youthful self-image. Many men become grandfathers at a time when they are heavily involved in their career. Thus their primary source of identity is still predominantly occupationally based and often they postpone involvement in the grandparent role until retirement.

The positive contribution made by older people within the family is rarely confined to the care of grandchildren. Older family members contribute to the care of other family members by means such as cooking meals, shopping, running errands or, in the case of older males, providing help with gardening and household repairs. This leads Townsend (1964, p. 63) to conclude that:

> it is clear that in general there were almost as many old people helping others as were themselves being helped during the weekly round. This evidence compels us to look more critically into the assumed burden of old age. We may be attaching too little weight to the contribution to society made by the aged and too much to their claims on it.

THE ROLE OF THE FAMILY IN THE CARE OF THE ELDERLY

Contact between the elderly and their families is extensive. This is in complete contradiction to the popular stereotype of the old as being neglected by their families. Following on from this is another popular image of the family as making little, or no, contribution towards the care and maintenance of older people. This attitude was particularly prevalent in the 1950s in the wake of the establishment of the British welfare state. McEwan and Laverty (1949), in a study of hospital provision in Bradford, were convinced that children were not prepared to care for their elderly parents. Consistently social commentators worried about whether the family still cared for its elderly and whether this responsibility was being undermined by the provision of domiciliary services. These questions and stereotypes remain in popular currency.

Empirical data suggests that this perception of the family as refusing to accept the care of their elderly is a myth totally without foundation. Consistently a stream of research reports from the 1950s onwards have demonstrated that it is the family which bears the brunt of the care of the elderly in the community (Equal Opportunities Commission, 1982a, b, 1983; Evandrou *et al.*, 1985; Jones, Victor and Vetter, 1983; Jones and Vetter, 1984; Green, 1988; Qureshi and Walker, 1989; Wenger, 1984). Contrary to popular stereotypes, there is very little evidence of families refusing to look after those elderly members who need such care and attention. Thus Lowther and Williamson (1966, p. 1460) wrote that 'belief in the decline in filial care of the elderly is unfounded'.

Table 10.6 Help with specific tasks (%) provided by family members (Abrams, 1980)

Task	Age of elderly person	
	65–74	*75+*
Bathing	78	69
Putting on shoes	95	90
Getting in/out of bed	95	82
Getting about house	100	58
Putting on socks	100	80
Washing self	80	59
Dressing	86	78
Getting to WC	100	69
Combing hair[*]	100	30
Shaving [**]	69	60
Feeding	78	53
Mean all tasks	90	66

[*] females only
[**] males only

Data from a survey carried out by Abrams, shown in Table 10.6, is representative of these research findings in demonstrating the importance of the family as a source of care for the elderly. These data show that even in the very oldest age groups the family are the main source of help for all household and personal care tasks.

The second fear expressed in relation to family care of the elderly was that the provision of services would undermine self-help and the family contribution. Little evidence has been provided to support this assertion. Indeed work by Townsend in particular has argued that the provision of services has increased the ability of the family to care for its old. Without the support of domiciliary services, Townsend (1964) has argued that many families would have had to abandon their elderly to an institution.

Research has consistently demonstrated that the family does care for its old and that this care is not undermined by the provision of domiciliary services. However many of these early studies, although clearly linking the role of caring with the female members of the household, did not question this essentially sexist state of affairs. It was taken for granted that it was the role of the family to care for its old and that this responsibility was best suited to women. However more recently feminists have started to question the assumption that the family is the natural 'caring' unit and have shown that these are socially defined norms rather than a natural order of things.

Who within the family provides this informal care to the older members? A variety of research reports have shown that, now as in the 1950s, the majority of carers of the elderly, probably about 70%, are females (Finch and Groves, 1983). Thus Walker (1981, p. 550) writes: 'care will be provided within families by women… men are not expected to look after themselves to the same extent that women are, nor are they expected to look after elderly or infirm relatives'. Whilst it is true that the majority of carers of the elderly are female it is wrong to see this as an exclusively female role. Research findings indicate that up to one-third of all carers of the elderly are male and their contribution should not be ignored (Arber and Gilbert, 1989).

Male and female carers differ in terms of their demographic characteristics, the type of household in which they live and their relationship to the person being cared for. In considering the role of particular family members in the care of the elderly it is necessary to distinguish between the different types of household in which elderly people live. Where the older person who requires help lives as a married couple then it is the spouse who takes over the prime caring responsibility. This divides equally between men and women. In this type of circumstance males make an important contribution to the care of the elderly. Where the older dependent person lives either alone, with siblings or with younger household members then the main carer is usually a younger female, normally a daughter. Jones, Victor and Vetter (1983), in a study of the elderly in south Wales, found that daughters were three times more likely to be identified as carers than sons. Consequently, where the carer is the same generation as the elderly dependent the role is undertaken equally as often by men as women, but when the carer is drawn from the ranks of younger family members then the role is assumed almost exclusively by women.

It has been suggested that it is inappropriate to identify main carers of the elderly as it likely that the elderly will be cared for by a 'network' of care. Data from South Wales strongly refute this suggestion (Jones and Vetter, 1984). Here it was found that few such networks could be identified. Rather the responsibility for caring for an older person would be assumed by a specific family member who would then receive little tangible support from the rest of the family, especially if the carer was of a different generation from the older person.

The strain felt by those caring for the elderly, especially the dependent and perhaps confused, is often acute (Sanford, 1975). However it is not characteristic of all those who maintain the elderly at home. Where the older person is being looked after by a spouse there seems to be less strain or psychological problems. This probably is because the role of carer is seen as the fulfilment of marriage vows taken many years earlier. The group most 'at risk' from the strain of caring seem to be daughters (or daughters-in-law) caring for an older person, especially if the elderly person is resident within the same household.

The amount of care provided by the family for their elderly is substantial in terms of both time and money. A survey of the carers of elderly handicapped relatives in Oxford reported that the average time spent caring was 3.5–4 hours a day or 1400 hours a year (Nissel, 1984). At 1983 prices the total value of this caring was £3500 a year. This calculation excludes the £6500 a year that the carer might have earned if she had been able to work outside the home. Thus the family are contributing between £3 000 000 000 and £5 000 000 000 a year to the care of their elderly relatives compared with the state contribution of £928 000 000. We return to some of these issues in Chapter 12 during the discussion of community care. However family care of older people is not without its problems, especially the problem of elder abuse, which exists, although upon what scale remains contentious.

WIDOWHOOD

At some time married couples, especially older couples, have to face the possibility of their own death or the death of their spouse. Widowhood is now a fact of married life which is confined to later life rather than being characteristic of all phases of the lifecycle.

Marriage is important both because of its intrinsic value and the links it provides to social networks and activities. A marriage relationship can provide affection and a sense of belonging and provide evidence to the wider world of social competence. All these are lost upon widowhood. The meaning of widowhood varies between cultures. The Hindu culture developed the tradition of *suttee*, the self-immolation of the widow upon her husband's funeral pyre. Other cultures isolate widows and demand that they dress in black and distance themselves from society.

Widowhood has strong negative consequences for the older person. The widowed demonstrate higher rates of mortality, morbidity and self-reported ill-health. However it is often difficult to establish the true effects of widowhood. For example it could be that the lower life satisfaction levels characteristic of widows may result from the factors which accompany widowhood, such as low income, rather than from widowhood itself.

Widowhood is predominantly a female experience. Whilst most widowed persons attain acceptable adjustment levels to their bereavement this process of adaptation seems to take some time. Studies from America indicate that two-thirds of widows take at least a year to come to terms with their new status, to learn to be alone and to be independent (Lopata, 1973). Widowhood disrupts, at least in the short term, established patterns of social relationships. At such times the widow usually turns to her family for help in coping with both immediate problems and establishing a new life. In particular, children are a first line of support. Typically daughters provide emotional help whilst sons provide financial help. However widows seem much less inclined to move in with their children after their bereavement.

Whilst widowhood disrupts wider social relationships the experience varies with both age and sex. Many social activities, at all stages of the lifecycle, are couple-based. Thus the widow of either sex may feel peripheral. However this feeling of being the odd one out is much more acute for males for whom widowhood is much rarer. For women, however, widowhood increasingly becomes the norm with age and thus may be a less socially disruptive experience. Indeed for very elderly women marriage may be perceived as the deviant status rather than widowhood.

THE WIDER SOCIAL NETWORK

Friends and neighbours form part of the wider social network and world of the elderly. The extent of this network may be influenced by a variety of factors including whether the elderly person has moved house around retirement age as well as their occupational status.

Contact with friends

A variety of surveys indicate that the elderly demonstrate extensive contact with friends. At least half of all elderly people are in contact with friends weekly. Females are more likely to see friends than males. Contact with friends does not decrease substantially with age. However the pattern of visiting does vary. The 'young' elderly are more likely to go and visit others, either family or friends, while the 'old' elderly are most likely to be the recipients of visits and visitors.

The elderly demonstrate a high degree of satisfaction with the amount of contact they have with friends. Almost 90% express satisfaction with the amount of contact they have with friends. Even in the very oldest age group, those aged 85 and over, three quarters state that they see enough of their friends. Those who would like to see more of their friends usually report that distance or health problems (either their own or the friend's) are the reasons that prohibit more social contact.

Neighbours also form part of the social network. The vast majority of older people report that they talk to their neighbours, although this percentage does decrease with age (Table 10.7). There is no difference in social contact with neighbours between the sexes nor between social classes. Up to the age of 80 a significant percentage of older people, approximately 20%, are engaged in various forms of voluntary work.

Table 10.7 Great Britain: contact with friends/relatives – visit to or from in previous 4 weeks (%) 1988 (Askham *et al.*, 1992, Table 7.1)

	60–64	*65–69*	*70–74*	*75–79*	*80+*
Yes	93	94	92	93	91

Visits to clubs

Another source of social contact and interaction is membership and participation in the events of various social groups and organizations. Included within this category are activities as diverse as church attendance or visiting the local public house. Two-thirds of the over-70s had participated in some form of social activity in the week before interview (Table 10.8). Even at the age of 85 years and over, 40% of people are still active in some form of social organization.

There is a marked difference between the sexes in the types of social clubs visited. Women are more likely than males to report attendance at church. In contrast males are more likely to frequent public houses. However at all ages, the church remains the type of organized social activity most frequently engaged in by older people. It will be interesting to see whether this remains a feature of ageing amongst future generations or whether this a cohort effect restricted to the generation of people who are now old. Certainly the lack of contact between older women and public

Table 10.8 Attendance by the elderly at clubs (%) (Research Team for the Care of the Elderly)

	70		*75*		*80*		*85*	
	M	*F*	*M*	*F*	*M*	*F*	*M*	*F*
Day centre	3	10	3	17	2	12	6	11
Bingo	15	15	14	12	9	10	0	5
WI		8		5		2		2
Church club	4	8	5	5	0	9	0	5
Masons	3	0	7	1	4	0	0	0
Sports	5	1	5	1	3	0	0	0
Church	25	33	25	35	15	33	19	29
Pub	27	9	21	3	27	2	16	1

houses probably reflects a cohort effect, especially as the data cited below derive from Wales where attitudes about women visiting public houses were very conservative.

Leisure activities

As well as visiting friends/relatives the elderly engage in a wide variety of leisure activities. Watching television and listening to the radio are popular leisure activities for men and women at all ages (Table 10.9).

Table 10.9 Great Britain: leisure activities of the elderly (%) 1988 (Askham *et al.*, 1992, Table 7.1)

	65–69	*70–74*	*75–79*	*80+*
Watch TV	98	98	97	96
Listen to radio	83	80	75	69
Listen to records	60	40	34	20
Read books	63	58	57	49
Gardening	56	49	47	25
DIY	38	24	18	7
Voluntary work	22	17	15	7

The fraction engaging in these types of activity shows little variation with age. Listening to records is popular with the young elderly but not with those in the older age groups. Gardening and DIY are activities popular mainly with younger males. Females are more likely to indulge in reading books than males. However the fraction of older people indulging in these forms of pursuit decrease with age.

TOTAL SOCIAL CONTACT

The perceived social isolation of older people has been a key component of many research studies of later life. This concern is indicated by the way that numerous studies of the elderly have attempted to summarize the levels of social contact amongst older people (Townsend, 1964). This is usually achieved by summing the number of contacts the elderly person had in a defined period with household members, family, friends and 'official' visitors, and attendance at social clubs and other gatherings. There are, however, two major problems inherent in this type of mathematical exercise. First, it is often difficult to differentiate between a pre-arranged social contact and the casual exchange of greeting between neighbours or acquaintances in the street. Second, the scoring systems used are often highly arbitrary. There are no good empirical data upon which to give a higher priority to contacts with family members as opposed to friends.

Bearing in mind these limitations this kind of exercise reveals that very few of the elderly, 2% or less, are totally devoid of social contacts. However the distribution of social contact scores tends to reflect the marital status, age and sex of the elderly. Men and the younger married elderly have the greatest numbers of social contacts, women, the single and older elderly the least. This relationship holds even when contacts within the household are eliminated.

Social isolation

The changed roles experienced with ageing, from employed to retired and from provider to dependent, it is argued, render the elderly particularly prone to the experience of social isolation. However social isolation is a rather nebulous concept consisting of both an objective and subjective component. Objective measures of social isolation relate to the extent of social contacts as described above. On a more subjective level social isolation relates to perceptions of isolation and loneliness and concerns the response of older people to the quality and quantity of their social contacts. As we saw above the groups most vulnerable to social isolation in its empirical sense are those who live alone, the never married, women and the very elderly.

The subjective component of social isolation is loneliness. Loneliness amongst the elderly has been an aspect of ageing that has received a great deal of attention and has contributed greatly to the negative stereotype of old age. Because this is a highly subjective state of mind it is a difficult dimension to research empirically. However a variety of studies have used a question which asks the elderly to rate how often they feel lonely and, generally speaking, the subjects involved in these investigations have seemed to understand the concepts underlying the question.

Application of this question to a study of the elderly in south Wales indicated that almost 90% of males and 75% of females aged 70+ reported that they never felt lonely. At the opposite end of the spectrum a variety of recent surveys have suggested that about 5% of the elderly perceive themselves as being lonely all, or most of, the time (Shanas *et al.*, 1968; Wenger, 1984). These findings are comparable with those produced by Sheldon (1948) in his study of Wolverhampton. The similarity of these results suggests that the prevalence of loneliness amongst the elderly has remained stable and not increased as is often suggested. However because researchers have largely perceived loneliness as a problem of old age this type of questions has rarely been asked of younger populations. Thus it is difficult to establish if the elderly feel more (or less) lonely than the rest of the population.

Within the elderly population the fraction reporting that they sometimes felt lonely increased with age (Table 10.10). However the proportion reporting that they always felt lonely showed no such trend. At all ages females were more likely to report that they sometimes felt lonely than males. However there was no consistent gender difference in the fraction stating that they always felt lonely.

Table 10.10 Perceived loneliness by age and sex (%) (Research Team for the Care of the Elderly, unpublished data)

	70–74		75–79		80–84		85+	
	M	F	M	F	M	F	M	F
Never lonely	89	79	90	76	80	70	79	69
Sometimes lonely	10	16	8	20	13	25	18	27
Always lonely	1	5	2	4	6	3	3	4

Isolation and loneliness

Social isolation and feelings of loneliness do not vary consistently with each other. Those who are most socially isolated do not, necessarily, express the highest rates of perceived loneliness. Thus Table 10.11 illustrates that a little over half of those who reported that they were always alone stated that they never felt lonely.

Conversely 10% of this group stated that they felt lonely sometimes or often. Similarly this table shows that the majority of those with very low

Table 10.11 The relationship between social isolation and loneliness (%) (Research Team for the Care of the Elderly)

	Never lonely	*Seldom lonely*	*Often lonely*	*Always lonely*
Always alone	57	33	5	5
Less than daily contact	74	19	4	2

rates of social contact, less than daily, express feelings of loneliness. These relationships hold for each of the major sub-groups into which the elderly population is usually disaggregated.

CONCLUSION

In this chapter we have demonstrated that the popular myths of the 'golden age' of elderly people when they lived in large family groups loved and venerated by all is an inaccurate and simplistic view of the past. Although most elderly live in households confined to members of their generation this seems to be an expression of their desire for independent living rather than a demonstration of neglect by their family. Those who extol the importance of co-residence are ignoring the wishes of older people and are denying them the pride which many elderly feel in maintaining and independent and autonomous existence.

The majority of older people are enmeshed in a complicated family network consisting of family, friends and neighbours. We have seen that where they are part of a kin network the elderly demonstrate high rates of social contact which seem to bring a large amount of satisfaction to them. However it is important to note that some elderly, either because they never married or have no children, have far fewer kin within their networks. This may have profound effect upon the ageing experience because it may limit their sources of support. Lack of an extensive kin network may also restrict the opportunities for the older person to make a positive contribution.

The family is not a static entity. Rather it is a social institution which is subject to almost continuous change. In the future the increased rates of divorce within society will inevitably affect the experience of ageing. For example divorce may severely restrict the extent to which older people may retain access to their grandchildren. Whilst the access rights of parents to children in the event of divorce are debated the problems of grandparents are ignored.

The family are an important source of care for the elderly. There are few data available that support the view that the family neglects the care of the old when services are provided by the state. However it is important to remember that the elderly also contribute to the life of the family by undertaking such activities as babysitting. Thus the flow of help and assistance is not just one-way.

Grandparenthood was identified as one role which is open to very many elderly. Over this century there has been a re-definition of the 'social age' at which grandparenthood arrives. At one time grandparenthood was seen as marking old age. Now it as seen as being part of middle age. Several factors influence the experience of grandparenthood. Firstly it is obvious, but not often stated, that the grandparent–grandchild relationship is influenced by the middle generation; the parent. Thus the norm is for grandparents to be passive and not interfere with the way that the parent raises the child and the rights of grandparents are seen as secondary to those of the parents. Whilst this often results in grandparents perceiving the role as comfortable it does raise problems and tensions between generations when issues of discipline are concerned. Gender also affects the experience of grandparenthood, with women pursuing the role more actively than men. This is perceived by many grandparents as being both right and natural, reflecting implicit gender assumptions about the caring roles of the sexes.

The availability of children to 'care' for the elderly is dependent upon family size. With the decrease in family size which has taken place over the last century there are going to be fewer potential carers available to future generations of elderly. The Family Studies Policy Centre (1984) calculated that in 1901 there were 2.77 women aged 50–59 for every elderly person aged 75 or over. By 1986 they estimated the same ratio at 0.86 to 1. This demographic trend has very profound implications for the current policy of caring for the elderly in the community. However it is a trend which has been given very much less publicity than the ones relating to the increase in the numbers of the very old.

We have demonstrated that few elderly live the socially isolated lives that popular stereotypes depict as the lot of the elderly. Whilst there are some elderly for whom this is an accurate portrait, for many older people later life is a time of considerable activity with clubs and church groups playing an important role in their social life in addition to contact with a wide network of family and friends. These social contacts are an important means by which the older person can retain autonomy and independence of action. They provide mechanisms by which the elderly can both give and receive help.

This interdependence between generations provides a way of integrating the elderly within society rather than casting them in the role of outside observers. Although these data are based upon cross-sectional rather than longitudinal data it would seem that the disengagement perspective is an inaccurate depiction of later life. In addition this theory may well have done much to generate the negative stereotypes of the family and social relationships in later life which we have sought to refute in this chapter.

11

Health and illness

The discussion of health and illness is basic to any consideration of the experience of ageing. In this chapter we examine the objective and subjective aspects of physical health and disability. The chapter concludes with a discussion of the psychological dimensions of ageing.

HEALTH

Health, although it is a factor of importance to both the individual and society as a whole, is a difficult entity to define. MacIntyre (1986) notes that there are no universally valid, comprehensive and agreed definitions of either the terms 'health' or 'illness'. Sociologists usually distinguish between 'disease' and 'illness' (Field, 1976). Disease usually describes the medical concept of a defect or abnormality in function or structure of any part, process, or system of the body. Thus, we have a situation where it is possible to imagine the doctor, using only signs based upon objective physiological indices, deciding whether disease is present or absent, irrespective of the state of perceived well-being of the patient (Dingwall, 1976). There are a number of problems with this theoretically 'objective' definition of disease. First, as we saw earlier in the section on the biology of ageing, there are few universally valid norms of physical functioning because of the enormous range of variability amongst individuals. Second, the 'objective' physiological measures may not correlate with subjective perceptions of health status, nor with features such as pain or debility. The correlation between physiological measurements and causes of death may also be poor. Third, using this type of objective approach, disease may be so prevalent that almost the entire group under study would have to be classified as 'diseased'.

Illness is a more subjectively defined state in that it usually refers to the feelings of the individual. The focus in research looking at illness is to identify perceived health status and the prevalence of features such as pain or disability. We may distinguish between disease, where the focus is upon objectively defined states, and illness, where the focus of attention is upon more diffuse and subjective manifestations of disease. The correlation between disease and illness is not perfect. Individuals may be diseased without feeling ill and *vice versa*.

Health is a more complex entity to define than either disease or illness. It is insufficient to think of health as simply being the absence of disease or illness. Culyer (1981) distinguishes between four main approaches to the definition of health: health as the absence of disease (a medical model approach); health as the absence of illness (a sociological perspective); health as an ideal state (the World Health Organization model); and health as a pragmatically defined entity. Health is a very broad concept that involves physical, social and psychological well-being.

The dimensions which constitute health and illness are subject to considerable social definition and negotiation. Consequently, the definition of health varies both historically and culturally. For example, epilepsy is now regarded as an illness. In ancient Arabic societies the epileptic was glorified and attributed extensive status; they were not, however, considered as ill. Another example is provided by homosexuality. Up until 1974 the American Psychiatric Association defined homosexuality as a mental illness.

Illness effects both society and the individual in a variety of ways. For society, ill health exacts a high cost in economic terms through both lost economic production and the provision of health care services. Illness also has consequences for the individual. Those who are ill are not required to perform their normal social roles but adopt what was termed by Talcott Parsons (1951) the 'sick role'. One of the distinguishing characteristics of this role is the adoption of a dependent rather than an independent status. This transition may be very distressing for the individual concerned given the heavy emphasis placed in our society upon remaining independent and autonomous. The sick role is not expected to be of long duration. The long-term sick, or those with particular illnesses such as epilepsy or various mental disorders, can come to acquire a highly stigmatized status because of the extensive duration of their illness.

Several sociologists have attempted to understand lay definitions of health and illness. A study conducted in Paris on a small sample of middle-aged and middle-class subjects reported that there was no single concept of health employed by the sample (Herzlich, 1973). Rather the group employed three concepts of health. First, there was health as the absence of disease. Second, there was a notion of health as a reserve of strength with which to resist the diseases. This was envisaged as a characteristic of an individual. Third, there was a definition of health as an equilibrium or balance in the lives of individuals.

Williams (1983, 1990) reports very similar ideas expressed by a sample of elderly living in Aberdeen. Firstly, he found that his subjects defined health as the absence of disease. Secondly, there was the rather more positive perception of health as strength or resistance. This idea is illustrated by comments such as people who are healthy being able to overcome disease. Third, health involved ideas of functional fitness such as being able to undertake 'normal' or conventional activities such as gardening or keeping house.

Health, in all its various manifestations, is of great importance to the elderly. Opinion polls of older people show that health (and the cost of health care in countries such as the United States) is a major concern. As an example of this concern we have already seen in an earlier chapter the importance of health status in defining age identity and effecting changes in perceived age status. Perceived health is of importance in the negotiation of a successful ageing.

THE HEALTH STATUS OF THE ELDERLY

Health is a wide-ranging notion encompassing more than the mere absence of disease. When we attempt to record the health status of populations, or of particular groups within defined populations, we are usually forced to use a disease-orientated definition of health. From this perspective health is perceived as the absence of disease rather than anything more positive. The use of this approach towards the definition of health reflects the difficulties involved in developing empirical measures of health status.

MORTALITY

Ideally we need to develop measures of health status that allow comparisons between individuals, groups, or different points in time. The index which comes closest to fulfilling these requirements is mortality.

Mortality is the probably the oldest and most widely used index of health status. As early as the 16th century, mortality statistics relating to epidemics of the plague were published in London. Mortality is widely employed as a health indicator by social researchers for a variety of reasons. The data are easily available in countries such as Britain which have compulsory and national systems of death registration. From these certificates it is possible to examine death rates within the different subgroups of the population. However when analysing mortality data for the elderly, we must be aware of the limitations imposed upon this type of analysis by inaccuracy in the certification of the cause of death amongst the older age groups.

The majority of deaths which occur annually in England and Wales, 78%, are of people over 65 years of age. The death rate increases sharply with age, as Table 11.1 shows. At all ages over 65 years, female death rates are substantially lower than those for males.

Table 11.1 England and Wales: deaths and death rates 1990 (Office of Population Censuses and Surveys, 1991, Table B)

	Deaths		Rate per 1000	
	M	F	M	F
under 1	3207	2357	9.1*	7.0*
1–4	593	434	0.4	0.3
5–14	671	450	0.2	0.2
15–24	3184	1088	0.8	0.3
25–34	3714	1702	0.9	0.4
35–44	6060	3875	1.7	1.1
45–54	13 342	8337	4.6	2.9
55–64	36 405	22 511	14.4	8.6
65–74	77 604	53 770	38.7	21.9
75–84	5539	102 440	93.3	58.1
85+	37 017	90 546	185.4	154.9
Total	277 336	287 510	11.2	11.1

* Rates per 1000 for under-ones expressed per 1000 live births

In Britain deaths are not equally distributed throughout the calendar year. McDowell (1981) reports that, for all age groups, there is a marked seasonality in the death rate with a considerable excess of deaths during the winter months. Table 11.2 shows that this seasonal excess of deaths is most marked amongst the elderly population. This marked seasonal variation in death rate is not a feature of other countries of western Europe, many of which experience considerably more severe winters than Britain.

Table 11.2 Great Britain: standardized seasonal mortality ratio – summer death rate = 100 (McDowell, 1981, Table 2)

Age	Male	Female
0	109	109
1–4	109	100
5–14	92	100
15–24	98	107
25–34	106	109
35–44	108	110
45–54	109	108
55–64	117	117
65–74	119	117
85+	122	119

Within Britain mortality is strongly associated with social class. This relationship has been well documented for the population of working age. Indeed publication of the latest data suggests that the differentials in mortality rates between the social classes are increasing rather than decreasing and the welfare state seems to have done little to bring about a decrease in them. This analysis has rarely been extended to the elderly population as it has been felt that the increased mortality of later life would overwhelm any social class differentials.

Table 11.3 demonstrates that, for males over the age of 65, there is a strong class-based gradient in mortality which mirrors that characteristic of younger age groups.

Table 11.3 England and Wales: standardized mortality of males by social class (Fox *et al.*, 1985, Table 2)

Age	15–64	65–74	75+
Class 1	66	68	73
Class 2	77	81	84
Class 3n	105	86	92
Class 3m	96	100	105
Class 4	109	106	108
Class 5	124	109	116

Consistently the elderly who were employed in professional occupations demonstrate a lower mortality than their counterparts who were engaged in manual occupations. Victor (1984) suggests that these differentials are preserved into the very oldest age groups. Even in retirement it seems that there are strong class-based inequalities in mortality for males. The data presented in this table do not indicate that these class-based differences in mortality decrease in potency with the onset of retirement and later life.

The position is less clear-cut for females, largely because of the inadequacy of the social class classification of older women. However it seems likely that there is a class-based mortality gradient amongst older women, although it may not be as strong as that for males (Victor, 1991)

MORBIDITY

Mortality is a useful index for comparing health status between groups or areas. However, its applicability as a measure of health is obviously limited in that it tells us nothing about the status of those who have not died. The use of mortality as an indicator of health status is predicated upon the assumption that it is a surrogate measure of morbidity. This means that it is assumed that causes of morbidity and mortality in the population are synonymous. This is a highly questionable assumption for studies of older age groups who experience much morbidity in terms of disabling illnesses such as arthritis and rheumatism which result in very few deaths.

To overcome these limitations various measures of morbidity have been defined. Four main approaches to the development of morbidity indicators have been described by Hunt and McEwan (1980). First, there has been the development of indices which attempt to determine the incidence and prevalence of various conditions via data such as absence from work. Second, there has been the widescale development of indicators of disability. Third, there are indices which describe clinical states, the ability to function in particular roles or the effect of illness or disability upon the individual. These indices are usually based upon the perceptions of a professional observer. Fourth, there has been the development of indicators which record consumer satisfaction with health care.

Of these approaches some of the most commonly used measures relate to the incidence of limiting illness amongst the population. These indicators usually differentiate between acute health problems and those of a more long-standing or chronic nature.

Acute health problems

Acute health problems are usually defined as self limiting conditions of short duration, usually 3 months or less. Included under this heading are such conditions as colds, influenza or accidental injuries. Usually, acute illnesses are characterized by symptoms or causes for which medical techniques or other forms of intervention may effect a cure.

Each year the General Household Survey asks its respondents about acute health problems that have restricted their normal level of activity in the 14 days before interview. Using these data, Table 11.4 reveals that there is an increase in the percentage of subjects reporting an acute illness with age.

Table 11.4 Great Britain: acute illness by age and sex 1990 (%)
(Office of Population Censuses and Surveys, 1992, Table 5.1)

Age	Male	Female
16–44	11	13
45–64	14	17
65–74	14	16
75+	15	22

In the 16–44 age range 10% of males reported suffering from an acute illness episode compared with 17% of those aged over 75. At all ages females consistently report a higher level of acute illness than males. However it is important to keep these data in context. Even in the very oldest age groups, acute illness only affects 20% of males and 25% of females, the rest remaining free of such health problems.

Chronic health problems

Chronic health problems are, by definition, long-term and not usually characterized by a cure. Medical intervention may (or may not) alleviate some, or all, of the associated symptoms. Examples of such long-term health problems are multiple sclerosis and arthritis. It is this type of health problem that is specifically identified by both the general public and many professional health workers alike as an integral, inevitable and universal feature of old age.

Again using data from the General Household Survey, we can compare levels of chronic ill-health within the population. The proportion of the population reporting that they have a long-standing illness or disability increases sharply with age (Table 11.7). A quarter of males and females in the 16–44 age group report that they have a long-standing illness compared with at least 60% of the over-75 age group. Only for the older age groups is there any difference in the reported prevalence of long-standing illness between the sexes.

Table 11.5 Great Britain: the prevalence of chronic health problems (%) 1990 (Office of Population Censuses and Surveys, 1992, Table 5.1)

Age	Long-standing illness		Long-standing limiting illness or disability	
	M	F	M	F
0–4	14	12	5	3
5–15	20	17	9	7
16–44	25	25	13	14
45–64	46	47	29	30
65–74	58	61	38	42
75+	66	70	47	53

The existence of long-standing illness or disability may not, however, impair the activity levels or lifestyle of the sufferer. Table 11.5 describes the percentage of the population reporting a long-standing limiting illness which they describe as restricting levels of normal activity in some way.

This demonstrates that the popular stereotype of old age as a time of universal and inevitable chronic health and impaired activity is far from correct. Whilst the prevalence of a long-standing limiting illness increases with age it is not a universal characteristic of latter life. Almost half the men and women aged 75 and over do not have a long-standing disability or illness that impairs their activity levels. Amongst the elderly limiting long standing disability rates are higher for females than males.

The percentage of older people reporting that they experience a long-standing limiting disability varies with social class from 37% of those from a professional occupation background to 47% from the semi-skilled and unskilled occupation groups (Victor and Evandrou, 1986; Victor, 1991)

Not only does the proportion reporting a chronic health problem increase with age but so does the number of such problems experienced. Ford (1985), using data from the longitudinal Aberdeen 'Lifestyles of Ageing' project, shows that there is a progressive increase in the number of chronic conditions an individual experiences with age from 1.6 for men aged 59–64 to 2.5 for those aged 85+. In addition there is a constant, if unspectacular, gender difference with females having an average of 0.5 more chronic conditions in all age groups.

Functional capacity

Another way of looking at chronic health problems has been via the collection of data about the ability of the elderly to undertake a variety of activities and tasks considered essential to an independent life in the community. These research instruments are loosely grouped together as measures of functional capacity. A large number of these measures have been devised. Much epidemiological study of the elderly has been almost solely concerned with the construction and validation of these measures. This interest in the functional capacity levels of older people stems, in part, from a desire to allocate services to those most 'in need'. The indices are not usually defined to demonstrate the independence of the elderly. Rather they concentrate upon measuring dependence and the 'need' of the elderly for services.

Typical of these measures of functional capacity is that described by Townsend (1979). This has been used in a large number of community studies of the elderly population (Bond and Carstairs, 1982; Vetter, Jones and Victor, 1984b). The nine items included in his list of activities cover all the different types of physical function the elderly might be expected to undertake when living at home such as bending, lifting, carrying and reaching. This is essentially a dictionary approach in which the ability of the older person to undertake a series of tasks is recorded upon a check-list.

Collecting data about such activities of daily living (often referred to in the literature as 'ADL') does pose some difficulties for the researcher. Asking the older person to perform tasks such as making a cup of tea in a test setting in a hospital may produce artificially high or low results. Collecting the data in a interview situation presents problems of sex bias. Survey work undertaken by the author and others in Wales encountered problems in getting older males to respond to questions about their ability to perform tasks such as ironing or cooking. Although many of the males interviewed were healthy and active, they almost universally reported that they could not possibly do the ironing for that was seen as the job of their wives.

Given these limitations, table 11.6 describes the ability of a sample of the over 70s in Wales to perform the nine activities included in the Townsend index.

Table 11.6 Ability of the elderly (70+) to undertake self-care and housecare tasks (%) (Research Team for the Care of the Elderly)

Activity	No difficulty	Some difficulty	Unable to do alone
Washing all over	87	7	6
Cutting toenails	64	17	19
Catching a bus	77	8	15
Going up and down stairs	77	16	8
Heavy housework	68	16	17
Going shopping	62	14	24
Cooking a meal	87	5	8
Reaching a shelf	73	12	15
Tying a knot	94	4	2

The majority of older people can undertake these activities without difficulty; only a minority are unable to undertake them without the assistance of another person. Thus we find that for the task which presented the most difficulty to this sample of elderly, going shopping, only a quarter were unable to undertake this alone and 60% were totally independent. Yet only 25% unable to undertake a task alone may mean more than 1 000 000 people needing support. The low percentages of elderly unable to perform these tasks has implications for the design of services to assist the continued independence of older people. Services which concentrate upon cooking and cleaning are clearly irrelevant to the needs of many older people.

When classifying the functional capacity levels of the population describing each of the nine tasks separately is rather time-consuming. Thus responses to the nine items are summed following a standard scoring procedure to produce an overall index of disability. Tasks which are performed without difficulty receive a score of 0; tasks which can be done only with difficulty are given a score of 1 whilst tasks which cannot be undertaken alone are scored as 2, giving the index a range of 0–18. According to their total score, the elderly are then classified into the following typology; not disabled (score of 0); mildly disabled (score of 1–7), moderately disabled (score of 7–11) and severely disabled (scores of 12 and over).

Applying this methodology to the elderly sub-sample included in the 1985 General Household Survey shows that the percentage classed as not disabled decreases with age (Table 11.7). At all ages females demonstrate a higher level of disability than males. Even for those aged 85+ and over, 14% of males and 11% of females are still classed as not experiencing any functional disability, whilst 24% and 45% respectively in this age group are classed as severely disabled.

Table 11.7 Great Britain: disability classification of the elderly (%) 1985 – excludes residents of institutions (Falkingham and Johnson, 1992, Table 3.7)

	65–69		70–74		75–79		80–84		85+	
	M	F	M	F	M	F	M	F	M	F
None	72	63	63	49	54	35	37	24	14	11
Mild	17	23	24	29	26	32	20	26	34	19
Moderate	6	9	8	14	10	17	22	25	29	27
Severe	5	6	4	7	11	15	11	24	24	45

We must be wary of assuming that an age-related increase in disability implies that older people cannot manage to care for themselves adequately in their own homes. Despite often severe limitations of activity, most older people develop coping strategies and modify their lifestyle to take these restrictions into account. This adaptation strategy is not unique to the elderly but rather applies generally to all those who experience long-term health problems.

As with acute illness and long-standing limiting disability, functional capacity demonstrates a relationship with the social class of the older person. Table 11.8 shows that the elderly from professional and managerial occupations are less likely to be classified as disabled than their counterparts from manual occupations. The fraction defined as severely disabled does not seem to vary with social class; rather it is the lesser categories of disability which seem to vary most markedly with the occupational status of the older person.

Table 11.8 Great Britain: disability by social class (%) 1980 (Victor and Evandrou, 1986, Table 6)

Disability	Social class			
	1 and 2	*3n*	*3m*	*4 and 5*
None	60	51	52	45
Mild	22	28	24	27
Moderate	13	14	17	20
Severe	5	7	7	8

If we examine the ways in which disability effects the lives of the elderly we see that the main effects are felt in the general area of mobility (Table 11.9). The distance and length of time that older people can walk, and difficulties with bending and stooping, seem to be the main implications of disability in later life.

Table 11.9 England and Wales: the effects of disability – percentage of elderly with difficulty undertaking activities (%) (Hunt, 1978, Table 10.6.1)

Activity	65–69		75–84		85+	
	M	*F*	*M*	*F*	*M*	*F*
Walking	17	14	26	17	39	24
Bending	7	10	10	13	13	14
Mobility	6	9	10	8	13	16
Housecare	1	8	2	11	4	8
Stairs	2	5	3	7	2	6
Lifting	4	4	5	3	2	2
Gardening	3	2	5	1	6	1
Self-care	1	2	2	2	0	2

There are also some interesting gender differences in the implications of disability illustrated in Table 11.9. Consistently, females are more likely to report difficulties with housecare than males. For gardening the opposite pattern is true. It seems unlikely that this is a difference brought about by disability itself. Rather it is a reflection of the social definition of gender roles and the tasks considered appropriate to those roles.

Multiple pathology

In addition to the increased prevalence of medical disorders in later life, the number of medical problems experienced by an individual increases.

Health and illness

One of the characteristics which the medical profession sees as distinguishing old age is multiple pathology.

Table 11.10 describes the percentage of elderly reporting that they have disabling conditions.

Table 11.10 Prevalence of disabling conditions (%) (Bond and Carstairs, 1982, Table 24)

No of conditions	65–69	70–74	75–79	80–84	85+
0	65	61	57	47	39
1	20	24	21	20	21
2	9	7	8	15	18
3+	6	8	14	17	23

The fraction reporting the presence of multiple problems does increase with age but again not to the extent which popular stereotypes would have us believe. For those aged over 85 years, a quarter have three or more disabling conditions. This should, however, be balanced against the 39% who do not experience any such conditions. The popular image of old age held by the medical profession that all elderly patients are typified by a whole plethora of medical problems and disabling conditions is again inaccurate.

Time trends in health levels

Old age is strongly associated with ill health by both professionals and members of the public alike. The data presented above indicate that whilst old age is not universally a time of poor health the reported incidence of ill health does increase with age. However it could be this is a cohort rather than ageing effect. Given the harsh circumstances that today's elderly experienced during their formative years, the levels of ill health we have observed may be a reflection of this. Future generations, which have experienced less privation and better health care, might demonstrate improved health status in later life.

It is not possible to test this particular hypothesis using cross-sectional data. In order to thoroughly investigate it we require extensive longitudinal data, which are not yet available. One method of considering this is to examine trends over time. Table 11.11 presents data from the General Household Survey from 1972–90. Interpreting this table is made yet more difficult by variations in the wording of the questions used to collect acute and chronic health status information. However it seems that there is some deterioration in health status in those aged over 75 now compared with their contemporaries 20 years earlier.

Table 11.11 Great Britain: health status of the elderly 1972–90 (%) (Office of Population Censuses and Surveys, 1992, Table 5.1)

Year	Long standing limiting illness				Acute illness			
	65–74		75+		65–74		75+	
	M	F	M	F	M	F	M	F
1972					10	10	10	14
1974	33	38	39	49	10	13	11	14
1976	38	40	48	53	9	11	10	11
1979	37	38	45	54	12	16	17	22
1980	39	42	45	54	14	17	17	21
1981	35	41	44	56	11	17	15	21
1982	41	39	43	54	14	15	16	19
1983	40	45	53	54	12	19	17	20
1985	38	38	43	51	12	19	17	20
1987	43	45	56	58	13	20	17	23
1989	37	36	44	53	13	19	17	26
1990	38	42	47	53	14	16	15	22

SUBJECTIVE HEALTH STATUS

Another approach towards the measurement of health status is to record the perception the individual has of her/his health. Many health status surveys of the population ask respondents to evaluate their health as good, fair or poor in the last year (or a specified period before the interview).

The percentage of older people of either sex who rate their health as not good increases with age (Table 11.12).

Table 11.12 Great Britain: reported health by age and sex 1988 (%) – health rated as good, fairly good or not good in previous year (Askham *et al.*, 1992, Table 6.1)

	60–64		65–69		70–74		75–79		80+	
	M	F	M	F	M	F	M	F	M	F
Good	45	48	46	42	39	37	38	31	33	28
Fairly good	32	36	36	38	41	40	36	40	39	38
Not good	23	15	18	20	21	24	27	30	27	33

Given the increased prevalence of chronic illness with age this is not surprising. Perhaps more surprising is that so few elderly rate their health as not good in the face of the high incidence of chronic illness and impair-

ments that afflict them. This anomaly probably reflects the highly subjective way we define and evaluate our own health status. For most people
health does not mean the complete absence of symptoms or morbid conditions but rather that these do not significantly restrict social interaction
or normal activity levels. Additionally, health is relative to the expectations of the individual. Blaxter and Paterson (1982) reported that working-class middle-aged women in Aberdeen regarded their health as good
when to the investigators these individuals displayed histories of chronic
disease.

As with the other dimensions of health status looked at earlier in this
chapter, perceived health shows a relationship with social class. Table
11.13 demonstrates that elderly from the professional and managerial
groups are more likely to rate their health as good than their counterparts
from manual occupations.

Table 11.13 Great Britain: subjective health rating by social class (%) (Victor and
Evandrou, 1986, Table 6)

Health rating	Social class			
	1 and 2	3n	3m	4 and 5
Good	49	43	34	31
Fair	35	37	42	42
Poor	16	20	25	28

The opposite pattern is evident for the fraction of older people rating
their health as poor. Almost a half of the elderly in the professional occupation groups rate their health as good compared with 30% of those elderly from the unskilled and semi-skilled occupation groups. This could
either reflect a 'real' difference in health status between the social classes
or a difference in social expectations.

INCONTINENCE

Incontinence is an aspect of health in later life which has received much
less attention than, for example, functional capacity or mental status for it
still remains rather a taboo subject. The causes of incontinence may be
both social or physical (or a combination of both). Whatever the causes
the results can be profound for the older person, causing strain amongst
carers, preventing admission to sheltered housing or residential accommodation and restricting the social activities of the sufferer.

Establishing the prevalence of incontinence amongst the elderly (or any
other part of the population) presents difficulties for the researcher. First,

we must define what constitutes incontinence and the degree of severity of the affliction. Thus, there has been considerable variation between surveys in both the definitions used and the questions used to solicit the information from respondents. Second, in interviews sufferers may be reluctant to admit to this problem because of its extreme negative connotations. There is some evidence that in interview surveys sufferers may be more reluctant to admit to their affliction than if the data are collected by other means such as a self-completion postal questionnaire (Victor, 1984). Consequently the data gathered in interview surveys may substantially under-estimate the true prevalence of incontinence within the population.

Table 11.14 presents estimates of the fraction of the elderly enumerated as incontinent of urine in a variety of community surveys. The differences between the figures presented in this table reflect the variations in question format used in these studies. Whilst there are substantial variations in prevalence between studies the data are consistent in indicating that this is a problem which is more common amongst females than males.

Table 11.14 Prevalence of urinary incontinence amongst the elderly (%)

Survey	Male	Female	Age
Vetter, 1981	7	18	70+
Sheldon, 1948	7	13	70+
Brocklehurst	17	25	65+
Milne, 1985	25	42	65+

Data from a community study of the over 70s resident in a rural and an urban area of Wales indicate that the prevalence of incontinence increases sharply with age (Table 11.15). At all ages women are more likely to experience incontinence than men. Incontinence is a substantial problem amongst the very oldest age groups. Almost a quarter of females aged over 85 report that they experience some degree of incontinence.

Table 11.15 Prevalence of incontinence by age and sex per 1000 population (Vetter *et al.*, (1981), table 1)

	70		75		80		85+	
Incontinent	M	F	M	F	M	F	M	F
Daily	17	40	18	75	50	94	63	138
< Daily	42	84	60	110	50	161	31	128

Incontinence has several consequences for the sufferer in addition to its status as a medical condition. Vetter, Jones and Victor (1981) have shown that the incontinent are often highly disabled and exhibit higher levels of anxiety and depression than non-incontinent elderly. In addition the incontinent exhibit lower levels of social contact and higher levels of loneliness.

HYPOTHERMIA

One of the characteristic physiological manifestations of ageing is a decreased ability to maintain a constant temperature. A young person can adapt her/his 'core' or deep body temperature in ways which an elderly person cannot. For the older person even a small exposure to low temperatures may bring about a fall in core temperature. Accidental hypothermia is defined as a core temperature of 35°C or less. It is given the prefix accidental to distinguish it from reductions in core temperature resultant from some therapeutic intervention.

Hypothermia is an aspect of ageing which attracts considerable interest in the media. The discovery of an older person dead from hypothermia during a cold spell will usually generate a considerable public outcry as it is a highly emotive issue.

Establishing the true extent of hypothermia amongst the elderly population (or any other age group) is rather difficult because of the problems of measuring core body temperature. A survey sponsored by the Royal College of Physicians (1966) of admission to 10 hospitals throughout England and Scotland during the winter of 1965 reported that 126 patients were defined as suffering from hypothermia. This represented 0.68% of all patients admitted. The highest rate of hypothermia was 82 per 1000 for those aged under 1. For patients over the age of 65 the rate was 12 per 1000. Extrapolating this rate to all hospital admissions of the elderly suggested that 3500 patients were admitted to hospital with hypothermia.

A national survey sponsored by the Nuffield Foundation indicated that 0.5% of elderly had a urine temperature of below 35°C (Fox *et al.*, 1973). A further 10% had a temperature in the range 35–35.5°C. Thus hypothermia, whilst it should not be ignored, is not one of the major health problems experienced by the old. Indeed in many cases hypothermia is probably the result of some other mishap such as falling rather than being a cause of such accidents amongst the old.

PSYCHOLOGICAL HEALTH

Although there is some general agreement on the biological changes which accompany ageing, such as decreased lung capacity, there is little agreement about the psychological dimensions of ageing. As with physical status the popular image of psychological health in old age is one of gradual, but inevitable, decline. However, this rather negative stereotype is, as will be demonstrated below, not supported by the evidence. Many of the studies upon which this rather pessimistic conclusion was based were of a cross-sectional design. Consequently many of the inferences attributed to ageing were, in fact, reflections of the study design.

Intellectual function

The most researched aspects of the psychology of later life are those relating to intellectual function: intelligence, learning, memory and problem-solving.

Several studies have shown a decreased performance in intelligence tests and psychomotor tests with age. The status of these kinds of finding remain highly contentious. This is a highly complex area of social investigation in which the methodology of the experiment used has great influence upon the resultant outcome. The identification of age differences in intellectual function does not reflect, necessarily, the process of ageing as most of the data are based upon cross-sectional research designs. Cross-sectional studies which have shown decreased intellectual functioning with age may well just reflect differences in levels of education between cohorts. It could be that intelligence itself does not change with age but that the skills and information held by older people has become obsolete.

Similarly it may be that, although older people do not perform tasks which measure learning as well as younger subjects, their capacity to learn may be just as acute. In psychological tests older people seem to sacrifice speed for accuracy, perhaps reflecting their general feelings of inadequacy. Indeed it seems that once the time limits are removed from experiments age differences in performance are much less marked.

The quality of the samples used in research which has looked at changes in intellectual functioning with age require critical examination. Volunteer samples drawn from the wives of Oxford professors tell us little about the normal course of development of psychological functioning with age. We should also question very closely the relevance of findings from the laboratory and experiment environments to looking at psychological development in the 'real world'.

Current evidence indicates that ageing does not bring about inevitable and profound declines in mental ability. Older people can learn and improve their intellectual functioning given the right sort of educational programme and setting. In particular older people learn best in a non-threatening environment in which they can regain confidence in their own abilities. The increasing popularity of the University of the Third Age in a variety of countries testifies to the general high level of intellectual functioning and desire for education amongst many older people.

A major problem related to the learning ability of older people is the expectations of the rest of society. There is a general societal expectation that older people should be incompetent. Consequently many older people become anxious in learning situations and avoid any chance of failure by not answering questions (even when they know the answer). They will often proceed very slowly and cautiously so as to minimize the risk of failure because they have taken on board the negative expectation that society has of them. A change in this expectation would greatly enhance the learning ability of older people.

Whilst no clear pattern of intellectual performance in old age has yet been established it is clear that there are enormous differences between individuals. Even when some degree of intellectual decline is found the influence this has upon the ability of that person to exist in the community has not been explicitly established.

Psychological disorder

As with any other age group the elderly suffer from various forms of mental illness. Mental illnesses are usually divided into organic syndromes, those which have a physical cause and functional disorders. However it is often difficult to separate these two types of illnesses and perhaps they should be perceived as a continuum rather than two distinctive categories.

Organic disorders of the brain are often referred to as senile dementia. This group of disorders are chronic progressive degenerations of mental function due to vascular or other conditions. Presenting symptoms include loss of memory and cognition and behavioural disturbances. Current estimates suggest that between 6% and 10% of the elderly living at home have some degree of clinically identifiable organic disturbance (Milne, 1985). It is, however, much more difficult to establish the proportion of the elderly population with mild impairment because of the difficulty of designing research tools to identify the condition.

The percentage with an organic disorder increases with age, doubling approximately every 50 years (Jorm, Korton and Henderson, 1987). Again even in the very oldest age groups only a third of all elderly experience some degree of organic brain failure and then usually not to such an extent that it impairs their ability to function normally in the community (Table 11.16).

Table 11.16 Prevalence of organic disorders amongst the elderly (%) (Bond and Carstairs, 1982, Table xliv)

	65–69	70–74	75–79	80–84	85+
None	98	96	91	82	71
Mild	2	2	4	8	10
Severe	0	2	5	10	19

Organic states are often referred to as senility, a term which is both inaccurate and emotive and implies that progressive deterioration which accompanies the disorder is a normal part of ageing. It cannot be stressed too strongly that organic brain syndromes are not part of normal ageing but a specific disease process which, as yet, we cannot treat or reverse.

Functional or affective disorders comprise a variety of states such as anxiety, depression and disturbances of mood. Table 11.17 shows that approximately a quarter of the elderly population have some form of affective disorder.

Table 11.17 Prevalence of affective disorders amongst the elderly (%) (Bond and Carstairs, 1982, Table xliv)

	65–69	70–74	75–79	80–84	85+
None	77	79	76	77	71
Mild/severe	23	21	24	23	29

Whilst more women than men suffer from this condition there is only a marginal increase in reported prevalence with age. It seems that it is fairly rare for a clinical affective disorder to manifest itself for the first time in old age. The major of psychiatric disorders are usually found in older people who have had a history of this type of problem in earlier life.

One manifestation of psychological ill health is suicidal behaviour. Data upon the prevalence of parasuicide and its relationship with age are not available. However mortality reports regularly publish deaths from suicide. These statistics must be interpreted with some caution for not all suicides are so classified for a variety of reasons.

Data from England and Wales indicate that of successful suicides 27% of males and 32% of females were aged over 65 years. Table 11.18 shows that, at all ages, females have a lower suicide rate than males. The suicide rate shows some increase with age. However, how well this actually corresponds with age related trends in suicidal behaviour remains unknown.

Table 11.18 England and Wales: death rate from suicide by age 1990 – rate per million population (Office of Population Censuses and Surveys, 1990, Table 3)

Age	Male	Female
15–24	117	20
25–34	160	38
35–44	171	45
45–54	164	51
55–64	133	53
65–74	136	61
75–84	187	60
85+	235	67

ILLNESS BEHAVIOUR IN OLD AGE

Illness behaviour is a complex aspect of social interaction which involves the individual in monitoring their body, interpreting symptoms, taking curative action and seeking help from the health care system. Even in Britain which has a national health care service which provides help free of charge, the vast majority of ill-health is not presented for consideration by medical authorities. The decision to seek medical aid is only one illness behaviour strategy out of a whole range of possible options which includes self-care, folk remedies and consultation with friends or relatives. Research has shown that between a quarter and a third of all illness episodes result in a medical consultation (Ford, 1985).

Typically sociologists have concentrated upon considering the illness behaviour of younger members of the population. However recently Ford (1985) has attempted to review illness behaviour in later life and its variation from that characteristic of younger age groups.

One of the enduring stereotypes about old age is that treatable illnesses are mis-ascribed to the process of ageing and therefore appropriate treatment is not sought. In support of this view a variety of studies have demonstrated that there are a large number of previously unidentified medical conditions to be found amongst the elderly living at home. Tulloch and Moore (1979), in the Oxfordshire town of Bicester, found that, on average, the elderly had a least one medical condition previously unknown to the medical practitioner. However the study of ageing in Aberdeen has shed some light upon this stereotype. These data suggest that the elderly do not ignore symptoms and are equally as likely to seek treatment for these health problems as any other age group. Ford (1985) also argues that illness behaviour in later life does not differ significantly from that in earlier life. The elderly are every bit as diverse in their illness behaviour as other age groups. However the lack of specialist training amongst physicians and general practitioners may mean that inadequate diagnosis and treatment is given to older people with health problems who do consult the medical profession.

Consultations

One aspect of illness behaviour is to seek medical attention by consultation with a general practitioner. In Britain this service is free to all. So there are no financial barriers to prevent the elderly (or any other age group) from seeking a consultation as often as they like.

The percentage contacting a GP increases with age as does the average number of consultations made per year (Table 11.19).

Table 11.19 Great Britain: GP consultations in the previous 14 days before interview 1990 (%) (Office of Population Censuses Surveys, 1992, Table 5.2)

Age	M	F	Contacts per year	
			M	F
0–4	26	22	9	7
5–15	10	13	3	4
16–44	10	19	3	6
45–64	14	19	5	6
65–74	17	19	5	6
75+	24	22	7	7

Although females have a higher consultation rate than males there is some evidence that they under-consult for their level of morbidity. The General Household Survey data also show that the percentage seeing their doctor at the surgery decreases with age whilst the fraction receiving home visits increases (Table 11.20).

Table 11.20 Great Britain: location and outcome of GP consultation (% of those consulting GP in previous 14 days) (Askham *et al.*, 1992, Table 6.11)

	60–64	65–69	70–74	75–79	80+
Location					
At surgery	76	83	69	56	40
At home	17	11	24	38	56
Telephone	5	2	8	4	5
Other	2	4	0	3	0
Outcome					
Prescription	71	74	78	73	75
Referral	13	13	17	10	8
Other/discharged	16	13	5	17	17

Canadian researchers considered whether this increased use of health care services by the older age groups represented an increased demand by the elderly in general as a result of increased acute and chronic illness or whether a minority of elderly consume a disproportionate amount of care. Their data lead them to conclude that a minority of elderly account for a disproportionate level of service use. Eight per cent of their sample accounted for 35% of all visits to the doctor and 10% accounted for 78% of all hospitalization.

Medicine taking and old age

Another aspect of health behaviour is the use of medicines. Such potions may be prescribed or purchased over the counter. Under the British

National Health Service people over retirement age do not have to pay for items of medicine that are prescribed for them by a medical practitioner. In 1981 the elderly received 37% of all items of prescribed medicines in England and accounted for 39% of prescription costs. The average number of items prescribed to them was 13.1 per year compared with 4.9 for the non-elderly population (Anderson and Cartwright, 1985).

A sample of one prescription per 200 is taken by the Department of Health to analyse trends in prescribing. The major prescribed drugs taken by the elderly are those acting on the cardiovascular system and musculo-skeletal systems. Use of preparations acting on the nervous system such as sedatives and tranquillizers has decreased slightly. However Skegg, Doll and Perry (1977) show that prescribing for the elderly has continued to increase whilst that for other age groups has declined.

Including both prescribed and non-prescribed medicines a survey by Dunnell and Cartwright (1969) showed that 85% of all elderly were using drugs of some sort. Non-prescribed medicines were used more frequently than prescribed ones. These data are similar to those from America which suggested that 89% of all elderly were taking drugs.

Given the large number of elderly taking medicines of different types there is the problem of polypharmacy. Several General Practitioners have tried to establish the extent to which the elderly are characterized by polypharmacy. Law and Chalmers (1976) found that a third of their elderly patients were regularly taking three or more medicines daily. Particularly prevalent was polypharmacy associated with the use of psychotropic drugs. Cartwright and Anderson (1981) indicate that at least 20% taking regular medication were also using psychotropic drugs.

In Britain three-quarters of prescriptions issued to adults are repeat prescriptions and it seems that the fraction receiving repeat scripts increases with age. Tulloch (1981) reported that half of the scripts issued to the over-65s in an Oxford general practice were repeats. Such treatment regimes are usually long standing although it is well known that certain drugs are not effective in the long term.

Not surprisingly those elderly using medicines are usually in poorer health than non-users. Symptom frequency and self-assessed health status are important features that differentiate between elderly users and non-users of drugs. Older women are more likely to be taking drugs than males and to take more items (Dunnell and Cartwright, 1972). This excess was almost entirely explained by the more extensive use of self-medication by older women. The fraction of people using medicines increases with age as does the prevalence of polypharmacy and repeat prescriptions.

The extensive nature of drug use and particularly polypharmacy amongst the elderly raises many problems. Cartwright and Anderson (1981) show that a third of older people taking prescribed medicine did not feel they knew enough about their treatment. A survey by the author of the elderly after discharge from hospital indicated that large fractions of the elderly using drugs acting on the cardiovascular and nervous systems had no idea what health problem their medicines were supposed to treat. Older people are less likely to use their prescribed medicines as directed and are more likely to experience adverse side effects from drug combinations. A study by Martys (1982) reported that 36% of the over-65s had a drug-related sign or symptom. Similarly research has indicated that, of the elderly admitted to hospital, up to 20% demonstrate evidence of adverse drug reaction (Williamson, 1978).

For older people the major problems associated with drug use seem to be:

1. the multiple pathology of the elderly;
2. multiple use of prescribed and non-prescribed medicines;
3 increased sensitivity to drugs and side effects;
4. lack of training amongst medical staff in prescribing for the elderly;
5. inadequate drug packing and instructions;
6. inadequate supervision of patients;
7. multiple sources of prescriptions, e.g. hospital and pharmacies;
8. inadequate testing of new drugs amongst older people.

CONCLUSION

In this chapter we have seen that health is a complex multi-dimensional phenomena. Although it is a difficult concept to define and describe empirically there is little doubt about the centrality of health and illness to the life of the individual whatever her/his age. Studies of older people have consistently shown that it is one of their major concerns. In particular Finch (1986) has shown that it is the fear of the loss of independence and autonomy, rather than the effects of illness itself, which is most prevalent amongst the elderly.

The popular stereotype of old age is of universal ill-health and a progressive, universal and inescapable decline in both physical and mental status. Clearly the empirical evidence does not support this proposition. Even amongst the very oldest age groups physical and mental ill-health are far from universal. We have shown that there is an increase in the prevalence of both acute and chronic conditions with age. However we must be wary of interpreting this an intrinsic ageing effect. Without good longitudinal data it is impossible to ascertain how much of this increased prevalence of disability is due to biological ageing, how much is socially and environmentally produced and how much is a cohort effect resulting from the harsh conditions experienced by many now elderly people when they were in their youth.

In particular we must wary of interpreting age related changes in health status as biologically determined 'facts'. The physical and social environment in which the older person lives will have a marked effect upon their health status and level of independence. The high steps up to buses may form a barrier to the mobility of older people. Low expectations of health in later life by older people may also influence their abilities. Classifying older people by their degree of dependency may facilitate efficient service planning but will have little positive effect upon the outlook of the elderly themselves.

The data upon which our analysis of the health status of older people has been based is largely cross-sectional in design. From this it is not possible to identify how much of the increased ill health found amongst older age groups is due to the effect of ageing *per se*. Rather it may well be that this is a manifestation of a cohort effect. The population who are now old experienced great privation during their formative years and few had access to medical treatment. With the establishment of the welfare state and socialized medicine older people in the future may display much lower levels of ill-health than the current generations of elderly. Additionally changes in lifestyle such as the decreased prevalence of smoking may well have a very profound effect upon the health status of future generations of elderly.

One method of improving the health status of the elderly is via the fostering of more positive images of health in later life. One method of achieving this objective could be via an extensive health education campaign. The scope for health education is extensive for it operates upon three main levels: advice about lifestyle; education about services; advice about 'normal' and pathological conditions. However, as with other aspects of ageing, a more positive attitude towards the health of older people will not be very fruitful if it is aimed solely at the elderly. Thus a radical programme of health education for later life would be aimed at altering the attitudes of the elderly, the wider society and professional groups to encompass a more positive perspective upon the health effects of growing older. Later life would then be seen as an integral part of a health education programme which stressed a lifetime approach, rather than concentrating upon specific isolated aspects of the lifecycle. Although such a programme would require a substantial input of resources it is likely that the benefits to both society and the elderly as a whole would be substantial.

12

Services for elderly people

As a society, Britain has developed a variety of services in response to the perceived needs and problems of elderly people. These will be examined in this chapter. In previous chapters we have sought to get away from the stereotyped emphasis upon ageing as a problem both for society and the individual. However, as we are examining service needs, delivery and use, in this chapter the problem-orientated approach will figure more heavily than previously. We start by offering a brief history of the development of health and welfare services for the elderly. This is followed by a description of current usage patterns.

THE DEVELOPMENT OF SOCIAL SERVICES FOR THE ELDERLY

Two major forms of health and welfare service have developed to cope with the perceived 'problem' of the elderly. The first service response has been concerned with the use of institutional care as a response to ageing. The second area of development has focused upon the care of the elderly in the community. Although the development of these two types of service response are inextricably inter-related we shall consider their early development separately.

THE INSTITUTIONAL SECTOR

The idea of caring for the elderly in institutions was not originated by the Victorians. The idea of institutional and custodial care as the correct response to the problems of the elderly has a long historical pedigree. As early as the 3rd or 4th century, Christian groups developed institutions called *gerontochia* to care for the elderly. In Britain, hospitals run by the monasteries contributed greatly to the care of the elderly during the medieval period. It was some time after the break-up of the monastic estates during the Reformation that the 1601 Poor Relief Act was passed. This Act was the culmination of a series of statutes passed in Tudor

England which laid the responsibility for the relief of what were termed impotent and able-bodied poor upon the parish. In turn, the parish could raise a rate to pay for the services they provided. Under these laws social casualties such as the poor, sick and elderly were to be cared for in custodial institutions known as houses of correction which were established in every city and county.

The system of poor relief remained largely unaltered until the amendment of 1834. Under this act the system of outdoor relief payable to the able-bodied poor was stopped and a system of workhouses developed. The first workhouses appeared in Britain in 1594 but they did not develop substantially until the passing of the 1834 Reform Act. The ideology underlying this reform was twofold. First, it was felt that the idle able-bodied poor, a British obsession, required to be shocked by a harsh punitive regime into supporting themselves and their families. Relief was denied to those who refused to enter the workhouse and undergo its harsh regime. Second, the Victorians felt that poverty was encouraged by the low rates of poor relief provided. Hence the refusal to provide help to those who would not enter the workhouse. Although the workhouse system has been rightly condemned for its harshness and naive assumptions about the causes and victims of poverty, it did provide a statutory right to assistance in times of need which was unique throughout Europe.

In the reform of the Poor Laws the elderly were not identified as a separate group of interest, they were lumped in with the rest of the pauper classes. At the turn of this century, services for the elderly were virtually non-existent. For those without family or friends to support them the only means of maintenance was the workhouse. Upon entering the workhouse, an institution which was viewed with terror by most of the populace, the elderly (and other inmates) lived in isolation from the rest of society, with little or no personal freedom, and totally cut off from their personal possessions. Consequently, the workhouse became a much feared institution. This is an image which still has important repercussions. Much of the reluctance with which older people enter residential care derives from the recollection of the workhouse regimes of old.

At the time of the Royal Commission into the Poor Law, which resulted in two reports in 1909, 140 000 elderly were resident in workhouses throughout the country. This represented about half of the total population resident in such institutions. The publication of the 1909 reports marked a change in the prevailing social attitude towards the care of the elderly. In combination with the passing of the 1908 Pensions Act these reports did much to convince the public that the old were a group which merited special treatment and should not be grouped in with other groups in poverty. These reports expressed concern about the wholesale consignment of the elderly to the workhouse, if only because of the expense involved. They thought that community social and health services might be a better response to the care of the elderly poor whose only 'crime' had been that economic forces, rather than personal failings, had meant that their old age was a time of great financial hardship.

Both the Majority and Minority Poor Law Reports of 1909 were scathing in their criticism of the Poor Law Guardians for failing to provide adequate nursing and medical care for the infirm elderly. As an alternative, it was suggested that domiciliary services be provided to bring care to the old living at home either on their own or with their families, thereby preventing admission to the workhouse.

Although much criticized, the workhouses remained a feature of the British social welfare system until the development of the welfare state in the immediate post-war years. The 1948 National Assistance Act, section III, laid a duty on local authorities to provide residential accommodation for all persons who because of age, infirmity or other reasons are in need of care and attention which is not otherwise available to them. Because this statutory duty was laid down in section three of the act local authority residential homes are often referred to as 'part III homes'. In the immediate post-war period, little money was available to build the new small homes envisaged by the act and the local authority homes sector developed around the basis of the old public assistance institutions or workhouses.

Townsend (1964), in his book *The Last Refuge*, strongly attacked the quality of residential care provided for elderly people in post-war Britain. He drew attention to the use of inappropriate buildings, inadequate facilities and a quality of life for the residents which was regimented and with little personalization. He wrote: 'communal homes of the kind which exist in England and Wales today do not adequately meet the physical, psychological and social needs of the elderly living in them... alternative services and living arrangements should quickly take their place' (Townsend, 1964, p. 222). His alternative policy response argued strongly that the community was the right and proper place to care for the elderly.

Since this date, the policy for the care of the elderly has concentrated almost exclusively upon community care (see below). However there have been some developments in the field of residential care. Increasingly, residential homes provided by the public sector have shed their 'workhouse' image and developed a much less institutional approach, with the creation of independent living units and a much more personalized service. The major policy initiative in the field of residential care has been the growth in private residential homes as a result of the direct encouragement of the 1979 and 1983 Conservative governments. These homes have been developed as profit-making concerns and great anxiety has been expressed by many at the quality of service offered by this sector. However homes in the private sector have been subject to statutory inspection which was not, prior to 1993, required in the local authority sector. Consequently standards in some public sector institutions fell into a very low level and this was as much a failure to develop an adequate inspection service as it was of lack of finance.

COMMUNITY CARE

The idea of community care for the elderly (or any other social group) is not new. However it has only really developed extensively in Britain since 1939. One major stimulus towards creating a policy for the care of the elderly outside of institutions was the social upheaval caused by the Second World War. The disruption to family life brought about by the mobilization of both men and women drew attention to the problems of who was to care for the elderly who remained in the family dwellings. The decline in the availability of cheap female labour for domestic service added to the perceived difficulties of caring for an increasingly elderly population. In addition this period was, as was shown in Chapter 6, the start of the increase in the percentage of elderly people in the population. Further concern was expressed about the elderly occupying hospital beds which were required by civilian or military casualties.

A second stimulus was the discredited image of the residential care sector. The large and impersonal nature of many of the existing institutions increasingly became a topic of social concern and disapproval. There was also an economic element in the discrediting of institutions as the 'appropriate' policy response to the needs of the elderly. Policy makers felt that it was expensive to care for the elderly in institutions, especially given the widespread pessimism about the numbers of elderly for which the institutional sector would have to cater. Almost from its inception, community care has been perceived by policy makers as a cheap option. Academic commentators have, to their credit, often pointed out that this is not the case (Walker, 1981). Providing good quality care in the community may be just as expensive as providing institutions.

Two main domiciliary social services, the home help service and mobile meals service, as we shall see below, constitute the basis of community care. Community care remains the favoured policy goal for the care of the elderly (Department of Health, 1989). Although the term 'community care' has remained the same over the last 40 years its meaning has undergone subtle alterations. At the outset community care meant the provision of domiciliary services of various types to care for the elderly at home and to prevent admission to an institution of some sort. Increasingly, however, this has been replaced by the idea of care by the community with the family and community assuming the main burden of support and caring with only minimal assistance from the state. Thus there has been a movement away from care in the community to a concept of care by the community.

The home help service

The origins of the home help service can be traced back to the Sick Room Help Society based in the East End of London. This was a model scheme which provided domestic help to new mothers. The perceived success of the scheme, combined with a shortage of domestic servants, led to local authorities being empowered to provide home helps under the 1918 Maternity and Child Welfare Act. This legislation permitted local authorities to provide domestic help to mothers during their lying-in period, regardless of whether the confinement had taken place at home or in hospital. The duties of the home help were those which were usually undertaken by the mother such as cleaning, cooking and washing. Thus the duties of the home help service were originally defined with the needs of new mothers rather than the elderly in mind.

The powers of the local authority to provide this service to the frail elderly was provided in 1944 through a Ministry of Health circular (179/44). This extension of the home help service to the elderly was provoked by a desire to keep as many elderly as possible out of hospital whilst compensating for the lack of family and domestic help due to the disruptions of the war. These powers were later enshrined in the 1946 National Health Services Act. However local authorities were generally slow to develop this type of service, largely because of problems with the recruitment of staff. It is difficult to estimate the extent of provision. Clarke (1984) suggests that by 1945, 19 local authorities had domiciliary domestic care schemes for the elderly. The powers of the local authority to provide home help services were made mandatory, rather than discretionary, under the 1968 Health Services and Public Health Act.

The home help service is now perceived as a vital component in the maintenance of the elderly in their own homes. The tasks undertaken by home helps still illustrate a very strong domestic bias with a heavy emphasis upon cleaning duties of all types. As we saw in Chapter 11, only a small percentage of elders experience difficulties with many of the housecare tasks, especially those such as dusting or sweeping. Yet it is precisely this type of task which the home help service has concentrated upon. Recently, there has been a clear trend for the development of a service which places greater emphasis upon providing a basic caring service rather than just a house cleaning service. To this end, a variety of authorities have deliberately widened the role of the home help and given them new titles such as 'home care attendants'. Many innovative services have been developed. Some, as in the Coventry project, proved a very intensive service. Others, such as a project in the Rhondda, provide a service to particular groups such as those recently discharged from hospital (Victor, Holtermann and Vetter, 1986).

The home help service is, however, beset with a number of problems. First, and foremost, it is a service which was not originally designed for older people. Its essential concentration upon domestic duties has not always been appropriate. Neither has there been much attempt to examine the expressed needs of the elderly and design an appropriate service response. Second, a key problem has been the allocation of resources, both within and between areas. Home help organizers are responsible for the assessment and allocation of home helps to appropriate clients. The available evidence suggests that assessment and allocation is not usually based upon any particularly sound or rigorous criteria. These criteria vary between places and there is some suggestion that, once initiated, services are not reviewed and reallocated where appropriate (Victor and Vetter, 1985). The service is usually provided infrequently for only a short period of time. Thus it has little opportunity to alter the ability of the elderly person to live independently at home. A further problem arises because of 'demarcation' disputes between those services providing care to older people in their own homes.

Another problem of the service is the debate about charging. Charges for services have existed since the 1950s. However the 1974 Local Government Act gave local authorities the power to introduce charges for domiciliary social services without needing ministerial approval. The decision about whether to charge for this sort of service is often related to the financial position of the local authority rather than to wider social policy concerns. There are a variety of policies towards charging. Some authorities provide all services free to all clients, others provide services free to those on low incomes whilst others charge for each visit. The most common form of charging is, however, a flat rate. Many authorities which do charge do this because they consider that the cost of collecting the income exceeds the income generated. There is some empirical evidence for this position. Hunt (1970) reported that charges covered only 9.5% of the cost of the service. In 1979 8% of the cost was recovered in charges (Clarke, 1984). Thus charges can only ever make a very small contribution to the financing of the service.

A major consideration of charging policy is the effect it has upon the elderly person, especially those with very low incomes or who are receiving supplementary pension, now that charges are no longer refunded to those receiving this benefit. The introduction of, or increase in, charges serves as a brake upon demand. A study from Redbridge in London suggests that approximately 10% of service users will cancel because of increased or introduced service charges (Clarke, 1984). It is not usually the less needy who withdraw. Another study from Cornwall indicates that the shortfall between ideal hours and actual allocated hours is greatest for those who have to pay for the service.

The Meals On Wheels service

The other major component of community care is the mobile meals service. This developed during the 1940s in response to the problems of meal provision created by the Blitz in London and may be seen as a development of the late 19th century mobile soup kitchens. From its inception it was the view of the government that this was an aspect of welfare provision that should be run by the voluntary rather than the public sector. There are rival claims as to the originator of the mobile meals service. Roberts (1970) suggests that it was initiated by the Woolwich Old People's Welfare Committee whilst Walker (1974) gives credit for the first schemes to the Women's Voluntary Service (WVS, now the WRVS). Whilst it is not important to decide who was the originator of the service, it is clear that the WVS soon became the main supplier of the mobile meals service. Initially, the emphasis of their efforts was upon children and those made homeless in bombing raids.

Concerns about the hardships and poor nutrition endured by older people as a result of post-war food restrictions, especially the rationing of bread, inspired the government to review the state of mobile meals provision. As a result of a series of conferences in 1947, local authorities were given the power to allocate grants to voluntary groups providing a mobile meals service and the need to expand and coordinate these efforts was generally accepted. The power for local authorities to develop their own meals services was provided by the 1962 Amendment to the 1948 National Assistance Act.

The development of the mobile meals service has also been under debate. It seems to be one of those services which is thought to be a 'good idea' by everyone except the consumers. There are a variety of criticisms concerned with the operation of the service, ranging from the quality of the food to the method of distribution. These arguments have yet to be resolved.

THE DEVELOPMENT OF HEALTH SERVICES

The other main type of service response to the problems of ageing and the elderly has come from the medical sphere. Health care in Britain is provided free of charge at the point of consumption. Under the National Health Service (NHS), established in 1948, there is, however, an important distinction between hospital-based health services and those provided in the community. The NHS is responsible for providing all aspects of health care to the elderly from preventive and health promotion activities to acute and long-stay hospital beds.

Hospital services

Prior to the creation of the National Health Service, three types of hospital existed in Britain: voluntary hospitals, public health hospitals and public assistance hospitals. Each sector catered for a different type of patient. Voluntary hospitals were run on a charitable basis. By the start of the 19th century, this type of hospital was beginning to exclude certain types of patients, mainly the incurably ill. By 1860 St Thomas' Hospital in London was concentrating upon curable cases to the exclusion of chronic conditions (Carboni, 1982), a precedent which was soon followed by most of the major voluntary hospitals throughout the country. This was an admissions policy which was soon followed by the main public health hospitals.

With the exception of a few hospitals established specifically for the incurably ill, the main provision for the chronic sick was through the Poor Law authorities. The Poor Law Act of 1834 stated that paupers were to enter the workhouse when their condition was rendered 'less eligible' than that of the lowest paid. Conditions in the workhouse were meant to be no worse than the conditions experienced by the poorest living outside the workhouse. It was never intended that the aged and chronic sick would be covered by this act. Rather, it was suggested that they should be housed in separate establishments away from the punitive workhouse buildings. This aspect of the act was never put into operation and the chronic sick, of whom large numbers were elderly patients, tended to languish in the hospitals which were still under the control of the public assistance committees. The chronic sick were treated in 'inferior' Poor Law institutions away from the mainstream medicine which was developing in the voluntary and public health hospitals. This separation of the chronic and acute sick is a feature which still pervades the modern organization of medicine in Britain, especially the exclusion of the chronic sick from general hospitals. It took the establishment of the Emergency Medical Service during the Second World War to 'rediscover' the plight of the chronically sick by drawing attention to the large number of beds, required to treat war casualties, that were occupied by this group of patients.

The hospital sectors were amalgamated with the creation of the NHS in 1948, but the history of the different types of hospital incorporated in the health service has continued to affect the development of medical care for the elderly. We still find that long-stay geriatric wards are to be found in the old Poor Law institutions. Medical staff in the newly unified hospital sector did not show an equal enthusiasm for all types of patient. In particular the treatment of the old was seen as both low in status, and low in priority in any competition for scarce financial or staffing resources. Consistently resources have been allocated, as a first priority, to acute and high technology medicine.

The stimulus for the creation of specialist medical services for the old came from a variety of sources. First, there has been a major trend over this century for medicine to become an ever more specialized occupation with the emergence of such specialties as paediatrics and cardiology. The emergence of geriatrics is a part of a general trend within the medical profession. Second, the immediate post-war period was characterized by a large number of qualified doctors seeking consultant positions which were not available in the traditional specialties. To this must be added the decreased demand for chest physicians once a cure for tuberculosis was demonstrated. Against this general background there was the perceived problem of 'bed blocking' by older patients. Many specialists felt that large numbers of elderly, although medically fit for discharge, could not be sent home because of inappropriate social circumstances, thereby 'blocking beds'. This remains a major, though probably widely over-rated, problem for many senior doctors today. Concerns about the costs of treating the elderly were also raised because of their long length of stay and its consequent economic implications.

The impetus to develop specialist geriatric medical services was not entirely negative. In the 1950s, the attention of the medical profession was being drawn to excellent and effective rehabilitative treatment which was being provided in some of the large municipal hospitals, most notably the West Middlesex Hospital under the aegis of Dr Marjorie Warren. Her work demonstrated that large numbers of elderly patients in institutions for the chronically sick were capable of a considerable degree of rehabilitation and subsequent successful discharge back into the community. At the same time Mr Cosin at Orsett in Essex was pioneering the policy of early mobilization and rehabilitation after surgery and Dr Brooke was establishing the principle of the home visit for potential geriatric hospital patients. It was argued that the creation of geriatric departments within general hospitals would improve the medical treatment of the sick elderly and decrease the blocking of beds and length of stay in hospital by such patients. Consequently geriatric medicine developed in a rhetoric of efficiency and cost-cutting.

Geriatrics, as now established as a medical specialty in Great Britain, is defined as the branch of medicine which concentrates upon the clinical, preventive, remedial and social aspects of health and disease in the elderly. To justify itself as a true medical specialty, geriatric medicine has to identify the principles of care that are unique to the clinical management of the elderly. Geriatrics as a medical specialty is characterized by an emphasis upon accurate diagnosis, comprehensive assessment, rehabilitation and continuing care of the patient once discharged back home. More recently there has been the development of psychogeriatrics, which concentrates upon the mental disorders of later life. This type of specialist service is still much less common.

Although there is still extensive debate amongst the medical fraternity about whether geriatrics should exist as a specialist branch of hospital medicine, most areas of the country now provide such a specialist service for the elderly. Academic departments with chairs of Geriatric Medicine are established in half of the medical schools in Britain. Education in geriatric medicine is a feature of the curriculum of all but two medical schools (Smith and Williams, 1983). The education of nurses and other health professionals in the health care of the elderly is fairly limited. A feature of the education that all these groups receive is a concentration upon the pathological aspects of ageing, rather than an investigation of 'normal' ageing. This educational bias probably provides at least a partial explanation as to why the old are perceived so negatively by many members of the medical and allied professions.

Despite the increased teaching in academic medical schools about health care of the elderly, geriatrics has continued to be seen as a 'low status' specialty. There is evidence that this trend is changing. A survey by Barker and Williamson (1986) indicates that half the consultants in geriatrics appointed during the period 1978–82 chose this specialty as their first choice. However, consultants appointed as general physicians with responsibility for the elderly were much less likely to report that this had been their first career choice. The main reasons cited for a career in geriatrics were the opportunities it afforded to work with a wide range of medical problems.

The precise way in which hospital-based health services for the elderly are offered, however, shows considerable variation within Britain. Some health districts operate specialist departments of geriatric medicine which treat all patients, acutely or chronically ill, above a defined age. In other areas the geriatric and general (internal) medical services are integrated, with certain consultants specializing in the care of the elderly.

Hospital-based services for the elderly have not developed extensively into the community as would be expected. The main exception to this has been the development of day hospitals as an adjunct to in-patient care. The first such purpose-built hospital was established in Oxford in 1958 at the Cowley Road Hospital. The role of these hospitals is to provide the therapeutic and medical aspects of geriatric treatment without the 'hotel functions' associated with in-patient care. Patients who require treatment but who can live at home are transported to the hospital to receive their rehabilitation and treatment. Typically, the types of patients using this dimension of hospital care are those with strokes, arthritis or chronic brain syndromes.

Primary health care services

Primary health care in Britain is provided via a system of general practitioners. Every member of the community is registered with a practice which may range from a doctor working on her/his own to a large health centre operated by several practitioners. Increasingly, doctors are grouping together in health centres which are providing a focus for primary health care. The development of health centres has been something of a mixed blessing for older people. The concentration of resources into centres means that the elderly are likely to have more difficulty in getting to their GP because of their reliance upon public transport. Such centres are usually run on a telephone-based rigid appointments system which may generate problems for older people who are less likely to have access to a phone. The main advantage of the larger size of these health centres is that a variety of services, especially of the preventive type, can be offered to patients.

Increasingly, health care at the primary level is being offered in terms of the primary health care team. This involves doctors, nurses, and health visitors working together to provide a comprehensive service to patients. For the care of the elderly the district nursing and, to a much lesser extent, health visiting services play a vital role.

The district nursing service

The district nursing service has its origins in the community nursing service established by William Rathbone in 1859 for the poor in Liverpool. Again this was a service which was not originally developed with the needs of the elderly in mind. The community nursing service is now made up of a variety of different grades of staff ranging from State Registered Nurses, who have completed a special course, to nursing auxiliaries. The roles of these different types of staff vary. District nurses spend a substantial amount of their time carrying out technical medical procedures such as changing dressings or giving injections whilst nursing auxiliaries concentrate upon the personal care of the patient.

Health visitors

Health visitors are a highly specialized group of nurses who have received training with a strong emphasis upon prevention and assessment. The majority of their work concentrates upon the provision of advice, referral to other services, and counselling rather than providing nursing care. They are not a specialist service for the elderly, rather they have a statutory duty to visit new mothers and babies. There has been recognition that they could play a vital role in the care of the elderly at home (Vetter, Jones and Victor, 1984a) and several authorities have developed specialist geriatrics-based health visiting teams.

THE ORGANIZATION OF SERVICES FOR THE ELDERLY

Even considering only the most basic aspects of the service response to ageing it is immediately obvious that a variety of agencies are involved, all of whom have varying professional objectives and modes of working. As originally organized, there was no division of responsibility between health and welfare services for the elderly. The social value of domiciliary domestic and meals services was recognized by their incorporation into the National Health Service when it was founded in 1948. The National Health Services Act of 1946 placed a duty upon the local authority to provide domiciliary nursing and domestic services. No guidelines were issued as to the number of district nurses or home helps to be employed. The Ministry of Health failed to specify the objectives and overall direction of the welfare services.

At the local authority level, the organization of services was extremely complicated and showed considerable variation between areas. The 1948 Act failed to identify who precisely within any local authority should run the welfare services. This led to a variety of responses. In some areas welfare committees separate from health committees ran the welfare services, whilst in others the two were integrated.

This was a rather unsatisfactory state of affairs and it was not long before great concern was being expressed about the lack of co-ordination and co-operation between the various agencies concerned with providing care to the elderly. The Seebohm Report (1968) recommended the establishment of a single social services department within the local authority, to be responsible for all the social needs of individuals and families. These departments were created under the 1970 Local Authority Social Services Act under the direction of a Social Services Director. The first departments came into being in 1971 and they are now responsible for the residential homes for elderly people, home help services, lunch clubs, laundry facilities and aids and adaptations. These departments remain responsible for such aspects of social welfare provision for the elderly. The responsibility for the provision of medical services remains with the health authority. There is now a split in responsibility for the care of the elderly at home which makes the development and implementation of comprehensive policies virtually impossible unless there is good coordination and cooperation between the various agencies.

This situation has been complicated still further in recent years with the emergence of private sector care agencies outside of the control of the state. We have already seen that there has been a substantial growth in the private sheltered housing sector. This has been matched by the growth of private nursing and residential homes as well as private home care agencies. These trends and their implications will be discussed later. The growth of care facilities outside the state system makes it difficult to quantify and catalogue trends in the care of the elderly, as private institutions are often outside the data-collecting machinery of the state.

CURRENT POLICY IN THE CARE OF THE ELDERLY

We have seen that, since the establishment of the welfare state in Britain, the institutional sector has been increasingly discredited. As the institutional sector has fallen out of favour it has been replaced by the alternative policy of community care. A further impetus towards the increased popularity of community care has been the expense of providing care in residential settings as compared with the perceived 'cheapness' of providing care at home. A less often quoted factor in the development of this policy has been the expressed wishes of the elderly themselves.

Community care is not a new policy objective. Townsend (1964, p. 196) quotes the then Minister of Health as stating that 'the best place for old people is in their own home'. The 1962 Hospital Plan for England and Wales recognized the importance of community care. This document also realized that, if this policy objective was to succeed, then there needed to be an expansion of community care services by a shift of resources from the institutional sector to the community. The principle of shifting resources from institutions to the community has been a feature of post-war social policy and community care is a well established priority.

The economic difficulties of the 1970s gave a new significance to the concept of community care. Although the term community care remained in use during this period, its meaning underwent a subtle change. Increasingly, a distinction has been drawn between care in the community and care by the community. Care in the community is best defined as the provision of care by the placing of professional and specialist personnel in the community to provide services to clients in their own home. Care by the community stresses the provision of care by lay/non-specialists on a voluntary or semi-organized basis. During the last decade, it is the concept of care by the community which has become the organizing principle for the provision of services to the elderly (and other groups such as the mentally ill or those with mental handicaps). In 1981 the DHSS White Paper *Growing Older* stated:

> the primary sources of support and care for elderly people are informal and voluntary. These spring from the personal ties of kinship, friendship and neighbourhood. They are irreplaceable. It is the role of public authorities to sustain, and, where necessary, develop, but never to displace such support and care. Care in the community must increasingly mean care by the community. (Department of Health and Social Security 1981, para 1.9)

The recent Barclay Report (1982) on the future of social work placed great emphasis upon a partnership between professional services and the community.

There is little evidence that resources have been transferred to any significant extent from the institutional sector to the community within the health service sector. Walker (1982) has shown that the targets for the provision of domiciliary services in order to make community care work effectively have never been achieved. He has shown that, within local authorities, the fraction of expenditure provided to residential care as opposed to community care actually increased during the period 1974–81.

Community care, in any of its manifestations, has consistently been presented as a method of reducing expenditure. Much of the rationale for community care has been based upon the premise that it was cheaper to care for people in the community than in institutions. Community care is only a 'cheap option' if it is calculated upon the basis of direct visible costs incurred by service-providing agencies. MacIntyre (1977) and Wicks and Rossiter (1982) have indicated that community care has consistently failed to take account of the indirect costs of this policy option. The practice of community care has failed to take account of the personal costs involved to those providing the care, has failed to understand the family and other responsibilities of carers and failed to make sufficient resources available to make community care a realistic policy option. Recent writings from authors working from the feminist perspective have indicated that community care, because of current patterns of gender responsibilities and dependency within the family, is a policy which has meant care by women (Finch and Groves, 1983). It is also a policy option that has not been costed to take account of the economic, social, emotional, psychological, physical, employment and opportunity costs involved in the community care of the elderly.

THE REFORM OF THE NHS AND COMMUNITY CARE

The passing of the NHS and Community Care Bill in June 1990 heralded a radical change in the way that health and social services are provided in Britain. The key changes in each sector of provision are briefly described below. A more detailed description may be found elsewhere (Victor, 1991).

The 1988 review of the National Health Service, which was published in 1989 as the White Paper *Working for Patients*, proposed a fundamental change in the structure and management of the NHS as the solution to the debate about the adequacy of the health care budget. At the heart of the proposals was the creation of an internal market for health care. This has been achieved by the separation of those who purchase care from those who provide it (the purchaser/provider split). The providing agencies consist of all NHS hospitals, private/voluntary hospitals and community health service. The purchasers are district health authorities and GPs who opt to become budget holders. The role of the DHA and other purchasers is to assess the health care needs of their population and to then purchase care which appropriately meets identified needs. Purchasers may 'buy' their care from whichever provider they chose. The assumption behind this change is that competition between providers will improve the range and quality of services provided. The full effects of these reforms, which were implemented in April 1991, are not yet clear; neither is it obvious that they have improved care for older people. However, they have served to stimulate debate about how services are 'rationed' or prioritized and in such debates it seems that services for older people do not attract the same amount of support as hi-tech interventions such as transplants or services for children.

Although the reforms which relate to the changes in community care were included in the 1990 Bill they were not implemented until April 1993. As noted earlier there has been a broad consensus in the post-war period about the desirability of community care as a social policy objective. However, several examinations revealed that community care had developed in a fragmented and slow fashion across the country (Audit Commission, 1986; Griffiths Report – Department of Health and Social Security, 1986). The Griffiths review, commissioned in 1986 and which resulted in the 1989 White Paper *Caring for People* (Department of Health, 1989), was both a follow-up to the Audit Commission report and a response to the spiralling cost of public payments via the social security system to those in private residential/nursing homes.

The White Paper made the assumption that a rigorous division could be made between those with health care needs and those with social care needs. The ideology underpinning these reforms is that for most people community care is the best form of care and this, by implication, means family care. The main organizational and philosophical changes may be summarized as follows. Local authorities, via their social services departments, have been given principal responsibility for the development of community care. They must draw up community care plans for their area, assess individuals' care needs, inspect private and public providers and purchase care as appropriate. So, as with the district health authorities, a market in social care is being created by the separation of purchasers and providers of care. A unified social care budget will be created so that, in future, there is no 'perverse incentive' to enter institutional care. From 1 April 1993 there has been a single method of entry into long-term care for those being supported by public funds. Another important change is the implementation of care management and assessment of individual needs, but there remain many questions marks about how these reforms will work in practice.

NORMS OF PROVISION

Health and welfare services for the elderly have developed in a piece-meal and pragmatic fashion over the last 100 years. In many cases, central government has been reluctant to formulate any detailed norms of provision for which local authorities should aim. Using a variety of sources, Table 12.1 indicates the accepted norms of provision for services for the elderly. However, with the introduction of internal markets for health and social care services the concept of service provision norms is seen to be outdated.

Table 12.1 Norms of provision for services for the elderly (Vetter *et al.*, 1980b)

Service	Provision norm
Hospital beds	10 per 1000 aged 65+
Day hospital	1 per 1000 aged 65+
Residential care	25 per 1000 aged 65+
Sheltered housing	5 per 1000 age 65+
Domiciliary nurse	1 per 2500–4000 total population
Health visitor	1 per 3000–4000 total population
Home help	12 per 1000 aged 65+
Meals	200 per week per 1000 65+

USE OF SERVICES

We describe the use by the elderly of health and social services in terms of three categories of service: the institutional sector; acute hospital services and community health; and medical services.

THE INSTITUTIONAL SECTOR

In Britain those elderly no longer able to live independently in the community may be housed in institutions. These are of two main types: long-stay hospital beds (including psychogeriatric beds) and residential homes. In theory, the residential sector caters for those who, though frail, only need care and attention whilst the hospital sector cares for those with more pressing medical needs. In practice this distinction is often blurred. The pattern has been given added complexity by the development of private institutions providing both residential and nursing care.

THE LONG-STAY HOSPITAL SECTOR

Long-stay hospital beds are provided through the National Health Service and are a relic of the services for the chronic sick inherited with the creation of the NHS. Britain is the only country which has hospital beds for which the length of stay is, in principle, indefinite. Countries which have systems of medical insurance usually have a maximum length of stay quoted in the insurance policy. Patients with mental disorders occupy long-stay beds in mental hospitals. These facilities are usually located well away from the main acute hospital buildings, often in the old workhouse, and are typified by a paucity of resources both in terms of staff and finances.

The residents of long-stay hospital beds are characterized by advanced age, with the majority of patients being aged over 75 years. As might be expected, females dominate this type of ward and all patients exhibit high levels of dependency and incontinence. The reasons for admission to long-stay hospital include strokes, confusion and extreme incontinence.

The efficacy of using long-stay beds to care for the very severely disabled and confused segment of the elderly population has been subjected to considerable scrutiny. The ethos of the hospital service is orientated towards acute medical problems which can be 'cured' and the patient then discharged. The existence of beds for long-stay patients, with little realistic chance of discharge home, does not conform with this philosophy. The type of regime characteristic of hospitals is, perhaps, more likely to foster dependence than independence. There are only a few nursing homes run by the NHS and, in response to the introduction of the 1989 NHS and Community Care Act, has started to divest itself of its responsibility for long-stay care.

The private sector is now a major provider of nursing and residential homes. These homes cater for medical, geriatric and convalescent patients. Fees in this type of establishment range from £200–350 a week, with additional charges for features such as chiropody and physiotherapy. This compares with an average of a NHS long-stay bed of £222 a week in 1983/84 (Capewell, Primrose and MacIntyre, 1986). Several recently published studies indicate that patients resident in private nursing homes do not exhibit the high degrees of disability found in NHS long-stay geriatric wards (Bennett, 1986; Capewell, Primrose and MacIntyre, 1986; Wade, Sawyer and Bell, 1983; Victor, 1992).

RESIDENTIAL HOMES

Three main types of residential home provision are found in Britain. The largest sector are local authority, or Part III, homes. These homes are constructed and run by local authorities as a service to the local community. In addition, residential homes may be provided by voluntary or charitable bodies such as the Methodist Homes for the Aged. These homes are run by the charities concerned and may cater for particular types of elderly such as the wives of the clergy. Finally there are homes provided by the private sector which are run as profitable businesses rather than charitable concerns. Although outside the state sector, they are subject to state legislation under the terms of the 1984 Registered Homes Act. Under the terms of this act, a registered home is 'any establishment which provides, whether for reward or not, residential accommodation with both board and personal care for persons in need of personal care by reason of age [or] disablement'. Only homes catering for four or more residents are required to register with the local authority and are subject to regular inspection of the standard of services provided. Inspectors are not empowered to look at the financial aspects of the private home; and in many areas there are insufficient numbers of inspectors to cover all the homes. In Suffolk in 1986 there were two inspectors and 100 homes (*Guardian*, 28/5/86).

Levels of provision in the local authority sector have remained essentially static since 1979 in response to restrictions in local authority funding and a greater emphasis upon community rather than institutional care. The number of voluntary sector homes has increased only slightly since 1976.

It is the private residential sector that has expanded considerably. There was a doubling of the numbers of places in the 5 years 1979–84. The most recent estimate indicates that there are 7118 homes registered to care for the elderly, mentally ill and mentally handicapped (*Guardian*, 28/5/86). Bornat, Phillipson and Ward (1985) estimate that the private sector now accounts for half of all available residential places. The growth in this area remain impressive. One estimate indicated that in England and Wales seven or eight new homes were being opened a week in 1983 whilst an article in the *Guardian* newspaper suggested that private homes were increasing at the rate of 1000 a year (*Guardian*, 28/5/86).

Taken overall in 1985 local authorities provided 47% of all long-stay places in England, the NHS 20% and the private sector the remainder (Victor, 1991).

Who are the proprietors of these new private care developments? Although there are few data available about the characteristics of these people, it is probably correct to speculate that there are several distinct types of person involved. Firstly, there are those who are simply business people attracted by the possibilities of an expanding market. Secondly, there are those motivated by a career change such as unemployment or transforming a less profitable hotel into a unit in what is perceived as the more profitable residential care sector. Thirdly, there are those with experience of nursing/caring who are taking advantage of the newly developing market.

Private residential care is not new. A number of private 'rest homes' or 'nursing homes' for the elderly have always existed. Additionally, hotels in some coastal areas have catered for older people on a long-term basis. The growth in private residential homes has been extensive since 1979.

What factors have brought about this increase? Firstly, the large proportionate increase in private homes has been brought about by a virtual
standstill in the construction of local authority homes. This lack of public
sector construction has been brought about by the strict control of local
authority funding by a central government committed to the reduction of
public expenditure and ideological objections to the public provision of
services. Second, a very positive inducement to expand private sector
places has been the payment of supplementary benefit 'board and lodg-
ing' allowances, subject to a means test, to those entering private care.
Thus private care came within reach of a wider spectrum of older people
and the fees paid by the DHSS to the private sector grew from £39 000 000
in 1982 to £1 000 000 000 a year in 1989. Such was the expansion
prompted by this change in DHSS policy that new ceilings for maximum
payments for private sector care were pushed through. Thirdly, there has
been a change in ideological climate. The 1979 and 1983 Conservative
administrations believed in the primacy of the 'free market' and did not
support very convincingly the need for state-provided welfare facilities.
However, the explosion of public sector funding of private care underpinned the review of community care undertaken by Sir Roy Griffiths
(Department of Health and Social Security, 1986).

The expansion of private sector residential care has also been encouraged by an ideological debate about the provision of welfare. The philosophy of the 'new right' is one of individual responsibility, a belief in the
efficiency of the market and a repudiation of state provision of welfare.
Private care has been justified by reference to five major themes. Firstly, it
is seen as meeting an existing, but unsatisfied, demand for care. Secondly,
it is seen as expanding the choices available to older people and their relatives in terms of the type of home available and their geographical location. Thirdly, private care is seen as decreasing the power of the
professional and increasing the autonomy of the older person as there is
usually no complex admission procedure for those wishing to enter private care. Fourthly, it is argued that the increase in private care reduces
inequality in old age. Private care has always been available to those with
a sufficient income. However the payment of fees by the DHSS, it is suggested, has reduced inequality between the elderly by making private
care available to a wider spectrum of the elderly. Fifthly, it is inherently
assumed that private care is better than public care, for the older person
has the freedom to move if (s)he is dissatisfied with the standard of care
provide. Sixthly, there has been the comparative failure of the public
sector.

The development of residential care as a means of increasing the choice
of older people is not as straightforward as protagonists of private care
suggest. Firstly, it assumes that there are waiting lists for public care.
Secondly, there are substantial regional and local variations in the

availability of private care. Consequently choice is highly dependent upon the area in which the older person lives. The use of public money to subsidize private care has undoubtedly made this available to a wider spectrum of elderly. However, it may be that such residents are not equally treated in homes because they are unable to pay for extra services provided by the home, such as hairdressing.

There are geographical variations in both types and levels of provision. The highest levels of public provision are to be found in the northern region and the lowest levels in the southern region. Private residential homes are concentrated particularly in the south and south-western regions of England, areas which, as we saw earlier, are the main focus of retirement migration.

Admission to residential care

An investigation of the routes by which older people are admitted to residential care highlights some of the differences between the public and private sector. Admission to public residential homes is usually based upon a waiting list. However a significant fraction of admissions are classed as emergencies and consist of individuals not previously on the waiting list. How many of these 'emergency' admissions result from poor case management is unclear. Admission to a public sector home usually implies some form of assessment of the 'need' of the individual and the appropriateness of residential care as a response to that need. It remains the case, however, that many elderly end up in residential care because there is nowhere else to cater for them. The only criterion for admission to private care is the ability to pay the weekly charge.

It was noted above that one argument for residential care was that it increased the choice and autonomy of the older person. This does not seem to be supported by the facts. Challis and Bartlett (1986) report that, in their survey of Bath, 5% of elderly had arranged their own admission. Doctors and professionals arranged 40% of admissions with relatives responsible for the remainder. They also report that the admission did not seem to have been planned. Rather, it was the response to a crisis in the pattern of care of the older person, usually precipitated by a change in her/his medical circumstances. How many of these admissions could have 'prevented' by the provision of community services remains unclear.

Challis and Bartlett (1986) report that there was little information available to enable the older person, or relatives, to make an informed choice of home. Few homes, they report, produced brochures or prospectuses detailing the care provided and charges levied. As homes vary so much, this could involve the relative in a considerable amount of visiting of homes in order to assess their suitability.

Lifestyles in residential care

Since the pioneering study by Townsend (1964), a variety of investigators have looked at the quality of life in residential homes. These studies have concentrated upon researching the public sector. However investigations are now taking in the newly expanded private residential sector.

Consistently, research has demonstrated that the vast majority of those living in residential care, either public or private, are women. Compared with female residents in these establishments, the males tend to be slightly younger but have largely spent more years in care.

Levels of disability in all types of residential care are high and estimates indicate that up to a quarter of those in residential care would be better cared for in hospital. Surveys have consistently identified a core of those within the residential sector who continue to demonstrate low levels of disability (Booth *et al.*, 1983). Data from a survey in Suffolk suggest that the residents of public residential accommodation demonstrate a higher level of disability than the private sector residents. This difference in the levels of disability found in public and private residential care may just reflect the more recent establishment of the private home. Consequently their residents may not yet have deteriorated in their levels of functional capacity. It could also be that the private homes 'cream off' the fittest elderly, who present the least problems, leaving the public sector to cope with the most severely disabled elderly.

There has been some debate as to whether the residents of public sector homes are becoming more disabled. The data are somewhat ambiguous on this point. A survey by Booth *et al.* (1983) established that there had been few changes in the fraction of residents who were substantially disabled. There did seem to be an increase in the proportion of residents classed as moderately dependent. Thus the perceived increase in dependency within homes is probably due to an increase in the number of residents with intermediate needs for care. This has obvious and very profound implications for levels of staffing and resources required to provide an adequate service within the public sector.

The stereotype of a residential home is of a group of older people sitting around doing nothing in particular. Unfortunately, this stereotype is still an accurate description of many homes where the activities undertaken tend to be indoor, communal and are very often staff-initiated. Independent and creative pastimes are conspicuous by their absence, as are outdoor pursuits of almost any kind. There is little contact with the wider community. Domestic activities are also restricted, with residents generally given very little control over most aspects of their lives. Interaction between staff and residents is characterized by the total dominance of staff, who have substantial power over the residents in almost every aspect of their lives.

Lack of privacy is one factor that seems to pervade residential living. Shared rather than private rooms remain the norm and small group living schemes, where residents live in small groups within the larger institution remain rare. Evidence from a study by Peace, Kellaher and Willcocks (1982) indicates that the majority of residents of residential care are being forced to live highly visible lives in a very public setting when the thing they crave above all else is privacy.

One argument advanced for the development of private residential care is that it offers a superior service to that offered in the public sector. As yet this issue has not been settled. Research has indicated that the private sector is characterized by homes which provide a very poor service to residents (National Union of Public Employees, 1986). It is true that the private sector can provide very good standards of care. The current evidence supports the view that the private sector is typified by levels of care which are more extreme, in either direction, than those found in public sector homes. Consumers of private residential care have no representation in management decisions and, as yet, there are inadequate channels by which residents may complain about the service offered. Apart from relatives or solicitors, there are no effective bodies through which private home residents may raise complaints about services and facilities. However residents of public care also have problems if they run into conflict with a powerful councillor or home manager.

There are some issues about the private sector which give cause for concern. Firstly, because of the lack of inspectors, it is possible for poor standards to exist in private homes for a long time. Secondly, the residents of these homes have no security of tenure: a change of owner or charging policy may force out existing residents. Thirdly, some homes charge exorbitant extra fees for additional services. Fourthly, the staff in private homes receive little or no training and staffing levels are often unacceptably low. Finally, it could be argued that the extension of support to private sector homes is in total opposition to the government's expressed policy objective of caring for the elderly in the community.

Should we abandon residential care?

Residential care has been under attack since the investigative efforts of Townsend (1964). He provided a vast wealth of empirical data to demonstrate the poor quality of life experienced by the elderly living in institutions. To this must be added the comment that residential care is very expensive. The existence of this type of home results in 'boundary' disputes between the health and social services as to with whom the responsibility for the frail elderly actually rests.

Peace, Kellaher and Willcocks (1982) felt that residential care, if suitably modified to provide residents with more privacy and autonomy, was one aspect of the care of the elderly and should be retained. Better design is one factor which has been consistently put forward as a way of improving residential care. However this seems a rather narrow concentration. Rather it would seem to be more appropriate to look at the concept of residential care for the elderly and how it fits in with the broader policy objective of community care. Townsend (1964) has consistently argued that residential care should be reserved for a minority of the most disabled elderly. This would be complemented by an increase in resources to the community to improve the potential for maintaining people at home. This seems to be in line with the wishes of the elderly but would require a substantial input of resources that is not likely to be forthcoming in the current political climate. This policy approach also neglects to take account of the private sector.

Several feminists, aware that community care has often been a code word for the exploitation of women, have argued that the expansion of residential care offers the best solution to the care of the elderly (Finch, 1984). This seems a rather extreme point of view. However, despite all the current emphasis upon community care, residential care has some contribution to play in the care of the elderly. However unfashionable it is to state it, it seems that there will always be a minority of elderly who, for whatever reasons, can be most appropriately cared for in an institutional rather than community setting (Higgs and Victor, 1993).

ACUTE HOSPITAL SERVICES

Data on the use of hospital services by the elderly (or any other client group) is provided in England by a 10% sample of patients published annually as the Hospital Inpatient Enquiry (HIPE). These data are probably typical of the pattern of usage of hospital services by the elderly within Great Britain as a whole.

The elderly are the major client group for hospital care, excluding maternity cases. Table 12.2 demonstrates that they are the main customer group for all of the major medical specialities. In addition, we can see that the fraction of elderly patients treated in these specialities has increased since 1969. Given the projected increases in the numbers of the very elderly, all of the major medical specialities will see an increasing fraction of older people amongst their patients.

Table 12.2 England: proportion of patients aged 65+ in each of the major medical specialties (Office of Population Censuses and Surveys, 1985e, Table S9)

	1969	*1983*
General medicine	34·	42
Ophthalmology	33	49
General surgery	21	31
Geriatrics	95	98
Orthopaedics	19	27
All	34	42

Admission rates of the elderly to hospital have been increased consistently since the creation of the NHS. The admission rate increases with age and is, at all ages, higher for males than females (Table 12.3). Overall 11% of the population aged 65–74 reports an in-patient stay in the previous year compared with 15% of those aged 75+ (Office of Population Censuses and Surveys, 1992).

Table 12.3 England: hospital admission rates of the elderly by age and sex 1983 (Office of Population Censuses and Surveys, 1985e, Table S1)

	Rate per 10000		*Mean duration of stay (days)*	
	M	*F*	*M*	*F*
65–69	1816	1269	12.3	14.6
70–74	2308	1565	14.9	20.7
75–79	2877	2032	17.5	27.2
80–84	3521	2598	21.7	32.4
85+	4471	3502	26.0	44.1

The length of stay by elderly patients in hospital has, as we noted earlier, been a consistent concern of the medical profession. Table 12.3 shows that mean duration of stay increases with age and is higher for women than men. Length of stay has decreased markedly in response to new methods of treatment, financial restrictions and policy directives. In 1974 mean length of stay for males aged 65–74 was 18 days compared with 13 days in 1983. Similar reductions in length of stay have been characteristic of all age and sex groups. Despite this, however, further reductions in hospital stay for older patients remains a major priority for the NHS.

At the inception of the NHS Amulree (1955) recommended the evaluation of the effectiveness of both the NHS and its newly created departments of geriatric medicine. There has been little research which has looked at the effectiveness of hospital treatment of the old (or any other patient group). A survey in Wales indicated that 3 months after discharge 13% of elderly were dead and 20% had experienced at least one re-admission (Victor, 1984).

How effective is hospital treatment in improving the ability of the elderly to live independently at home? Compared with their levels of functional capacity before admission, the majority of elderly demonstrated no change in their functional capacity 3 and 12 months after discharge; 20% were improved and 9% worse (Victor, 1984). However it is difficult to establish precisely what these research findings mean, as we do not know whether they are better (or worse) than would be expected given the amount of resources involved. Given these caveats it does seem that hospital treatment contributes little to the wider policy objective of increasing the independence of the elderly.

COMMUNITY SERVICE PROVISION

The home help and Meals on Wheels services are now almost exclusively services for the old. Currently 85% of all home help service goes to those aged 65 years and over. Despite this heavy emphasis upon the elderly, Table 12.4 shows that the percentage of elderly receiving these services is small, although the usage rate increases with age.

Table 12.4 Great Britain: use of service by elderly people (%) 1985 (Victor, 1991, Figs 8.4, 7.12)

	65–69	70–74	75–79	80–84	85+
Health visitor	2	2	4	8	10
District nurse	2	2	5	10	20
Home help	1	5	11	22	36
Meals on Wheels	0	1	3	6	11

Community health services are also used extensively by the elderly; 45% of home nursing clients, 20% of health visitor clients and 20% of all GP consultations are accounted for by elderly people. The visiting rate of district nurses to the elderly has increased from 166 visits per 1000 population aged 65 and over in 1979 to 219 per 1000 in 1984. The comparable rate for health visitors, 85 and 70 per 1000, shows a decrease over the same period. However, again these services are only used by a minority of older people.

FAMILY AND STATUTORY CARE

State services are received by only a minority of older people. This indicates that the bulk of the responsibility for caring rests with the informal sector. Data from Evandrou *et al.* (1985) can be used to assess the relative contributions made by formal and informal sectors to those elderly with particular needs. These data indicate that, for those elderly who require help with specific activities of daily living, the family is the primary source of help. The largest contribution made by statutory services was to the elderly who required help with bathing. For this group 23% were helped by statutory services. However the vast majority, 76%, received help with this task from informal carers. Only for specific medical tasks did the contribution of the statutory sector overtake that of the informal sector.

INEQUALITIES IN SERVICE PROVISION

Both health and social services are inequitably distributed throughout Great Britain. The National Health Service has been attempting to redistribute money and resources to some of the more deprived areas of the country but to little effect. Social services illustrate a marked variation in levels of provision between local authorities. Bebbington and Davies (1982) observe that the variation between authorities in service provision is large and has remained remarkably stable over time. They observe that in 1977/78 Devon and the Isle of Wight spent £25 per person aged 65 and over compared with £137 in the London boroughs of Islington and Camden. Historical circumstances, political ideology and relative costs combine to produce an inequitable distribution of resources. The distribution of resources between different types of services also varies between authorities. For example, the London borough of Greenwich spent 37% of its resources for the elderly upon residential care compared with 70% in the counties of West Sussex and the Isle of Wight. This tendency for retirement areas to spend a higher fraction of its resources for the elderly upon residential care has been reported for Wales as well as England (Vetter, Jones and Victor, 1980a).

CONCLUSION

The history of service development for the elderly has been one of responses to a variety of factors, including a disenchantment with institutionalized care, the expense of providing such care, fears about the numbers of elderly who might want such care and a perception that community care is a 'cheap' option compared with institutional provision. Perhaps the most interesting feature of the development of policy for the elderly is the way that it has evolved in a highly pragmatic fashion with little reference to the needs and wants of the consumers of care. Policy developments for the elderly are characterized more by the needs of professional groups than the expressed wishes of the elderly. The power of the vested interests of professional groups remains a powerful influence upon policy development. In particular there is still a tendency to deny the autonomy of older people and to provide them with the sorts of services we think are good for them, rather than responding to their expressed wishes.

Both health and social services are united by the policy objective of community care. However, the administrative split between health and social services has resulted in a fragmented approach to the development of policy. There is little coordination between these two types of service, which results in the haphazard development of policy and provision of care.

The elderly are the major client group of the NHS. In addition to the specialty of geriatrics, the elderly are the main 'customers' of the specialities of surgery, medicine, ophthalmology and orthopaedics. Within the health service geriatrics remains a low status specialty. Given current patterns of health service use and demographic predictions, all of the major specialities are going to become even more dominated by the care of the elderly. This has important implications for medical education. It would seem obvious that future generations of medical students should receive a better and more extensive training in the medical care of the old.

The major policy initiative has been that of community care. Although the term has remained the same over the last 40 years its meaning has been subtly altered. In its original conception, community care implied a massive input of resources by the state. Now the policy involves only a residual role by the state with the emphasis upon individual responsibility and the role of the family. The policy as now manifest is based upon an essentially sexist premise that women will undertake the caring. Most policy documents omit to mention that, in the future, decreases in family size over this century mean that there will be fewer carers available to care for a greater number of elderly. One response to this shortfall of 'informal' carers has been the idea that the young elderly should care for the old elderly. However, as we saw in Chapter 6, there is also going to be a decrease in the numbers of young elderly. Simple demography would, therefore, suggest that there will have to be an extensive increase in the role of the state sector in the care of the elderly.

Volunteers and the free market are seen as being the means by which community care can be made a reality. However, volunteer groups, whilst making a useful contribution to the local provision, cannot provide adequate and reliable services on a national basis. A reliance upon the 'free market' to provide care only serves to increase and preserve current patterns of inequality of provision and makes the development of rational policies impossible. Demographic trends which suggest more elderly and less carers indicate that services should be expanded rather than contracted. However, these are essentially political decisions and as yet there is no indication that the state is prepared to expand its commitment to the care of the elderly. It seems likely that the full implementation of the Community Care Act of April 1993 will not greatly expand the amount of services provided for older people or tackle any of variations in the level of quality of services provided.

13

Issues in the politics of ageing

In this book we have sought to describe the diversity of the experience of old age in modern society. Factors such as age, gender and social class have been shown to have a marked influence upon the experience of later life. In this chapter we shall consider some of the main issues which now confront the position and status of older people. Finally we shall conclude with an examination of the politics of ageing in Great Britain.

PENSIONS POLICY

The 1980s have been characterized by economic recession and high unemployment. Estes (1986) terms this 'austerity' and distinguishes between objective and subjective austerity. The objective reality of austerity is the worldwide recession in economic activity which has resulted in unemployment and decreases in demand. The subjective basis of austerity is socially constructed and relates to the idea that the cause of economic recession is state spending upon welfare. This approach proposes that it the old who are to 'blame' for current economic difficulties. The 'greying' of the welfare budget is an issue which has attracted considerable interest.

The ability of the state to pay pensions at a realistic rate to the elderly has been questioned by the 'new right' which favours the dismantling of the welfare state. The rhetoric employed by the protagonists is based upon the irrational use of demographic data predicting a 'massive' increase in the fraction of older people. As we saw the actual numbers involved are rather small and current projections suggest that there will be little alteration in the ratio of workers to dependants in the coming decades.

Using these fears about the 'ageing' of the population the 1983 Conservative administration failed to fully maintain the levels of state pensions paid to the elderly and espoused the cause of private pension schemes. Whilst these may well be helpful to the well paid, occupational pension schemes do little to reduce inequalities in old age. The extension of private schemes, combined with a reduction of the state pension, will inevitably lead to an increase in poverty in old age (Arber and Ginn, 1992).

However, the breakdown of the consensus between the political parties in their attitudes towards pensions is not mirrored by the population at large. Studies have consistently demonstrated that the British population favours the payment of welfare benefits to the elderly (Victor, 1984). Additionally, whilst current pensioners accept low living standards without much complaint, it remains to be seen whether future generations of elderly will be so compliant. Consequently future administrations may well find that they have to substantially change their policy towards the provision of pensions by both expanding the role of the state in providing pensions and paying this at a level which enables the elderly to be fully participating members of society.

ISSUES IN SERVICE PROVISION

The provision of care to the elderly in the community is a topic which has been the subject of considerable debate. Here we will focus on six main concerns; class and the allocation of services; sexism and community care; changes in levels of service provision over time; implications of demographic trends for service provision, the attitudes of the elderly to the services they receive and the privatization of care.

Class and service use

The establishment of the welfare state was seen by its protagonists as one method of diminishing the class-based inequalities which pervade British society. The working class, who could not afford health, welfare and education services, were seen as being the prime beneficiaries of state welfare. However in reality it is the articulate middle class who have fared best in the state allocation of welfare. Several studies, most notably the report on *Inequalities of Health* (Department of Health and Social Security, 1983), have demonstrated that class-based health inequalities have been little altered by the creation of the welfare state. The centrality of social class to the understanding of modern British society has been recognized by its inclusion as a key variable in most social investigations, with the exception of those concerned with the elderly. In particular, there has been little consideration of how class influences the receipt of welfare services in later life.

Recent evidence suggests that there is no relationship between the social class of the older person and receipt of medical services, even though it is known that the elderly in classes 4 and 5 experience a lower health status than those in classes 1 and 2 (Victor and Evandrou, 1986).

Similarly, receipt of the mobile meals service is not related to class. In contrast the receipt of the home help service is inversely related to class. Elderly in classes 4 and 5 are more likely to receive this service, at all levels of disability, than their counterparts from classes 1 and 2. This may reflect a positive bias in allocation amongst service providing agencies. However it seems more likely that those elderly from the professional classes, because of their greater affluence, are using private rather than public services.

Sexism and service allocation

We have noted earlier that the community care of the elderly has been a policy objective for several decades. A variety of authors have drawn attention to the essentially sexist premise upon which this policy has been developed. Studies by Walker (1981), Finch (1984) and Finch and Groves (1980) have demonstrated that family care is a euphemism for care by women because of gender inequalities in caring roles. However we must acknowledge, as was noted earlier, that in the care of the elderly men do play a significant part. This is, however, very largely confined to the care of their spouse rather than of an elderly person of a different generation.

Apart from identifying the essentially sexist nature of the rhetoric of community care some authors suggest that it is sexist in its application. Feminists have suggested that women experience a double disadvantage under community care. Firstly they are more likely to be carers and secondly they are likely to receive less support than male carers (Charlesworth, Wilkin and Durie, 1984). These authors have suggested that, in a time of scarce resources, women are discriminated against in the allocation of services. The evidence for this assertion is not, however, conclusive for several reasons. Those studies which have demonstrated allocative bias are small-scale and therefore do not provide sufficient numbers for detailed analysis. Secondly, such studies have not always controlled for disability and household composition. Recent analysis by Arber *et al.* (1986) has suggested that sex is not the basis of discrimination in service receipt. Rather they suggest that it is household composition which is the key variable, the elderly living alone receiving more services than those who had a carer available, regardless of sex. However this debate has not yet been resolved and there is much research to be undertaken before the matter is finalized.

Trends in the provision of services

An integral part of the policy of community care has been the implied transfer of resources from the hospital sector to the community. This should be reflected in an increase in the availability of community care services. However, as table 13.1 demonstrates, the fractions receiving services show only slight increases up to 1978 and seem to have remained constant since.

Table 13.1 Comparisons of elderly receiving services (%) (Bebbington, 1978, Table 7; Victor and Evandrou, 1986)

	AWS 1962	SWE	EAH	GHS 1980
Home help	4.5	4.5	8.6	9
Meals	1.1	1.1	2.4	2
District nurse		2.3	5.5	5
Health visitor		1.6	1.7	2

In Chapter 6 we saw that there is going to be a large proportionate increase in the numbers of 'old' elderly over the next two decades. As this is the group which makes most use of health and social services this demographic trend has obvious implications for the provision of services. As this age group is not evenly distributed across the country the demands for services will vary geographically. However Table 13.2, drawn from the work of Vetter, Jones and Victor (1985) indicates the scale of increases in service provision that will be required just to keep provision levels at current levels.

Table 13.2 Projected increases in the demand for services in two areas of Wales by 1991 (%) (Vetter *et al.*, 1985, Tables 2–6)

	Urban	Rural
GP visit	27	15
GP home visit	42	18
District nurse	55	20
Home help	50	22
Meals on Wheels	42	17

Attitudes of the elderly towards service provision

Services for the elderly have developed in a highly pragmatic way over the last century. A plethora of interested parties ranging from the government to the medical profession have been instrumental in these developments. However the group which has been conspicuous by its absence have been the consumers. Rarely have the views of the clients of these services been sought. Most evidence indicates that the elderly express a high level of satisfaction with the services provided (see Table 13.3).

However it is difficult to interpret exactly what these data mean. It could just be that the elderly are much less ready to criticize than younger members of the population. However it does seem important that the views of the elderly should be taken into account when planners and policy makers are developing their strategies to care for them.

Table 13.3 Satisfaction with services by age (%) (British Social Attitudes Survey, 1983, unpublished data)

	< 65	65–74	75+
GP	78	86	87
Dentist	79	63	56
Health visitor	52	47	53
District nurse	65	64	62
In-patient	73	85	83
Out-patient	58	81	75

The privatization of care

Much of the current ideological debate about service provision centres upon the issues of private versus public sector care. We saw in the section on residential care that the private sector has expanded considerably. Private sector domiciliary services are now developing. The key to the ideological debate seems to be the notion of 'freedom of choice' allied with feelings that private services are inherently better than public services because the consumer has the ability to withdraw from unsatisfactory arrangements. However, we saw that with residential care the notion of freedom of choice is more illusory than real. The 'free market' is an insecure place for elderly people who often lack power in the decision making process. The idea that a free market will necessarily bring high standards of care, either domiciliary or residential, is both naive and dangerous whilst one outcome of the free market – business failure and bankruptcy – carries important implications for the residents of private homes and those reliant upon private care to maintain themselves at home.

TOWARDS A POLITICS OF AGEING

There is no politics of ageing in Britain, unlike the United States where age advocacy groups challenging the prevailing attitudes towards old age and the elderly have emerged. The post-war period has, in Britain, been characterized, until very recently, by an all party consensus over pensions and services for the elderly.

Walker (1986) suggests that five main factors account for the way that pensioners in Britain acquiesce to policies of central government, even when these policies are a direct assault on their diversity of the elderly population. The elderly are deeply divided along lines of class, race and gender. Consequently it is too simplistic to expect that there will be a single 'politics of old age'. Secondly, there is the powerlessness of the elderly. Retirement removes many older people from the workplace, which is often their only source of political power. Thirdly, there is the lack of formal political organization for the elderly. The structures of the main political parties preclude the active participation of the elderly. Fourthly, there are barriers to political activity such as disability, poverty and ill health. Finally, there is the conservatism of the current cohort of older people.

As yet there are few signs that the political process has been influenced by the increase in the fraction of the population classed as elderly. However there are ageing advocacy groups in Britain such as Age Concern, Pensioners Voice and Help the Aged which are currently active. Overall, however it seems that in later life older people retain their pre-'old age' voting patterns and political allegiances.

CONCLUSION

Ageing in modern society is a richly diverse experience. Factors such as age, sex and social class contribute to make the elderly a heterogeneous segment within the total population. The popular negative stereotypes of later life are clearly inappropriate and later life is best seen as a continuation of earlier phases of life.

The elderly are, however, a group which is under threat. The widespread fears about the 'greying' of the population and the welfare budget have brought about a sharp attack upon the living standards of a group who are, in comparison with the rest of society, already deprived. State expenditure upon the elderly (and other groups) is depicted as a major 'cause' of current economic difficulties. However these are essentially ideological views which are not supported by the 'facts'. The increase in numbers of the very old is nowhere near the crisis proportions many commentators would have us believe.

The persistence of inappropriate negative stereotypes about later life results in both discrimination and prejudice against the old. Society consistently displays ageist attitudes that demonstrate a marked lack of concern about its older members. However it is not only the elderly who lose out because of the existence of ageist attitudes. Only by changing attitudes across society will we be able to ensure that future generations of elderly experience old age as fully participating members of society, instead of as observers confined to the margins. To achieve this end we must stress the common interests between age groups instead of seeing the old (or any other marginal group) as fundamentally different from ourselves. The main goal for an ageing society must be to replace notions of independence and dependence with a social framework which emphasizes interdependence between generations.

References

Abrams, M. (1978) *Beyond Three Score Years and Ten: First Report on a Survey of the Elderly*, Age Concern England, Mitcham, Surrey.

Abrams, M. (1980) *Beyond Three Score Years and Ten: Second Report on a Survey of the Elderly*, Age Concern England, Mitcham, Surrey.

Achenbaum, W.A. (1978) *Old Age in the New Land*, Johns Hopkins University Press, Baltimore.

Ascadi, G. and Nemeskeri, J. (1970) *History of Human Lifespan and Mortality*, Akademial Kiado, Budapest.

Agate, J. and Meacher, M. (1969) *The Care of the Old*, Fabian Research Series 278, Fabian Society, London.

Age Concern (1974) *The Attitudes of the Elderly and Retired*, Age Concern England, Mitcham, Surrey.

Amulree, Lord (1955) Modern hospital treatment and the pensioner. *Lancet*, **17 September**, 571–575.

Anderson, M. (1972) Household structure and the industrial revolution: mid-nineteenth century Preston in perspective, in *Household and Family in Past Time*, (ed. P. Laslett), Cambridge University Press, Cambridge, pp. 215–235.

Anderson, M. (1977) The impact on the family relationships of the elderly of changes since Victorian times in governmental income maintenance, in *Family, Bureaucracy and the Elderly*, (eds E. Shanas and M. Sussman), Duke University Press, Durham, NC.

Anderson, R. and Cartwright, A. (1985) The use of medicines by older people, in *Self Care and Health in Old Age*, (eds K. Dean, T. Hickey and B.E. Holstein), Croom Helm, London, pp. 167–203.

Apple, D. (1956) The social structure of grandparenthood. *American Anthropologist*, **58**, 656–663.

Arber, S., Dale, A., Gilbert G.N. and Evandrou, M. (1986) *Provision of Formal Care to the Elderly at Home: Is it Gender Blind?* Paper presented at the Annual Conference of the British Sociological Association, University of Loughborough, Loughborough.

Arber, S. and Gilbert, G.N. (1989) Men, the forgotten carers. *Sociology*, **23**(1), 111–118.

Arber, S. and Ginn, J. (1991a) The invisibility of age: gender and class in later life. *Sociological Review*, **39**, 260–291.

Arber, S. and Ginn, J. (1991b) *Gender and Later Life*, Sage Publications, London.

Arber, S. and Ginn, J. (1992) The transmission of income inequality, in *Responding to an ageing society*, (ed. K. Morgan), Jessica Kingsley, London pp. 63–83.

Aries, P. (1962) *Centuries of Childhood*, (trans. R. Baldick), Cape, London.

Atchley, R.C. (1976a) *The Sociology of Retirement*, Schenkman, Cambridge, MA.

Atchley, R.C. (1976b) Selected social and psychological differences between men and women in later life. *Journal of Gerontology*, **31**(2), 204–211.

Askham, J., Barry, C., Grundy, D., Hancock, R. and Tinker, A. (1992) *Life After 60*, Age Concern Institute of Gerontology, London.

Audit Commission (1986) *Making a Reality of Community Care*, HMSO, London.

Baker, S. and Perry, M. (1983) *Housing for Sale to the Retired*, Housing Research Foundation, London.

Baker, S. and Perry, M. (1984) *Housing for Sale to the Elderly, Second Report*, Housing Research Foundation, London.

Baker, S. and Perry, M. (1986) *A Review of the Retirement Housing Market and Future Trends*, Housing Research Foundation, London.

Barclay, P.M. (Chairman) (1982) *Social Workers: Their Role and Tasks*. Report of a working party set up by the National Institute of Social Work, Bedford Square Press, London.

Barker, W.H. and Williamson, J. (1986) Survey of recently appointed consultants in geriatric medicine. *British Medical Journal*, **293**, 896–898.

Bebbington, A.C. and Davies, B. (1982) Patterns of service provision for the elderly, in *Perspectives on the Elderly*, (ed. A.M. Warnes), John Wiley, Chichester, pp. 355–374.

Beltram, G. (1984) *Testing the Safety Net*, Occasional Papers on Social Administration 74, Bedford Square Press, London.

Bengtson, V.L. (1967) *The Social Psychology of Ageing*, Boobs-Merrill, Indianapolis.

Bennett, J. (1986). Private nursing homes: contribution to long stay care of the elderly in Brighton Health District. *British Medical Journal*, **293**, 867–870.

Berger, P.L. and Berger, J. (1976) *Sociology: A Biographical Approach*, Penguin, Harmondsworth.

Berger, P.L. and Luckmann, T. (1967) *The Social Construction of Reality*, Doubleday, New York.

Beveridge, W. (1942) Social Insurance and allied services, *Cmnd 6404*, HMSO, London.

Blau, P.M. (1964) *Exchange and Power in Social Life*, John Wiley, New York.

Blau, Z.S. (1973) *Old Age in a Changing Society*, Franklin Watts, New York.

Blaxter, M. and Paterson, E. (1982) *Mothers and Daughters*, Heinemann, London.

Bond, J. and Carstairs, V. (1982) *The Elderly in Clackmannan*, Scottish Health Service Studies 42, Scottish Home and Health Department, Edinburgh.

Booth, T.A., Barritt, S., Berry, S. *et al.* (1983) Dependency in residential homes for the elderly. *Social Policy and Administration*, **17**(2), 46–62.

Bornat, J., Phillipson, C. and Ward, S. (1985) *A Manifesto for Old Age*, Pluto Press, London.

Bosanquet, N. (1978) *A Future for Old Age*, Temple Smith, London.

Breen, L.Z. (1960) *The Aging Individual*, in *Handbook of Social Gerontology*, (ed. C. Tibbitts), University of Chicago Press, Chicago, pp. 145–162.

Briggs, E. and Rees, A. (1980) *Supplementary Benefits and the Consumer*, Occasional Papers in Social Administration 66, Bedford Square Press, London.

Broad, P. (1977) *Pensioners and their Needs*, Office of Publication Censuses and Surveys, HMSO, London.

Burgess, W.W. (1960) *Aging in Western Societies*, University of Chicago Press, Chicago.

Bushell, R. (1984) *Great Britain: The Job Release Scheme* (mimeo), Organization for Economic Cooperation and Development, Paris.

Butler, A., Oldman, C. and Greve, J. (1983) *Sheltered Housing for the Elderly*, George Allen and Unwin, London.

Capewell, A.E., Primrose, W.R. and MacIntyre, C. (1986) Nursing dependency in registered nursing homes and long term geriatric wards in Edinburgh. *British Medical Journal*, **292**, 1719–1721.

Carboni, D.K. (1982) *Geriatric Medicine in the United States and Great Britain*, Greenwood Press, Westport, CT.

Carter, H. and Gillick, P.C. (1970) *Marriage and Divorce: A Social and Economic Study,* Harvard University Press, Cambridge, MA.

Cartwright, A. and Anderson, R. (1981) *General Practice Revisited,* Tavistock, London.

Central Statistical Office (1986) *Social Trends,* HMSO, London.

Challis, L. and Bartlett, H. (1986) The paying patient: customer or commodity: surveying private residential homes for the elderly, in *Dependency and Interdependency in Old Age,* (eds C. Phillipson, M. Bernard and P. Strang), Croom Helm, London, pp. 270–278.

Charlesworth, A., Wilkin, D. and Durie, A. (1984) *Carers and Services: A Comparison of Men and Women Caring for Dependent Elderly People,* EOC, Manchester.

Child Poverty Action Group (1984) *Estimates of Benefit Take-up,* Child Poverty Action Group, London.

Chudacoff, T. and Haraven, T. (1978) Family transitions in old age, in *Transitions, the Family and Life Course in Historical Perspective,* (ed. T. Haraven), Academic Press, New York, pp. 217–243.

Clarke, L. (1984) *Domiciliary Services for the Elderly,* Croom Helm, London.

Clayton, S. (1978) *Sheltered housing.* Occasional Papers in Health and Welfare 1, Department of Social Administration, University of Lancaster, Lancaster.

Cowgill, D. (1974a) The aging of populations and societies. *Annals of the American Academy of Political and Social Science,* **415**, 1–18.

Cowgill, D. (1974b) Aging and modernization: a revision of the theory, in *Late Life: Communities and Environmental Policy,* (ed. J.F. Gubrium), C.C. Thomas, Springfield, IL, pp. 123–146.

Cowgill, D.O. and Holmes, L.D. (1972) *Aging and Modernization,* Appleton-Century-Crofts, New York.

Craig, J. (1983) The growth of the elderly population. *Population Trends,* **32**, 28–33.

Culyer, A.J. (1981) *Health Indicators,* University of York, York.

Cumming, E. and Henry, W.E. (1961) *Growing Old,* Basic Books, New York.

Cunningham-Bowley, S. (1986) Becoming a grandparent. *New Society,* **7/2/86**, 22–23.

De Beauvoir, S. (1972) *Old Age,* Penguin, Harmondsworth.

Department of Employment (1985) *Family Expenditure Survey 1983,* HMSO, London.

Department of the Environment (1979) *English Housing Condition Survey,* HMSO, London.

Department of Health (1989) *Working for Patients,* HMSO, London.

Department of Health and Social Security (1978) *A Happier Old Age,* HMSO, London.

Department of Health and Social Security (1981) Growing older, *Cmnd 8173,* HMSO, London.

Department of Health and Social Security (1983) *Inequalities in Health* (the Black Report), HMSO, London.

Department of Health and Social Security (1985) Reform of social security, *Cmnd 9516–9518,* HMSO, London, 3 vols.

Department of Health and Social Security (1986) *Community Care: Agenda for Action,* HMSO, London.

Dingwall, R. (1976) *Aspects of Illness,* Martin Robertson, London.

Dowd, J. (1980) *Stratification Amongst the Aged,* Brooks-Cole, Monterey, CA.

Dunnell, K. and Cartwright, A. (1972) *Medicine Takers, Prescribers and Hoarders,* Routledge and Kegan Paul, London.

Elder, G. (1974) *Children of the Great Depression,* University of Chicago Press, Chicago.

Elder, G. (1975) Age differentiation and the life course, *Annual Review of Sociology*, **1**, 165–190.

Equal Opportunities Commission (1982a) *Caring for the Elderly and Handicapped: Community Care and Women's Lives*, Equal Opportunities Commission, Manchester.

Equal Opportunities Commission (1982b) *Who Cares for the Carers?*, Equal Opportunities Commission, Manchester.

Equal Opportunities Commission (1983) *Carers and Services: A comparison of Men and Women Caring for Dependent Elderly*, Equal Opportunities Commission, Manchester.

Erikson, E. (1950) *Childhood and Society*, W.W. Norton, New York.

Estes, C.L. (1979) *The Aging Enterprise*, Jossey-Bass, San Francisco.

Estes, C.L. (1986) The politics of ageing in America. *Ageing and Society*, **6**(2), 121–134.

Estes, C.L., Swan, J.S. and Gerard, L.E. (1982) Dominant and competing paradigms in gerontology. *Ageing and Society*, **2**, 151–164.

Eurostat (1981) *Europe: Demographic Statistics*, European Economic Community, Brussels.

Evandrou, M., Arber, S., Dale, A. and Gilbert, G.N. (1985) *Who Cares for the Elderly? Family Care Provision and the Receipt of Services*. Paper Presented at the 1985 British Society for Gerontology Conference, University of Keele, Newcastle-under-Lyme, Staffordshire.

Eversley, D. (1982) Some new aspects of ageing in Britain, in *Ageing and Life Course Transitions*, (eds T.K. Haraven and K.J. Adams), Tavistock, London, pp. 245–265.

Fairhurst, E. (1976) Sociology and ageing: an alternative view. *Concord*, **6**, 43–54.

Fairhurst, E. (1977) A sociologist looks at ageing. *Residential Social Work*, **17**(7), 188–190.

Falkingham, J. and Victor, C.R. (1991) The myth of the woopie. *Ageing and Society*, **11**(4), 471–493.

Family Policy Studies Centre (1984) *The Forgotten Army*. Briefing paper, Family Policy Studies Centre, London.

Feeney, R.J., Galer, J.D. and Gallagher, M.M. (1974) *Alarm Systems for the Elderly and Disabled People*, Institute for Consumer Ergonomics, University of Loughborough, Loughborough.

Fennell, G. (1985) Sheltered housing: some unanswered questions, in *Ageing: Recent Advances and Creative Responses*, (ed. A. Butler), Croom Helm, London, pp. 178–191.

Fiegehen, G.C. (1986) Income after retirement. *Social Trends*, 13–18, HMSO, London.

Field, D. (1976) The social definition of illness, in *Introduction to Medical Sociology*, (ed. D. Tuckett), Tavistock, London, pp. 334–368.

Finch, H. (1986) *Health and Older People*, Research Report 6, Health Education Council, London.

Finch, J. (1984) Community care: developing non-sexist alternatives. *Critical Social Policy*, **9**, 6–18.

Finch, J. (1989) *Family Obligation and Social Change*, Polity Press, Cambridge.

Finch, J. and Groves, D. (1980) Community care and the family: a case for equal opportunities? *Journal of Social Policy*, **9**(4), 487–514.

Finch, J. and Groves, D. (1983) *A Labour of Love: Women, Work and Caring*, Routledge and Kegan Paul, London.

Fisher, D.H. (1978) *Growing Old in America*, Oxford University Press, New York.

Fisk, M.J. (1984) Community alarm systems: a cause for concern. *Housing Review*, **33**(1).

Fisk, M. J. (1986) *Independence and the Elderly,* Croom Helm, London.

Ford, G. (1985) Illness behaviour in old age, in *Self Care and Health in Old Age,* (eds K. Dean, T. Hickey and B.E. Holstein), Croom Helm, London, pp. 130–166.

Fox, R.H., Woodward, P.M., Exton-Smith, A.N. *et al.* (1973) Body temperatures in the elderly. A study of physiological, social and environmental conditions. *British Medical Journal,* 200–206.

Fuller, R.C. and Meyers, R.R. (1941) Natural history of a social problem. *American Sociological Review,* 321–328.

Gardner, M. and Donnan, S. (1977) Life expectancy: variations amongst regional health authorities. *Population Trends,* **10**, 10–12.

Gibson, H.B. (1992) *The Emotional and Sexual Lives of Older People,* Chapman and Hall, London.

Glenn, N. (1974) Ageing and conservatism. *Annals of the American Association of Political and Social Science,* **415**, 176–180.

Goffman, E. (1963) *Stigma,* Prentice-Hall, Englewood Cliffs, NJ.

Gray, J.A.M. and Wilcock, G. (1981) *Our Elders,* Oxford University Press, Oxford.

Green, H. (1988) *Informal Carers.* Office of Population Censuses and Surveys General Household Survey Series 16, HMSO, London.

Grimley-Evans, J. (1981) Demographic implications for the planning of services in the UK, in *The Provision of Care for the Elderly,* (eds J. Kinnaid, J. Brotherston and J. Williamson), Churchill-Livingstone, Edinburgh, pp. 8–13.

Groves, D. (1986) *Occupational Pensions.* Paper presented at the Annual Conference of the British Society of Gerontology, University of Glasgow, Glasgow.

Gubrium, J.F. (1974) *Late Life: Communities and Environmental Policies,* C.C. Thomas, Springfield, IL.

Guillemard, A.-M. (1983) The making of old age policy in France, in *Old Age in the Welfare State,* (ed. A.-M. Guillemard), Sage Publications, Beverley Hills, CA, pp. 75–100.

Hagestrand, G.O. (1985) Older women and inter-generational relationships, in *The Physical and Mental Health of Older Women,* (ed. M. Haug), Springer, New York.

Harman, D. (1956) Aging – a theory based on free radical and radiation chemistry. *Journal of Gerontology,* **11**, 298–300.

Harris, D.K. and Cole, W.E. (1980) *Sociology of Ageing,* Houghton-Mifflin, Boston.

Havighurst, R. (1963) Successful aging, in *Process of Aging,* (eds R.H. Williams, C. Tibbitts and W. Donahoe), University of Chicago Press, Chicago, vol 1, pp. 311–315.

Havighurst, R.J. and Albrecht, R. (1953) *Old People,* Longman-Green, New York.

Hayflick, L. (1977) The cellular basis for biological aging, in *Handbook of the Biology of Aging,* (eds C.E. Finch and L. Hayflick), Van Nostrand, New York, pp. 159–188.

His Majesty's Stationery Office (1909) Report of the Royal Commission on the Poor Laws and Relief of Distress, *Cmnd 4499,* HMSO, London.

Herbst, K. (1981) *Mental Disorder and Illness in the Elderly at Home.* Research Report, Department of Applied Social Studies, Polytechnic of North London, London.

Herzlich, C. (1973) *Health and Illness,* Academic Press, London.

Hess, B. (1971) Stereotypes of the aged. *Journal of Communication,* **24,** 76–85.

Higgs, P. and Victor, C.R. (1993) Institutional care and the lifecourse, in *Ageing, Independence and the Lifecourse,* (eds S. Arber and M. Evandrou), Jessica Kingsley, London (in press).

Hill, M. (1982) *Understanding Social Policy,* Martin Robertson, Oxford.

Hillhouse, K. (1983) A geographical perspective on the relocation of elderly persons to sheltered housing in Glasgow. University of Glasgow BSc Thesis.

Homans, C.G. (1961) *Social Behaviour: Its Elementary Forms*, Harcourt, Brace and Wald, New York.

House of Commons Social Services Committee (1982) *Third Report*, HMSO, London.

Hunt, A. (1970) *The Home Help Service in England and Wales*, HMSO, London.

Hunt, A. (1978) *The Elderly at Home*, HMSO, London.

Hunt, S. and McEwan, J. (1980) The development of a subjective social indicator. *Sociology of Health and Illness*, **2**, 231–246.

Isaacs, B., Livingstone, M. and Neville, Y. (1972) *Survival of the Unfittest*, Routledge and Kegan Paul, London.

Itzin, C. (1984) The double jeopardy of ageism and sexism, in *Gerontology: Social and Behavioural Perspectives*, (ed. D.B. Bromley), Croom Helm, London, pp. 170–184.

Jefferys, M. (1983) The over eighties in Britain: the social construction of a moral panic. *Journal of Public Health Policy*, **4**, 367–372.

Jerrome, D. (1990) Intimate relationships, in Bond J. and Coleman, P. (eds) *Ageing in Society*, Sage, London, pp. 181–208.

Johnson, P. (1987) *The Structured Dependency of the Elderly: A Critical Note*, Centre for Economic Policy Research Discussion Paper 202, Centre for Economic Policy Research, London.

Johnson, P., Conrad, C. and Thomson, D. (1989) (eds) *Workers Versus Pensioners*, Manchester University Press, Manchester.

Johnson, P. and Falkingham, J. (1992) *Ageing and Economic Welfare*, Sage Publications, London.

Jones, D.A. and Vetter, N.J. (1984) A survey of those who care for the elderly at home: their problems and their needs. *Social Science and Medicine*, **19**(5), 511–514.

Jones, D.A., Victor, C.R. and Vetter, N.J. (1983) Carers of the elderly in the community. *Journal of the Royal College of General Practitioners*, **33**, 707–710.

Jorm, A.F., Korton, A. and Henderson, A.S. (1987) The prevalence of dementia. *Acta Psychiatrica Scandanavica*, **76**, 465–479.

Karn, V. (1977) *Retiring to the Seaside*, Routledge and Kegan Paul, London.

Kerr, S.A. (1982) Deciding about supplementary pension: a provisional model. *Journal of Social Policy*, **11**, 505–507.

Kuypers, J.A. and Bengtson, V.L. (1973) Competence and social breakdown. *Human Development*, **16**(2), 37–49.

Laczko, F. (1986) *The Social Implications of Rising Early Retirement Amongst Men Aged 60–64*. Paper presented at the British Sociological Association Annual Conference, University of Loughborough, Loughborough.

Laczko, F. and Phillipson, P. (1991) *Changing Work and Retirements*, Open University Press, Milton Keynes, Buckinghamshire.

Lamb, M.J. (1977) *The Biology of Aging*, John Wiley, New York.

Laslett, P. (1983) *The World We Have Lost Further Explored*, Methuen, London.

Laslett, P. (1989) *A Fresh Map of Life*, Weidenfeld and Nicholson, London.

Law, C.M. and Warnes, A.M. (1980) Characteristics of retired migrants, in *Geography and the Urban Environment*, (eds D.T. Herbert and R.J. Johnston), John Wiley, Chichester, vol. 3, pp. 175–222.

Law, R. and Chalmers, C. (1976) Medicines and elderly people: a general practice survey. *British Medical Journal*, 565–568.

Lawton, M.P. and Herzog, A.R.C. (eds) (1989) *Special Research Methods in Gerontology*, Baywood, New York.

Lemon, B.W., Bengtson, V.L. and Peterson, J.A. (1972) Activity types and life satisfaction in a retirement community. *Journal of Gerontology*, **27**(4), 511–523.

Lopata, H.Z. (1973) *Widowhood in an American City*, Schenkman, Cambridge, MA.

Lowther, C. and Williamson, J. (1966) Old people and their relatives. *Lancet*, **31 December**.

McCauley, W.J. (1987) *Applied Research in Gerontology*, Van Nostrand Reinhold, New York.

McDonnell, H., Long, A.F., Harrison, B.J. and Oldman, C. (1979) A study of persons aged 65 and over in the Leeds Metropolitan District. *Journal of Epidemiology and Community Health*, **33**, 203–209.

McDowell, M. (1981) Long term trends in seasonal mortality. *Population Trends*, **26**, 16–19.

McEwan, P. and Laverty, S. (1949). *The Chronic Sick and Elderly in Hospitals*, Bradford Hospital Management Committee Report, Bradford.

McGoldrick, A. and Cooper, C. (1980) Voluntary early retirement: taking the decision. *Employment Gazette*, **August**, 859–864.

MacIntyre, S. (1977) Old age as a social problem, in *Health Care and Health Knowledge*, (eds R. Dingwall., C. Heath., M. Reid and M. Stacey), Croom Helm, London, pp. 41–61.

MacIntyre, S. (1986) Health and illness, in *Key Variables in Social Investigation*, (ed. R. Burgess), Routledge and Kegan Paul, London, pp. 76–98.

McKeown, T. (1979) *The Role of Medicine*, Blackwell, Oxford.

Macnicol, J. (1990) Old age and structured dependency, in *Aspects of Ageing*, (eds M. Bury and J. Macnicol), Social Policy Papers 3, Royal Holloway and Bedford New College, London, pp. 30–52.

Mannheim, K. (1952) *Essays in the Sociology of Knowledge*, Oxford University Press, New York.

Martys, C.R. (1982) Drug treatment of elderly patients: a general practice audit. *British Medical Journal*, **285**, 1623–1623.

Mauss, M. (1954) *The Gift*, Free Press, Glencoe, NY.

Meacher, M. (1972) *Rent Rebates: A Study of the Effectiveness of the Means Test*, Child Poverty Action Group, London.

Mead, G.C. (ed.) (1934) *Mind, Self and Society*, University of Chicago Press, Chicago.

Merton, R.K. (1957) *Social Theory and Social Structure*, Free Press, Glencoe, NY.

Middleton, L. (1981) *So Much for So Few*, Institute of Human Ageing Research Paper, University of Liverpool, Liverpool.

Middleton, L. (1983) Friendship and isolation: two sides of sheltered housing, in *Ageing in Modern Society*, (ed. D. Jerrome), Croom Helm, London, pp. 255–268.

Milne, J.S. (1985) *Clinical Effects of Ageing*, Croom Helm, London.

Ministry of Housing and Local Government (1969a) *Council Housing: Purpose, Procedures and Priorities*, Central Housing Advisory Committee (the Cullingworth Committee), HMSO, London.

Ministry of Housing and Local Government (1969b) *Housing Standards and Costs: Accommodation Specially Designed for Old People*, Circular 82/69, HMSO, London.

Ministry of Pensions and National Insurance (1966) *Financial and Other Circumstances of Pensioners*, HMSO, London.

Moser, C.A. and Kalton, G. (1975) *Survey Methods in Social Investigation*, Heinemann Educational Books, London.

National Council on Aging (1975) *The Myths and Realities of Aging*, National Council on Aging, Washington, DC.

National Union of Public Employees (1986) *The realities of home life*, NUPE/West Midlands County Council Economic Development Unit.

Neugarten, B. (1974) Age Groups in American Society. *Annals of the American Academy of Political and Social Science*, **415**, 187–198.

Neugarten, B.L., Havighurst, R.J. and Tobin, S.S. (1968) Personality and patterns of aging, in *Middle Age and Aging*, (ed. B.L. Neugarten), University of Chicago Press, Chicago, pp. 173–177.

Neugarten, B.L., Moore, J.W. and Lowe, J.C. (1965) Age norms, constraints and adult socialization. *American Journal of Sociology*, **70**, 710–717.

Neugarten, B.L. and Peterson, W.A. (1957) A study of the American age grading system, in *Proceedings of the 4th Congress of the International Association of Gerontology*, vol. 3, pp. 497–502.

Neugarten, B.L. and Weinstein, K.K. (1964) The changing American grandparents. *Journal of Marriage and the Family*, **26**, 199–204.

Nissel, M. (1984) The family costs of looking after handicapped elderly relatives. *Ageing and Society*, **4**(2), 185–205.

Office of Population Censuses and Surveys (1982) *General Household Survey 1980*, HMSO, London

Office of Population Censuses and Surveys (1992) *General Household Survey 1990*, HMSO, London.

Olson, L.K. (1982) *The Political Economy of Aging*, Columbia University Press, New York.

Oppenheim, A.N. (1966) *Questionnaire Design and Attitude Measurement*, Heinemann, London.

Palmore, E. (1965) Differences in the retirement patterns of men and women. *Gerontologist*, **5**, 4–8.

Palmore, E. (ed.) (1970) *Normal Aging*, Duke University Press, Durham, NC.

Palmore, E. (1971) Attitudes towards aging as shown by humor. *Gerontologist*, **3**, 181–186.

Palmore, E. (1978) Compulsory versus flexible retirement, in *An Ageing Population*, (eds V. Carver and P. Liddiard), Hodder and Stoughton, Sevenoaks, Kent, pp. 87–93.

Palmore, E., Burchett, B., Fillenbaum, G. *et al.* (1985) *Retirement: Causes and Consequences*, Springer, New York.

Palmore, E., Cleveland, W., Nowlin, J. *et al.* (1979) Stress and adaptation in later life. *Journal of Gerontology*, **34**, 841–851.

Palmore, E. and Whittington, F. (1971) Trends in the relative status of the elderly. *Social Forces*, **50**, 84–91.

Pampel, F. (1981) *Social Change and the Aged: Recent Trends in the United States*, Lexington Books, Lexington, KY.

Parker, S. (1980) *Older Workers and Retirement*, HMSO, London.

Parsons, T. (1951) *The Social System*, Free Press, Glencoe, NY.

Peace, S. (1990) *Researching Social Gerontology*, Sage Publications, London.

Peace, S., Kellaher, L. and Willcocks, D. (1982) *A Balanced Life*, Survey Research Unit, Polytechnic of North London, London.

Phillips Report (1954) Report of the Committee on the Economic and Financial Problems of the Provision for Old Age, *Cmnd 933*, HMSO, London.

Phillipson, C. (1982) *Capitalism and the Construction of Old Age*, Methuen, London.

Phillipson, C. and Strang, P. (1985) Sheltered housing: the warden's view, in *Ageing: Recent Advances and Creative Responses*, (ed. A. Butler), Croom Helm, London, pp. 192–203.

Phillipson, C. and Walker, A. (1986) *Ageing and Social Policy*, Gower, Aldershot.

Quadagno, J. (1982) *Aging In Early Industrial Society*, Academic Press, New York.

Qureshi, H. and Walker, A. (1989) *The caring relationship*, Macmillan Education, Basingstoke, Hampshire.

Reid, I. (1977) *Social Class Differences in Britain*, Fontana, London.

Riley, M. (1971) Age strata in social systems, in *Handbook of Aging and the Social Sciences*, (eds R. Binstock and E. Shanas), Van Nostrand Reinhold, New York, pp. 189–217.

Riley, M., Johnson, M. and Foner, A. (1972) *Aging and Society*, vol. 3: *A Sociology of Age Stratification*, Russell Sage, New York.

Roberts, N. (1970) *Our Future Selves*, Allen and Unwin, London.

Rose, A.M. and Peterson, W.H. (1965) *Old People and their Social World*, F.A. Davis, Philadelphia.

Rosow, I. (1974) *Socialization To Old Age*, University of California Press, Berkeley, CA.

Royal College of Physicians (1966) *Report of the Committee on Accidental Hypothermia*, Royal College of Physicians, London.

Royal Commission on Population (1949) *Cmnd 7695*, HMSO, London.

Russell, C. (1981) *The Ageing Experience*, George Allen and Unwin, Sydney, Australia.

Sanford, J.R.A. (1975) Tolerance of debility in supporters of the elderly at home. *British Medical Journal*, 471–473.

Seebohm, J. (Chairman) (1968) Report of the Committee on Local Authority and Allied Personal Social Services, *Cmnd 3703*, HMSO, London.

Shanas, E., Townsend, P., Wedderburn, D. *et al.* (1968) *Old People in Three Industrial Societies*, Routledge and Kegan Paul, London.

Sheldon, J.H. (1948) *The Social Medicine of Old Age*, Oxford University Press, Oxford.

Simmons, L. (1945) *The Role of the Aged in Primitive Society*, Yale University Press, New Haven, CT.

Simmons, L. (1960) Aging in pre-industrial society, in *Handbook of Social Gerontology*, (ed. C. Tibbitts), University of Chicago Press, Chicago, pp. 62–91.

Sinfield, A. (1979) *What Unemployment Means*, Martin Robertson, Oxford.

Skegg, D.C.G., Doll, R. and Perry, J. (1977) Use of medicines in general practice. *British Medical Journal*, 1561–1563.

Smith, R.G. and Williams, B.O. (1983) A survey of undergraduate teaching of geriatric medicine in the British medical schools. *Age and Ageing*, **12**, 2–6.

Sofer, C. (1970) *Men in Mid Career*, Cambridge University Press, New York.

Sontag, S. (1978) *The double standard of aging, in An Ageing Population*, (eds V. Carver and P. Liddiard), Hodder and Stoughton, Sevenoaks, Kent, pp. 72–80.

Stearns, P.N. (1976) *Old Age in European Society*, Holmes and Meir, New York.

Strehler, B.L. (1962) *Time, Cells and Aging*, Academic Press, New York.

Taylor-Gooby, P. (1974) Means testing and social policy. University of York MPhil Thesis.

Taylor-Gooby, P. (1979) Rent benefits and tenants attitudes: the Batley rent-rebate and allowance study. *Journal of Social Policy*, **5**, 33–48.

Thane, P. (1978) The muddled history of retiring at 60 and 65. *New Society*, **3 August**, 233–236.

Thane, P. (1983) The history of provision for the elderly to 1929, in *Ageing in Modern Society*, (ed. D. Jerrome), Croom Helm, London, pp. 191–198.

Thomas, K. (1976) Age and authority in early modern England. *Proceedings of the British Academy*, **62**, 205–248.

Thompson, P., Itzin, C. and Abendstern, M. (1990) *I Don't Feel Old*, Oxford University Press, Oxford.